EVERYTHING
BY DESIGN

EVERYTHING BY DESIGN

My Life as an Architect

ALAN LAPIDUS

ST. MARTIN'S PRESS 🔀 NEW YORK

www.stmartins.com

Design by James Sinclair

Author's note about the jacket photograph:
In 1978 I was commissioned to design the Benihana Casino, pictured on the jacket— a six-hundred-room hotel and casino in Atlantic City that was to incorporate the existing Shelburne Hotel, the only building in that city on the National Register of Historic Places. Researching the existing structure, I located the original blueprints. The sheet showing the building's façade was beautifully rendered, and instinctively looking at the title block, I noted that it had been drawn by "ML" (my father's initials). I called my father, who confirmed that while working at the firm of Warren and Whetmore in 1926 he had for the first time been given the opportunity to design the casino's exterior. It was right down the boardwalk from the Atlantic City Convention Hall, the only other building he had worked on in Atlantic City, which I connected to my Trump Plaza (see the photo insert).

Library of Congress Cataloging-in-Publication Data

Lapidus, Alan.
   Everything by design : my life as an architect / Alan Lapidus.—1st ed.
      p. cm.
   ISBN-13: 978-0-312-36166-2
   ISBN-10: 0-312-36166-1
   1. Lapidus, Alan. 2. Architects—United States—Biography. 3. Architecture— United States—20th century. 4. United States—Civilization—20th century. I. Title.

NA737.L319 A2 2007
720.92—dc22
[B]

                                                                      2007028251

First Edition: October 2007

10 9 8 7 6 5 4 3 2 1

To Caroline,
in all things, in all ways,

My foundation

CONTENTS

Acknowledgments   ix

Introduction   1

1. Donald Trump's Architect   9

2. Growing Up Lapidus   20

3. You're in the Air Force/Marines/Army Now   38

4. At Columbia (and Almost Prematurely Ejected)   42

5. The Son Also Wants to Rise   56

6. Eye of the Beholder   68

7. A Swimming Pool Grows in Brooklyn   76

8. Go Tell It on the Mountain   90

9. What Happens in Vegas . . .   116

10. Donald Down the Shore   139

11. "It's the Magic Kingdom and Magicians Never
    Give Away Their Secrets"   160

12. The Four Mouseketeers   170

13. "The Most Gorgeous Building in All Manhattan"   195

14. The Ungrateful Living   211

15. A Walk on the Wild Side   229

16. "A Little Favor"   238

17. The Return of *Gospodin* Lapidus   243

18. Rich and Famous   248

19. A Way Out   257

20. End of the World   269

21. *Ryokan*   285

Epilogue   289

Index   297

ACKNOWLEDGMENTS

I would like to thank Phil Revzin, my wonderful, understanding, and above all knowledgeable editor at St. Martin's Press. For a first-time author, his guidance and wise council made this experience a joy.

The Lake Region Writers Guild was an asset to be treasured. This group of talented Maine writers listened patiently and offered much appreciated guidance as I developed this book.

My talented son, Adam, who showed me, by example, that becoming a writer was achievable.

Lee Moulton, the resident computer guru, who guided me through the mysteries of the IT world.

And my clients, who taught me the sometimes-painful lessons in the ways of the REAL world. But who enabled me to build my buildings.

Thanks.

EVERYTHING
BY DESIGN

Introduction

M rs. Axelrod wanted an ocean view from her bidet.

That presented a problem. The master bedroom was located at the back of the beach house so that its French doors would open onto a very private garden. The toilet was in a bedroom attached to the master bedroom. But the ocean was inconveniently located at the front of the house.

I began to reassess the wisdom of my decision to become an architect.

People have been known to lie to their shrinks but never to their architects. Hell, you can always get another shrink, but you are going to have to live with and in your house. This leads to some fascinating insights into the kinks and twists of clients. Normally I am willing to accede to any of these little foibles as long as they don't result in the destruction of the environment, the collapse of civilization, or violations of the local building code.

Houses, to be sure, are not my specialty. Hotels and casinos are. But I have, on occasion, planned out homes for friends of mine like Mrs. Axelrod. Since all of my clients who wanted houses were friends, I knew how to design a home that would perfectly fit each one. "Fit" is an appropriate word; I consider a custom-designed home the architectural equivalent of a bespoke suit. Years later one of my client-friends, in an interview in *The New York Times*, described my creation as "a work of art on the Eastern end of Long Island."

There are times, such as while I was drawing up plans for the Axelrods' house, that I ponder the vast differences in architecture as it is idealistically taught in school, largely unfettered by reality and fettered by unreality, and the profession that is practiced by too many architects chasing too few commissions. Architecture has been called the second oldest profession, but sometimes it bears a close resemblance to its older sister.

When I entered the School of Architecture at Columbia University in 1959, Dean Kenneth Smith, looking as old and wrinkled as the steelpoint engravings that we were to study, welcomed the three dozen of us with his standard speech: "The practice of this ancient craft will not bring you worldly riches, but should you successfully complete your six years of study and your three years of apprenticeship and pass the rigorous licensing exam, you will be privileged to be part of that ancient group of artisans who are the only ones to have left behind the chronicle of mankind, speaking to future ages in a universal language that explained to generations yet unborn, how they lived, how they labored, and in what they believed."

Mrs. Axelrod believed in feminine hygiene in a scenic environment. Let future ages chew on that one.

Over the course of more than forty years, I have been an architect based in New York City, working here and throughout much of the world with and for the likes of Donald Trump (prompting *The Wall Street Journal* to label me "Donald Trump's Architect"); Michael Eisner and his Disney Corporation; Bill Zeckendorf; John Tishman (who told one interviewer that I'm "probably the most knowledgeable architect . . . in the operation of hotels"); Aristotle Onassis; Sophia Loren and Carlo Ponti; Mayor John Lindsay as well as his counterpart, the latter-day mayor of Moscow; Bob Guccione; Rocky Aoki of Benihana Steakhouses; and assorted mafiosi. You'll meet most of these—any many other— people later.

I've been asked countless times, "Exactly what does an architect do?" and "What is it like to be an architect?" As time passed, I came to realize that not only are the answers to these questions of interest to many people, but that, to the best of my knowledge, there has never been a book that offers an insider's account of the life and motivations of a "working" architect, written for lay readers. This book is about real buildings and real clients, many of whom, to be candid, wanted me to draw up plans for ever higher and gaudier buildings that would make clear to the whole world that "mine is bigger than his." As a matter of fact, one Mob operative who was part of a group that wanted me to design an Atlantic City casino for them announced during a rather unusual business meeting around a table of his compadres at a Frank Sinatra concert that my plans to erect the structure were giving him an erection—not his exact words.

Hollywood seems to regard architects, at least male architects, as iconic and interesting figures—for example, Gary Cooper in *The Fountainhead*; Paul Newman in *The Towering Inferno*; Richard Gere in *Intersection*, with Sharon Stone cast as his wife; and Woody Harrelson in *Indecent Proposal*, with Robert Redford as the rich man willing to pay $1 million for a night with Harrelson's wife, played by Demi Moore. Although *Indecent Proposal* is hardly *Citizen Kane*, Harrelson does deliver a monologue that is one of the best descriptions I've ever heard of being an architect. Even Ralphie on *The Sopranos* said he had planned to be an architect until he got diverted into the "family" business.

"Pilot, skydiver, author, chef, one-shot Central Intelligence Agency operative, and, oh, yes, hotel architect" is the way one magazine has described me. (The CIA mention refers to the time in the mid-1990s when I was enlisted to travel to Havana, ostensibly to help restore an old synagogue there, and take with me several "associates" whose backgrounds were definitely not in architecture and whose mission was to gather as much information about the situation in Fidel's Cuba as they could. See Chapter 17.) But it's the last credit in the list, hotel architect, that is dearest to my heart and has constituted the majority of my life's work. Designing resorts and casino hotels is what I find most satisfying, because it means involving the guests in what I call "participatory theater" and trying to indulge and fulfill their fantasies.

Among the more than one hundred thousand working architects in America, plus at least as many who are unregistered (over half of the graduates of our 139 accredited schools of architecture don't go through the process of becoming registered), there are dozens if not hundreds of outstanding architects. What sets the small group of A-list architects apart from the rest is not necessarily that the A-listers are more talented than others but that the people they meet and the clients they deal with are also A-listers. At the upper echelons of architecture, who you know becomes as important as what you know and how skilled you are. If one mover and shaker introduces you to another, that one in turn might introduce you to a Donald Trump.

There's no question I got a running start. My father, Morris Lapidus, who, with his design of Miami's Fontainebleau Hotel in 1954, more or less "invented" postmodern architecture, was the most popularly known architect of his time. Professionally reviled during his life, late in 2006 he was picked by *The Atlantic* magazine as one of the five most influential architects of our time. Being his son was a decidedly mixed blessing. I became his apprentice and eventually his partner. Because of this I had opportunities that were quite unusual for a young designer, but I always worked in his shadow. Even after I started my own firm, I was always "Morris's kid." At first it was an irritation, but eventually I took great pride in that sobriquet.

My father was an extremely prickly character. I have used his teachings in all my work, and he and I were partners for many years. But our relationship had countless ups and downs. I won't characterize it as a love-hate association, because I never hated him, but anyone who has had a rocky history with a parent, much less has worked with one, will be able to identify with my account of how the Lapidus family interacted. I must make clear that being the son of Morris was not always an advantage. A professor of mine at Columbia, Gerhard Kallmann, a leader of the New Brutalism school that abhorred the flourishes my father was known for, noticed my surname on the first day of class and stopped at my worktable. "Lapidus?" he inquired. "Any relation to Morris Lapidus?" "Yes," I answered. "He's my father." "Gott help us!" was all Kallman could say.

As Ada Louise Huxtable, the renowned architecture critic of *The New York Times*, observed thirty-five years ago (in a praise-filled story about a public swimming pool I designed in a poor area of Bedford-Stuyvesant at the direction of Mayor John Lindsay), "The architect is . . . victim and fall guy. . . . Everything is rigged to make him responsible for everyone else's sins, and he is treated as the one potential crook. No one shares his concern for good design and everything is stacked against it."

Moreover, one aspect of the architect's glamorous life, which few outsiders understand, is that a majority of the projects any architect works on never make it off the drawing boards. The reasons are many and varied, from the client's inability to obtain financing, to the client's changing his or her mind after the plans have been drawn, to shifting economic conditions that render a project not viable, to terrorist attacks such as the one on the World Trade Center that ruined the business of many a New York City architect. This reality is something that most architects, sadly, do not realize until they have been in business for a while. About 35 percent of the buildings I designed got built, which I believe is one of the highest success ratios in the business.

In many ways, often thanks to sheer luck and to no particular planning or intent on my part, my career and my life have been unique. Through the luck of the draw, two of my schoolmates at Midwood High School in my native Brooklyn were Erich Segal and Allen Konigsberg—better known in his adult years as Woody Allen. Woody Allen was one year ahead of me, but both Erich Segal and I graduated in 1954—yet it was I who was named best writer in the class! Woody's film *Zelig* was about a character who keeps turning up at many historical moments, and as you will see, mine has been a Zelig-like life, throughout which I've encountered an almost unbelievable cast of characters.

A case in point: At a social gathering many years ago in the Central Park West apartment of my lifelong friend Mike Kenin, I was introduced to Lee Strasberg, the founder of the world-famous Actors Studio in Manhattan. When I told Strasberg I was an architect, he asked if I could possibly help him fix a problem in the fireplace flue at his Upper West Side apartment. Although this is not the type of request that I usually respond to, hey—it was Lee Strasberg. After I solved his problem,

Strasberg asked if I could design some modifications to the studio itself. The Actors Studio is in a former church in midtown Manhattan, and it was critically short of backstage storage and wardrobe space. I ended up doing set design for some of the productions and working with some remarkable people. (Among the perks was having a very happy secretary, because Paul Newman called periodically to discuss my work at the Actors Studio.) One of the reasons I loved set design was that it provided instant gratification. As an architect designing hotels and other high-rise structures, there is usually a minimum of four years' gestation between the time I design a building and when I actually see the finished product at streetside. At the studio, I would design a set, and in less than a month it was in place. Another advantage was that if I had second thoughts, I could always say "a little to the left." Try doing that with a fifty-story building. One other Strasberg story: The first movie he ever acted in was *The Godfather Part II* (1974), in which he played the role of Hyman Roth—based upon the real-life figure Meyer Lansky.

Shortly after the Depression, my father designed one of New York's most glamorous speakeasies, the Palais Royale, for two clients he always identified as "Mr. Walters" and "Mr. Siegel." When the club opened, *The Times* gave it a glowing review, mentioning him as the designer, and the souvenir program for opening night stated in bold type: "Entire decoration conceived and designed by Morris Lapidus." Morris saved and cherished both items.

But opening night almost didn't happen. When the club was nearly finished, a city building inspector showed up with a list of violations that would have prevented the opening. To the horror of my gentle father, "Mr. Siegel" pulled a gun and was about to negotiate, when Morris stepped in, handed the functionary a hundred-dollar bill, and the violations disappeared. To the best of my knowledge, my father was unaware that Siegel's first name happened to be "Bugsy." Morris remained friendly for many years with "Mr. Walters," whose first name was Lou and who owned the French Quarter nightclubs in Boston, New York, and Miami. Morris often commented that Mr. Walters had a nice-looking daughter who wanted to break into broadcasting but would never be successful because she had a speech impediment when it came to pronouncing *r*'s. He never realized that the Barbara Walters on TV was Lou's daughter.

By the mid-1990s, well over thirty years into my career as an architect, an immutable truth finally dawned on me: The people who make money from hotels, which has been my specialty, are not the architects but the owners. So I set out both to design and own a hostelry. My pitch to investors that all my experience in the hotel industry had put me in a position where I knew what it took to be successful paid off, and I assembled an investment group in which I was a participant. The result is the Holiday Inn Wall Street, at the corner of Gold and Platt streets, way downtown, the first new hotel in the Financial District in almost fifty years and the first hotel in New York City to be built with the business traveler as its primary client. I designed the seventeen-story, 138-room boutique hotel to offer singular accommodations, featuring ultrafast Internet service in every room. It has been a hit since opening day in 1999, with exceptionally high rates of occupancy and return customers. The Holiday Inn is also unique for its imaginative use of real estate, "an example of how much can be crammed onto a 4,000-square-foot trapezoid site that was formerly a parking lot," in the words of *The Times*.

In view of the success of the Holiday Inn Wall Street, I've become picky about the buildings I work on, usually insisting that I receive an ownership share as part of my fee. My current pet project, in the Catskills, is another new concept in hospitality, at least in the United States. It is a world-class spa to uplift both the body and the psyche called a *ryokan*, or traditional Japanese inn, meant not just as shelter from the storm but also as a place to restore one's *wa* (spirit), outfitted with peaceful gardens, shaded walkways, and relaxing baths, and featuring a level of personal service unknown in this country along with exquisite food, both American and Asian. Ironically, a site under consideration was once home to the famous Concord resort, one of my father's earliest hospitality projects, as was Grossinger's. Just as he designed those places, and even more so the Fontainebleau, for people like himself, the *ryokan* is a place where I would want to stay. As I told *Newsweek*, my dream hotel is one that's "no place like home" and will "get the heads in the beds." Otherwise "it's a failure, no matter what the other architects say."

1

Donald Trump's Architect

The voice on the phone had a tone of easy familiarity: "Hey, Alan, howyadoin', it's been a while."

It had indeed been a while since I last talked to Donald Trump. His call would lead to me becoming "Donald Trump's Architect," to quote *The Wall Street Journal*, and being intimately involved in the design and construction of Trump Plaza, his first casino in Atlantic City or, for that matter, his first anywhere. It amounted to my having the opportunity to see Donald in action before he was *The Donald*, to watch him evolve from his first persona into his second, like a moth into a butterfly. Or, perhaps more to the point, from a run-of-the-mill butterfly into a spectacular creature.

During the late 1950s, a man named Fred Trump vacationed at one of my father's early and smaller Miami Beach hotels, the Sans Souci. Trump fell in love with the design of the lobby. He felt that if he added a "classy" lobby to the otherwise drab middle-income high-rise apartments he was planning to build on Ocean Parkway in Brooklyn (still known as Trump Village), he could beat the competition. Trump called our office, only to have Morris turn him down cold: "I don't do lobbies!"

Fred Trump was a man who got what he wanted—a family trait his son Donald inherited and of course perfected. This apartment complex was to contain more than three thousand units, and if Morris would design the lobby, well, then Fred would hire him as architect for the whole complex. It was an offer my father couldn't refuse. Fred specified that the structures were being built under a federally subsidized housing program, meaning that by necessity and regulation, they had to be plain boxes with punched windows. We could choose any brick we wanted, as long as it was red, unglazed Hudson Valley brick. But the lobbies—they would be terrific! *And* the generous fees for such bland and mindless work were irresistible. Trump Village was a smash hit, immediately filled with eager renters and later successfully converted to condos.

At that time I was just starting to work in the firm, and I occasionally accompanied Morris on his site visits, where we encountered Fred Trump. Fred was tall and lean, with high cheekbones and piercing eyes set in an angular face. He was gruff and yet very likable at the same time. He had a relatively modest office on Avenue Z in Brooklyn (our home had been on Avenue J), and it reflected his down-to-earth, outer-borough persona: The sole decoration in the place was a large wooden cigar store Indian.

Fred believed in maintaining political connections and using them to access programs that subsidized the production of sensible, solid apartments for working-class people. He also believed in avoiding anything having to do with Manhattan—a trait his son would not share, of course. It was during one of these visits that Fred introduced me to one of his sons, a cocky fourteen-year-old lad ten years my junior with sandy blond hair and a round face. The kid, who was watering down a pile of dusty construction rubble, was Donald. During the early stages of my relationship with the Trump family, I became friendly not with Donald but with his older brother, Fred Jr., a pilot for American Airlines. Since I was a newly minted pilot, he and I talked flying, not real estate.

Many years later, in the early 1980s, the grown-up Donald acquired a parcel on Atlantic City's Boardwalk, next to the Convention Hall, a site that I had worked on for another developer who had been unable to secure funding. But Donald had gone my former client one step better by assembling the rest of the block. Having seen my name on the plans for the initial attempt, he learned that I had already designed two other Atlantic City casinos that had won full approvals and that I was very much involved in the whole scene there. I of course had been following his meteoric rise in Manhattan real estate circles.

Now he spoke to me as an old family friend. Explaining that he had become owner of the site and seen my work, he felt it would be ideal for us two old "buddies" to work together. After all, we were both second generation, and each of us was going to show his father a thing or two. And, by the way, he added, because we were practically "family," I couldn't charge him the fancy fees that I charged my other clients.

I was charmed.

Donald had put together several notable packages by then, but he had never been the sole principal. One such deal was the Grand Hyatt Hotel, which he created out of the old Commodore, in a brilliant piece of brinkmanship. During the mid-1970s, New York City was on the verge of bankruptcy, thanks in part to the ineptitude of his father's old political cronies, and Forty-second Street was starting to look like a third-world thoroughfare. The boarded-up Commodore Hotel, once one of the city's finest, was now a deserted eyesore that greeted passengers leaving Grand Central Station. Public confidence in the city had reached an all-time low.

Donald walked the neighborhood and noticed that on the opposite side of Forty-second was the headquarters of the Dime Savings Bank. Never afraid to go fishing in troubled waters, he brashly informed Dime executives that the value of their real estate was down the tubes, facing the derelict Commodore as it was. But, he promised, if they backed him he would transform their location from a quickly devaluating pit into the centerpiece of the city's renaissance. They bought into the idea. Trump eventually was able to win spectacular concessions from a desperate municipality, and even better terms from the state. The reborn hotel, the Grand Hyatt, did indeed accomplish all that Donald had promised. It was the shot in the arm the city needed, a sign that someone was still willing to bet that there was a future. In the annals of municipal chutzpah, if not municipal planning, it was pure genius. But it was the state's superagency, the Empire State Development Corporation, not Donald Trump, that actually owned the building. That arrangement was a necessary formality in order to obtain state subsidies, but it was Donald who made the big bucks. Likewise, Trump Tower, another thoroughly audacious development, was done under the aegis of the Equitable Insurance Company.

By the time he approached me about his Atlantic City property, Donald hungered for a deal that would be his very own. When I asked why he was planning to do a development in Atlantic City, since all his financial and political connections were in New York City, his reply was the same as the one given by noted bank robber Willie Sutton when asked why he robbed banks: "That's where the money is."

Donald and I made a date to go down to A.C., and I offered to fly him in my airplane. This was before the days of his private jets, helicopters, and yachts, and he was delighted. My airplane was a solid, reliable, single-engine propeller craft, which, although mechanically perfect, left something to be desired in the cosmetics department. We met at Teterborough Airport, my home base, and headed south. Donald sat next to me in the right seat, and his COO, Harvey Freeman, sat in back working on *The New York Times* crossword puzzle. Donald chattered away as we flew down the Atlantic coast. Navigating from the outskirts of New York City to A.C. is quite simple: Fly to nearest ocean, turn right, keep going until you see a bunch of high-rise buildings, land. So his conversation didn't distract me at all. In the midst of talking, he became aware of the less than pristine upholstery, then looked over at me and inquired, "Hey, Alan, is this plane safe?"

My reply amused him: "Donald, my epitaph is not going to be 'Donald Trump and two others die in plane crash.'"

As the months went by, I began to fully appreciate why Donald was such a force to be reckoned with. He was street smart in a way that distinguished him from other developers I had worked with. Donald was a young WASP in a field dominated by aged Jews. Not just Jews, but German Jews. New York's real estate dynasties were not founded by turn-of-the-century immigrants from Eastern Europe. That group landed on our shores for the most part religious, penniless, and, except for their Hebrew education, illiterate. The German Jews had arrived much earlier and were mostly coming *to* something rather than fleeing *from* something. Polished and urbane, they and their descendants used their education and drive to found enduring businesses. The Tishmans, the Zeckendorfs, and the Silversteins (all my clients or to be my clients) were prime examples. In his book *Our Crowd*, Stephen Birmingham did a brilliant study of these folks. Temple Emanu-El, *the* temple of this set, was such an Episcopal wannabe that for a long time few if any bar mitzvahs (disdained as a trashy Eastern European custom) were performed there. A standing joke, at least among all of us "Johnny-come-lately" Jews, was that at Temple Emanu-El they were so WASP that they were closed on *Shabbos* (the Jewish Sabbath).

At that time, the established real estate guys kept an extremely low profile. Relatively unknown to the public, they wanted to maintain their ability to fly below the radar and generally avoided publicity. The reason was straightforward: Big real estate deals were dependent on the proper political allies. There were government subsidy programs, subtle shifts of zoning entitlements, and myriad other ways that a politician could smooth the path of a real estate transaction. Bear in mind that during this era before Watergate and "open government," meaningful public forums, rights of disclosure, and investigative reporters were comparatively rare; the fabled "smoke-filled back rooms" were no fable.

Then along came this kid from Queens who had been raised by a low-key, in fact damn near invisible, WASP developer of a father and steeped in the timeless tradition of political patronage and rock-solid developer smarts. Young Donald Trump was brash, smart, driven, and, above all, clever. He did not give a fiddler's fart for the aloof old boys' world of Manhattan developers. He had a feel for the times he lived in. He knew that his future customers would have the same sensibilities he did. Donald instinctively understood that regardless of how much people professed admiration for "culture" and the refined taste of the ads in *The New Yorker*, what they really wanted was glitz and glamour.

At least *his* market did. And, as history has shown, his market is quite large.

The old guard reacted with loathing and derision. Harry Helmsley, one of the leading Manhattan developers, was publicly scornful: "The kid can talk, but he can't build." Ironically, Helmsley's own membership in the old guard was threatened during the years before his death in 1997, as he became somewhat marginalized socially after his 1972 marriage to Leona Helmsley, "the Queen of Mean." I met her at a couple of social occasions and found it easy to see why she was so widely disliked.

Donald was really the first to grasp the sea change in how Americans bought real estate. It wasn't only about getting solid value for your money—it was also about celebrity. He understood that if he made himself a star or, in our world of hyperbole, a *superstar*, he could enhance the value of anything he had to sell, including himself. Circular logic, perhaps, but, oh, so true!

Years later, when he owned three Atlantic City casinos, Trump's enterprises did quite well because people wanted to associate with a star, hoping some of the glamour would rub off on them. I once walked with him across the gaming floor of his Taj Mahal, watching in amazement as hordes literally flocked around him, hoping to be acknowledged as they heaped adulation upon his meticulously coiffed head. As the two of us moved along, Donald with his signature black cashmere overcoat draped over his shoulders like an Italian movie director, and I practically invisible, I realized that for him it was a case of mission accomplished.

Yes, Donald had actually succeeded in turning his name into a brand!

By sheer coincidence, I had two groups of clients named Trump during the mid-1980s. One pair was Donald and his brother Robert. The other pair, unrelated to Donald and Robert, was a Jewish brother duo named Julius and Eddie Trump. Each team of brothers was developing real estate on a grand scale. Moreover, their Manhattan offices were a scant half block apart; the offices of Julius and Eddie were at 9 West Fifty-seventh, while Donald's headquarters were at Trump Tower on Fifth Avenue between Fifty-sixth and Fifty-seventh. Julius and Eddie were building a complex in north Miami Beach called Williams Island. Full-page ads for this venture appeared frequently in *The New York Times*, stating that it was a project of the Trump Group.

The result was almost inevitable: Donald sued Julius and Eddie for using *his* name. To be sure, Julius and Eddie, in contrast to Donald, were Orthodox Jews of South African descent; their name was either Afrikaner or Dutch and had been theirs for many generations.

Donald won.

All of Julius and Eddie's subsequent advertising had to display the disclaimer that they were *not* a part of the Trump Organization. Donald, aware that I was architect for the other Trumps as well, confided in me, "Hell, if I liked their stuff I would claim it was my project, but it's too low-class for my name."

Donald was also quick to grasp the idea that if you embellished a story enough times, loudly enough, and with squinty eye and furrowed brow, *and* if you had the best publicist in New York (Howard Rubenstein) to make sure you were quoted in the popular press almost daily—all the while repeatedly denying that you had a publicist—you were whatever you said you were. Truth was a self-fulfilling prophecy. As the Cary Grant character, an ad executive in one of my favorite movies, *North by Northwest*, declared, "In the world of advertising, there's no such thing as a lie. There's only expedient exaggeration."

The same holds true in real estate, and condemning a real estate developer for exaggeration, hyperbole, and even outright lies is like condemning a fish for swimming. Such is the nature of the business—as it was in the beginning, is now, and ever shall be. That's how Atlantic City started as a resort, created by developers using absurd claims from medical doctors about the ability of Absecon Island's sea breezes to cure everything from cancer to dropsy. Likewise, America's West was settled by pioneers lured to the frontier by developers and land salesmen claiming that the cold, dangerous, and forbidding prairie was the Garden of Eden. Compared to those statements and countless other similar ones, Donald's claims seem modest indeed.

A developer's objective is to sell what he or she develops. You don't have to be a rocket scientist to understand that that's how developers make their money, often tons of money. Developers are not in the business of improving the human condition or elevating the masses. The biggest difference between Donald Trump and other developers is that Donald has carried the business to its logical conclusion. If his name is on a project, it sells; he has literally and officially morphed into a franchise. He may not quite be McDonald's, but many of his most recent deals do amount to him "selling" his name to other people's developments for millions of dollars and a cut of the take. He doesn't own, and never has owned, the Trump International Hotel, Trump Place, and other big "T" icons. His lucrative type of no-investment, no-risk business deal has earned him a hallowed niche in the developers' hall of fame.

One example: Trump Place on the Upper West Side. It opened in 1998, and most of the tenants were young women. Quite a few were just starting their careers in New York City and were supported or at least subsidized in part by their parents. As she was moving her daughter into an apartment there, one lady explained to me why she chose this particular building. To her, the name Trump meant that it was safe, clean, and secure, and offered prestige they could be proud of. "When I tell my friends that Cindy lives in Trump Place, they don't think we're being reckless by letting her live in New York City." Again, it's called "branding."

I was there because I was renting one of the apartments myself, after my second marriage broke up. My business setbacks had forced me to declare bankruptcy in 1992, which made me an untouchable in the eyes of leasing agents. I called Donald and he quickly fixed that problem and ordered his people to rent me an apartment. I paid him full freight—and on time every month.

And so it was that I attended and was singled out at the 1998 Christmas party Donald hosted there, about two months after the building opened and quickly filled to capacity. In one of his patented PR coups, Donald had announced that his soiree for the tenants would feature food, wine, music, and, last but definitely not least, The Donald. In person.

Several hundred tenants gathered in the beautifully decorated lobby to feast on endless platters of sushi and other delicacies, drink imported champagne, and listen to a string quartet featuring performers from the nearby Juilliard School of Music. Finally, coat draped over shoulders, He (that's not a typo) arrived and shared with the adoring throng details of his painful, heroic, uphill battle, lasting more than a decade, to transform a rusting, rotting, rail yard into this splendid statement of sophisticated urban living.

Then, noticing that his audience was mostly young and female, Donald pointed at me and bellowed, "And another thing—living in this building is one of America's greatest architects. His wife just threw him out, so, ladies, let me present the newly single Alan Lapidus." Totally blown away, I turned red, waved, took a bow—and wound up receiving about a dozen business cards from young lovelies over the course of the evening.

Donald's attempt to help with my love life pretty much made us even. I helped him out once by escorting Marla Maples to a retirement dinner in honor of Andy Goldman, whose wife, Susan Heilbron, was Trump's general counsel. The affair was at the Winter Garden in the World Trade

Center, and after the main event Marla and I and a few others went to a small, chic bistro in Little Italy. When I arrived in the limo Donald had provided, accompanied by Marla wearing a short purple dress that somehow looked both sedate and very sexy, and we made our grand entrance, it was as if the whole world had come to a stop. The women at the restaurant seemed to wish to have Marla cut into little pieces and then have all the parts burned, while the kitchen crew pushed open the kitchen door, the better for them to stare and gape. The waiter brought us a complimentary bottle of wine, and when, trying to appear cosmopolitan, I said, "*Grazie!*" Marla turned to me and said, "I'm impressed. I only speak two languages, Yankee and Southern." She was absolutely delightful, down-to-earth, and with no pretensions whatsoever. One of the stories she told me that night was about an evening when she and Donald were at his Mar-a-Largo estate in Palm Beach, walking on the sand, and she looked at Donald and asked him to give her his shoes. When he asked why, she just repeated her demand. He reluctantly took off his wingtips and handed them to her, and she threw them into the sea, telling him, "It's a beautiful night, we're walking on the beach, so for God's sake, just relax!"

By the way, when I called my then (second) wife that day to tell her I wouldn't be home for dinner because I was taking out Marla Maples, her answer was, "That's nice. See you later."

As the Atlantic City project started to take shape, Donald and I found ourselves spending more and more time together. When it became apparent that the project was a "go," he asked me to submit a contract for my services so we could negotiate the terms. A couple of weeks later I received the call I was expecting. But it wasn't from the person I anticipated. Fred Trump was on the line. He invited me to Donald's office so we could talk about my contract.

Fred had aged very gracefully. He still had his great shock of hair, bristling mustache, and ready smile. As we sat down at a spare desk in a small office, he reached into his briefcase and brought out an architectural contract but not the one I had sent to his son. It was the one he had signed with my father for Trump Village back in 1957.

"Alan," Fred said, "just take this contract—you remember this one, don't you?—and put Donald's hotel project in the job description, with the same financial terms that you sent to him, and we'll sign it tomorrow. This contract worked for your father and me, and it should work just as well for the two of you." It must be said of Fred that he was a man whose simple values worked quite well.

Fred and I went on to chat about how my father was doing, and we reminisced at length about the "good old days." We also had a long talk about Donald, although it was mainly Fred doing the talking. He was obviously proud of his son, although he was mystified as to why he wanted to do all these buildings in Manhattan. Fred mentioned in particular the glass-sheathed Grand Hyatt, along with the new Trump Tower that was then under construction across the street, also with a glass curtain wall. At one point Fred looked at me and asked earnestly, "Alan, can you suggest to Donald that good old redbrick is much more efficient, less expensive, and doesn't leak?"

I said I would.

I never did.

Later that year I got a call from Fred, who seemed to regard me as a bridge between the old guard and "the kids." Fred asked if I could hint to Donald that he didn't have to waste electricity by leaving Trump Tower's Christmas tree lights on during the day.

I said I would.

I never did.

Two years after we executed the contracts, when the building, ultimately to be known as Trump Plaza, was under construction, I got an irate call from Donald demanding that I come over to his office *at once*. When I arrived, he was fuming about how I had been overcharging him for the "reimbursables."

Reimbursable expenses in an architectural contract are those costs that the architect pays for and the client later repays him for. These include the price of blueprinting and reproduction, postage, travel expenses, and the like. On a project of this size, the reimbursable expenses will run several hundred thousand dollars. Donald had noticed that I had been adding a 10 percent surcharge to these items. Such a surcharge is commonly added to cover the cost of all the bookkeeping and accounting and billing that my office has to do to keep track of all these items.

How dare I try and "cheat" him by adding this 10 percent, he fumed. Never, he declared, would he agree to such an arrangement.

Trying to look as innocent as I felt, I answered, "Donald, it's in the contract that your father signed with me, because it was in the contract my father signed with him twenty-five years ago. Your father insisted on the exact same contract."

For what may have been the first and last time, Donald Trump had been trumped.

2

Growing Up Lapidus

Some of my colleagues have looked at my career and thought I was blessed to have Morris Lapidus as a father. But a curse came along with the blessing. The Lapidus household, with Morris and especially my mother, Bea, running the show, was an uncommonly dysfunctional one. I joined Morris in his practice for the first thirteen years of my career, and no doubt working for him helped open certain doors for me. But for the thirty-five years after that, I spent much of my time trying to free myself from my parents' shadows.

The story starts chez Lapidus on East Eighth Street between Avenues J and K in Brooklyn. Until 1954 or so, when I was in my late teens and finishing high school, I had no idea what an architect actually did. At home, my father had no interest in talking about what he did for a living, or precious little interest in talking with me at all. My awakening came while Morris was involved with his magnum opus, the Fontainebleau Hotel in Miami Beach. When the hotel opened in December 1954 (I was eighteen then), its sweeping curve and ornate interiors brought him popular acclaim and professional scorn. The grand-opening ceremonies and the storm of publicity that ensued from the opening piqued my curiosity.

The gala celebration itself was overwhelming to a kid from Brooklyn. All sorts of celebrities, including the mayor of Fontainebleau, France, were there. Most everyone was bedecked in what passed for Miami Beach "ultrachic" circa 1954. The brand-new hotel was such a hot spot that only registered guests were allowed inside for weeks after the doors opened. A few days after the Big Event, trying to impress a local teenager of the feminine persuasion, I offered to give her a tour. My "passport" was being the son of the great man who had designed this edifice. I stood at the front door, explaining to the security guard that, no, I was not a guest, but I was the son of . . . Which is as far as I got before my date and I were hustled away from the building. So much for reflected glory.

Still, all the attention paid to the Fontainebleau imbued in me for the first time an understanding of and appreciation for what my father did: He put something onto paper, and his drawings were transformed into visible and sometimes large additions to the landscape. I was also impressed by the gravitas that many people afforded his every word. At college I started writing papers for various classes, usually working in an architectural angle. Even after I enrolled at Columbia's architectural school, I wasn't sure whether I would actually practice architecture or just write about it.

Many beginning architectural students and members of the public may have an image of architects like Paul Newman in *The Towering Inferno*. In the opening scene, we see him helicoptering out of a primeval forest, complete with hard hat, to his San Francisco penthouse office, which closely resembles Mission Control, then entering his private suite where a negligee-clad Faye Dunaway awaits him on peach-colored silk sheets. Wow! That sure beats the heck out of processing insurance claims. It was Ayn Rand's *The Fountainhead*, an epic as both a novel and a movie starring Gary Cooper, that helped guide me into architecture as a profession. The opening line is, "Howard Roark laughed." Roark stands, stark naked, on the edge of a limestone quarry and dives into the water far below. Instead of toweling off, he breaks into the nearby mansion of his boss, the quarry owner (also an architect), and ravishes his willing and ravishing daughter, Dominique, amid the quarry dust. Now, *that* will put any thoughts about dental school on your back burner. But I still had a problem reconciling that concept with my conservative, middle-aged real-life father. Mom was okay, but not quite Faye or Dominique.

I, and my four-years-older brother Dick, were not the only family members without a handle on architecture. My grandfather Leon was a

Russian peasant who brought my grandmother and infant father to the *goldena medina*, which translates as "golden land" or, in our case, Manhattan's Lower East Side, in 1903. Grandpa Leon was a coppersmith who came from a very poor family in Kurland. Having too many mouths to feed, his father indentured Leon to a coppersmith when Leon was nine. Leon apparently never saw his family again. From what I can gather, his was a literal Cinderella experience. He slept by the fireplace and never got enough to eat. As a result, he didn't grow taller than five foot three or four. My grandfather was delighted to have been drafted into the Russian army, because he finally got enough to eat. Many details of Leon's life are a mystery to me; for example, there was no official record of when he was born and he was never certain exactly how old he was. Both my grandmothers died before I got to know them, and my maternal grandfather died before I was born. My parents believed, as a general rule, that children were to be seen but not included in conversations. As a result, what little I know about family history comes from Morris's memoir, *Too Much Is Never Enough*, which wasn't published until 1996 when I was sixty, and from my father's youngest brother, my uncle Sol. Sol and his wife, my aunt Evelyn, were the only members of my family for whom I felt real affection. It was as though Morris and Sol had been switched at birth. Sol and Ev were warm, funny, loving people.

After serving in the Russian army, Grandfather Leon moved to Odessa, opened a coppersmith shop, and married his true love. The following year, 1902, Morris was born, and the year after that the three set off for the New World, where Leon pursued his trade on the Lower East Side. Apparently he was a terrific craftsman. Eventually he opened his own shop, which grew into a factory that manufactured automobile accessories. In those days, the 1920s or so, when you bought a car, you got the stripped-down model. Period. If you wanted headlights or a rearview or side mirror or even license plate frames, you bought them separately. This is what Leon specialized in. His company was Yankee Metal Products, located on Atlantic Avenue in Brooklyn, near the Brooklyn Navy Yard. When World War II got going, the navy put out a RFP (request for proposals) for the design and construction of a signaling searchlight for the ships of the fleet. Because things were a tad slow in my father's practice at that moment, for the first and only time he set to work with his father and his two younger brothers, Ben, the middle brother, and Sol. My father designed a model of a searchlight and my grandfather built it by hand. When it came time to submit the prototypes, all the competitors for the contract gathered at the Brooklyn Navy Yard, where a young engineering officer named Hyman Rickover, later to be known as the father of America's nuclear submarines, oversaw the proceedings. Rickover asked whether all the prototypes had been stress tested. The representatives from all the major manufacturers assured him that they had been. According to Uncle Sol, my grandfather, with his heavy Yiddish accent, asked "So vat's a stress test?" Rickover grinned and declared, "This is a stress test!" and threw all the prototypes out the window, sending them crashing down fifteen floors to the concrete courtyard below. Grandpa's hand-built lamp was the only one still in one piece. Our family won the contract and, to the great pride of my immigrant grandfather, the firm was awarded the Army-Navy "E" (for excellence), which was a *very* big deal during World War II. (My son now has that very prototype. You can see these lamps in every single World War II movie when ships are blinking Morse code messages to each other.)

Although his skill as a metalsmith eventually enabled him to send my father, his firstborn, to NYU and Columbia, Grandfather was never at ease with the English language. He did speak Russian, Yiddish, Polish, and German, the languages of the New York ghetto at the beginning of the twentieth century.

As Dad's fame turned into an avalanche, he tried to impress his father by showing him his glowing press clippings. But Grandpa held the peasant's firm belief that unless a man worked with his hands or was a doctor or a professor, he was a thief. Therefore, his sense of propriety inhibited him from ever speaking of whatever it was his eldest son did to earn a living.

Finally, one Sunday afternoon when I was eighteen, my grandfather looked up from his glass of schnapps after the traditional weekly family dinner at the unpretentious home in Brooklyn where he lived with his third wife, Gussie, and proclaimed, "Mine son Moishe is a famous man."

All of us were dumbfounded.

It was at that moment we learned that New York's Yiddish-language newspaper, *The Jewish Daily Forward*, had run a feature article on Morris. Never before had it occurred to any of us that because Grandpa could not read English, this was the first he had learned of his son's accomplishments. And he was curious; it seemed possible to Grandpa that the family honor might *not* be in jeopardy. My father, too, was delighted that at last *his* father had seen Morris's name in print.

"Moishe, so tell me, you do something with the buildings?"

"Yes, Pop, I do buildings."

"So, you build the buildings?"

"No, Pop, I'm an architect. I design the buildings."

(Shaking his head in incomprehension): "You lend the money for the buildings?"

(Sighing): "No, Pop, I don't lend the money."

(Head tilted and squinting): "You maybe own the buildings?"

(Despairing): "No, Pop."

(Leaning forward in high squint): "Moishe, so what do you do with the buildings?"

(For the first time trying to explain to a family member what in fact he does do): "Pop, I sort of draw pictures of the buildings."

"And from this you make a living?"

"Yes, Pop."

"Moishe, YOU'RE A DEVIL!"

I've always thought of this as a pretty good definition of the profession. So have some of my clients.

If your parents don't meet and fall in love and have children, you don't get born. That's indisputable. But having made that statement, I must add that my parents never should have had kids. My mother was all about status, perception of status, and feeling superior to everyone in her world. Both of my parents were completely self-absorbed, and I'm sure they had kids simply because in middle-class Jewish society in the 1930s having two perfect children was a social imperative. They had little or no interest in my brother Richard and me, seizing every opportunity to leave us in the care of assorted uncles and aunts and housekeepers. The four of us took exactly one vacation as a family, and that was in part because my father was working on a job in D.C., so we all piled into the car and went to Washington, and then on down to Virginia.

Morris (known as Mo), my father, was movie-idol, drop-dead gorgeous. About five foot eight and slightly paunchy, he dressed in conservative suits, white shirts, and—always—a bow tie. That was his signature. The lobby of the Fontainebleau, his most famous creation, has a white marble floor with inlaid black marble bow tie shapes. He once admitted to me that he wore bow ties because he could never figure out which tie to wear with which suit. With a bow tie, it makes no difference. Morris had brown eyes and thick black hair that he always wore brushed straight back, revealing a pronounced widow's peak. He never engaged in any sports when I was growing up, but, according to my brother, he used to go to Coney Island and play handball when he was younger. His sole recreation that I remember was to go off by himself and sketch and do watercolor paintings.

My mother, Beatrice or Bea (when she died I found out her birth name actually was Bertha), was about five foot six, with a conventionally pretty face and a pronounced gap between her two front teeth. My father was always painfully shy as a young man, he once told me, and Bea was the first and only girl he ever dated seriously. She was fifteen and filled with self-confidence when they met; he was twenty-three but, even so, overwhelmed by her. Like my father she always wore the nondescript conservative clothes of that era (1930s to 1950s), complete with gloves and hats with veils, as did many women of that place and time. Her affirmation of "self-expression" was to wear gaudy fake jewelry. Ironically, years later, when my parents were living in Miami Beach and the good times were rolling, she finally got the real stuff. My father was retained to replace a famous London restaurant, the Trocadero, that was being torn down to make way for a new road or some other model of progress, and the owners hired him, "the guy that did the Fontainebleau," to design a new Trocadero. The clients were Jewish and well-connected, and offered to get my mother "such a buy!" on emeralds. She commissioned an elaborate emerald necklace with matching earrings, probably the most expensive item she would ever buy. When the two of them got back to Miami, she had cheap paste copies made and wore them all the time. She was paranoid about wearing the real jewels, convinced that if she did, someone would "hit her on the head and steal them." Fancying herself a connoisseur of everything, she always said that no one could tell the difference between the paste and the real gems. What she meant was that *she* could not tell the difference. Later I learned from my sister-in-law, Dick's wife, that everyone could tell my mother's "jewels" were paste, and people wondered why the wife of a rich and famous architect was wearing cheap costume jewelry.

Bea was not raised as an observant Jew. The family was well-off, manufacturing and selling Perlman Pianos. My mother and her parents lived in the Bay Ridge section of Brooklyn, a WASP area. My grandmother was a little old Jewish lady who never spoke English and dressed entirely in black. My grandfather was a regular "Yankee" who wore spats and insisted that his youngest daughter was to be raised as a princess. I have a picture of her in full riding habit, sitting on her stoop in Brooklyn. According to my mother, her father lived most of the week in Manhattan to be near the factory and would come back to Brooklyn for *Shabbos*, bearing all sorts of smoked fish, bagels, and other Jewish culinary delights not then obtainable in that section of Brooklyn, and then return to Manhattan on Sunday morning. My mother hated him.

My mother and father met at a party on Avenue J in Brooklyn. We wound up living just a few blocks from where they first encountered one another. She was quite conniving even as a teenager. As she liked to boast, "All my friends were going with doctors, lawyers, and accountants, so going with an architect was something special and unique." How's that for a noble reason for wedlock?

My mother graduated from Hunter College. I don't believe she actually ever worked, except for one year during World War II when there was a critical need for teachers. That I remember because I transferred to the public school where she taught so she could take me with her to work.

Nor did she do much housework or cooking, since we always had a *"shvartse"* for that. I ended up relating to these nice black maids far more than I ever did to my own mother. I remember that when she fired one, named Mary, who had been with us for a long time, I cried inconsolably for days. My mother berated me for being such a sissy, saying she would just hire another one.

Ironically, my mother, coming from a comfortable background, was one of the cheapest human beings on the planet. It was my father, after a childhood spent in the New York ghettos, who never gave much of a damn about money. Bea always bought fruit and vegetables that were going bad because "they are much cheaper and they taste the same." If there were four leftover Del Monte canned string beans from supper, she would save them and then at the end of the weekend combine all this sodden dreck with leftover scraps of meat and stale bread, and mash them together to make "hamburgers." Not surprisingly, in general I tried to avoid food. Early pictures of me show a rail-thin little boy. When I was in high school, some friends and I stopped at a luncheonette, and my friends all ordered hamburgers. I couldn't imagine why anyone would voluntarily eat one of these noxious concoctions, having experienced only my mother's version. Being desperately hungry, I took a bite out of one and had an epiphany, realizing instantly that there was a world of great-tasting food outside my home. My mother, of course, considered herself the world's best cook, so she disdained ever eating out. She could cook better than any restaurant, so why spend all that money? The only type of cooking even she could not fake was Chinese food, which we, like many others in our neighborhood, had every Sunday evening. That's why I later learned to cook, and specialize in, Chinese cuisine.

In 1940, when I was four, my parents bought a modest three-story wood-frame house in the Flatbush section of Brooklyn, a middle-class house on a block of similar middle-class structures. It stood out in the neighborhood because Morris had it painted red, white, and blue. What was truly unique was the interior, which Morris transformed into a temple of Art Moderne. There was a bay window on the first floor in the living room, and inside that window my father made a planter faced with real, original Delft tiles that he scrounged from some of the original Dutch homes that were then being torn down in the Flatlands section of Brooklyn. He designed all of the furniture and had everything in the house custom-made. At the time he was still working for a contractor and had his own construction crew. Morris hand-painted designs on the wooden armoires and headboards. There was a wall of beautifully designed wood paneling, and when you pressed a certain area, a hidden door materialized, which allowed you to go from the living room to the kitchen without walking through the dining room. The dining room had a black-and-white zebra-striped linoleum floor, and the back wall was a mirror, which made the room look enormous. Running the length of the mirrored wall was an invisibly supported glass shelf, which itself disappeared, so that dishes placed on it seemed to float on air. This was a variation of the display windows he installed in the storefront businesses he designed.

The kitchen was my father's masterpiece. He had designed a showroom for the linoleum industry and he loved working with this "new" material. He curved the floor up to the underside of the kitchen cabinets so there would be no corners to catch the dirt. He had also designed a pavilion at the 1939 World's Fair where samples of the then relatively new line called Fiestaware were displayed, and as a result at home we had an extensive set of this most colorful (and today, recently resurgent) type of crockery. The dining area of the kitchen (where all our meals were taken) was a three-quarter circular form with vertical stripes of red and white linoleum, while the circular settee at its base was blue leatherette. Yep, it was Uncle Sam's hat. No question about the loyalty of the Lapidus family.

I think my father was so inventive with the house and poured his soul into this creation because it was the first one he could design for himself without a client to satisfy or the need to "sell" anything. He often lamented that his architecture, whether retail or hospitality facilities, was always out there "selling." With our house, his only goal was to express himself. When I designed my own co-op in Manhattan in 1985, I experienced the same sense of freedom. For an architect, being your own client is wonderful and liberating.

I must confess that I never really appreciated how special our house was during my childhood. What we grow up with seems "normal" and often is taken for granted. I was always surprised by my friends' reactions when they first entered our house. Their jaws dropped; they had never seen anything like it. Conversely, I always thought their homes, furnished in typical middle-class Brooklyn frumpy styles, were kind of exotic. I look at the photos of my home—long since demolished—and am awestruck by the brilliantly innovative design. It was my father's work at its best. I can but wonder at the creativity and, yes, wonderfully playful humor that this man possessed. It was clear that his whole being was expressed in his work, and I almost never saw the personal side of him. What a pity. He was a brilliant architect and a lousy father. I'd say I broke even in the overall scheme of things.

My world was Dickensian in its rules, strictures, and terrors. My brother and I were not allowed in the living room unless we were invited. In our dining room, with the zebra-striped floor, Dick and I were not permitted to step on the white linoleum, only the black portions. Nor were we allowed to talk when my father came home; he was not to be disturbed. I do not remember ever having a conversation with him when I was a boy.

For the most part, other than making sure Dick and I obeyed their rules, Morris and Bea ignored us. I didn't exactly go out of my way to make them notice me, either, as their "attentions" usually were unpleasant. When I was about twelve, for example, I decided to become a Cub Scout. Because I joined Cub Scouts just one year before I "graduated" to full-fledged Boy Scout, I didn't have time to earn any merit badges during the cub year. To my surprise, my parents actually showed up at the ceremony where I graduated from Cub Scout to Boy Scout—no doubt because the event took place on the next block. Noting that the other cubs had won numerous badges, my father's only comment was, "What's the matter with you? How come you're the only one with no awards?" His disparaging remark still bothers me.

Actually, Morris and Bea didn't seem to treat Dick and me all that differently from the way they dealt with one another. They struck me as being devoted to theirselves as individuals, not as a couple. I never saw any demonstration of affection between them, and looking back, I have the impression they didn't particularly like each other.

Although I had very limited contact with my father, even when he was in the house, there were lots of one-way conversations with my mother, who gave commandments in the form of advice. I think she started lecturing me on the necessity of marrying a rich girl when I was ten.

My brother and I were shipped off to summer camp every year from the age of six, and my parents frequently took extended vacations, some as long as two months, leaving us in the care of any family member who could be dragooned into the task. My mother's favorite "caregiver" was her older sister Rose, who never married. Aunt Rose was either marginally impaired or simply bone stupid; I have never been able to figure out which.

When I was nine, my parents left for another of their long trips, and Rose moved in with us. One day Dick started having severe stomach pains, and they kept getting worse. Dick, the more intelligent of the two of us (he became a very successful lawyer in Miami), got out his Boy

Scout manual and started reading about first aid. He quickly realized that he was having an attack of appendicitis and asked Rose to call our family physician. Dr. Berner lived on the next block, and in those happy days, physicians made house calls.

Rose insisted that all Dick had was a bellyache. She said she wasn't about to waste money on a doctor when all Dick needed was an enema, which she gave him. This caused his appendix to burst. I remember the ambulance coming to the house. They somehow reached my parents, who came rushing back, arriving when Dick had already been admitted to intensive care with peritonitis.

Looking at my critically ill brother, my mother, with one of her typically theatrical flourishes, cried, "Dick, you must live! If you recover, you can have anything you want."

"Anything?" he asked.

"Anything!"

They had always forbidden us to have pets.

"I want a dog!"

My mother, ever the drama queen, and probably expecting him to die, promised, "If you get well, we will get you any kind of dog you want."

Dick, thirteen and at death's door, already was the nascent lawyer. Sensing triumph, he rallied and recovered.

True to her word, we got a dalmatian.

Years passed. Domino the dalmatian became a part of our household, beloved by my brother and me as much as he was despised by my parents.

When Dick went away to college, Domino, deprived of his master, became more and more unruly.

One day, no Domino.

My mother explained that Domino was so unhappy, cooped up in the house without Dick, that she had found a farm in Connecticut where the farmer wanted a good watchdog. She told us that Domino loved his new home, where he could run over the fields and play all day long.

We were kids; we bought the story.

About forty years passed.

One evening when I was visiting in Florida, we all went out to eat. In the restaurant, my mother was telling some boring story that I was only half listening to. Then she said, ". . . like the time we put Domino down."

My fifty-eight-year-old brother looked like someone had hit him between the eyes. "YOU DID WHAT TO MY DOG?"

And so childhood ended.

A year or two later I was on vacation with some friends in their condo on St. Croix. My host Jerry came down to the beach to tell me I had a telephone call from my brother. Dick, like my parents, lived in Miami. He and I usually speak only about twice a year when we exchange birthday greetings, so I knew something was up.

When I picked up the phone, Dick said, "Alan, Mom's gone to a farm in Connecticut."

Jerry came into the room to find me literally rolling on the floor, laughing so hard my sides were hurting.

"What's up?" Jerry asked me.

Between guffaws, I replied, "My mother just died!"

Jerry has never regarded me as completely normal ever since. But then again, he never met Beatrice Lapidus. After recovering from my floor show and pulling myself together, I made my way to Miami for the funeral. If the greatest gift a parent can bestow is to not burden his or her children with sorrow when the end arrives, Beatrice was the gold standard mother of all time.

My salvation as a child was the refuge of the homes of friends. I was always amazed to be in an atmosphere where parents actually liked and interacted with their children. When I was five, my best friend was David Davis, who lived across the street. David and I were inseparable; I spent more time in his house than in mine. His father was a writer for the *Truth or Consequences* radio show. In 1946, when David and I were ten, the Davises moved to California, where there were more opportunities for scriptwriters. I grieved as I would a death. As I wasn't much for writing letters—and my mother could care less that I had one fewer friend— I lost track of David.

About a quarter century later, when I was thirty-five or so and newly divorced, I was watching television with my son. *The Newhart Show* was on, and Bob's next-door neighbor was a divorced airline pilot named Howard who cared for his six-year-old son between trips. The pilot was talking to his son and asking him how things were going, and the kid answered, "I had a lot of fun. 'Uncle Harry' stayed over for three nights."

"Uncle Harry?"

This was a joke that could have been written only by someone my age who had recently been divorced. I looked at the credits and saw that the show's writer/producer was David Davis. I sent a letter to David at MTM Productions, asking if he was the same David Davis who had moved away from Brooklyn in 1946, and had he taken my model PT boat with him? I had been lonely in the bathtub ever since.

I received back an immediate reply: "Sorry about the PT boat, but it was wartime, and anything goes."

David suggested that since he would be coming to New York soon to film the main title for his new show, *Rhoda*, we should meet in the lobby of the St. Moritz the following Wednesday morning at 9 o'clock. Arriving at 8:30, I realized that I hadn't seen David for twenty-five years. I wondered if I would recognize him. I did. We ended up hugging and kissing amid all the scurrying businessmen who probably had us pegged for a couple of lovers. Bringing ourselves up to date, we learned that our lives had paralleled. David, too, was divorced and was going with a lady who turned out to be a virtual clone of the lady I was seeing at the time. That was before he and Julie Kavner, who played Rhoda's younger sister on the TV show and would later play Marge and her sisters on *The Simpsons*, became husband and wife. Most important, despite the long break, our renewed friendship endured.

I discovered girls when I was about fifteen. I began practically living at the house of Shelly Greenberg. Shelly was not quite the girl next door, but she did live on the next block, at Avenue K (which was the dividing line between single-family houses and duplexes) and East Eighth Street. She was tall, about five foot ten, had ice-blue eyes, high cheekbones, and black hair. I fell in love with her as soon as I grew about as tall as her. Her parents were loud, argumentative, and very loving. My mother just about had a stroke, because Shelly's father drove a taxicab. My father, as usual, was totally disengaged. Because of my mother's attitude toward her, Shelly and I spent most of our time at her house. Thoroughly intimidated by my parents because she knew my mother hated her and was giving me grief about seeing her, Shelly visited my house only during afternoons when my parents weren't home.

Shelly and I were classmates at Midwood High School. Midwood was everything a school should be. It opened in 1940 as an "experimental" school and, as such, attracted the best and the brightest teachers in the New York City school system. Creativity was emphasized and independent scholarship rewarded. To this day, even in an ethnically changed neighborhood, it remains at the top of the list for students receiving science prizes and the best college placements. It was there that my earliest attempts at writing bore fruit and gave me a sense of identity. I was the editor of the school paper, wrote the class play, and was literary editor of the yearbook. At graduation I was voted "Class Writer." My classmate, Erich Segal, the future author of *Love Story*, was voted most likely to succeed. Erich actually lived outside the Midwood district but had some sort of pull, as I recall, which enabled him to attend Midwood. His father was a rabbi, and Erich had an air of self-assured authority. He was elected "mayor of the city of Midwood," which would have been class president in a more conventional school, except that Midwood's student government organization was modeled loosely on the New York City government. Shelly was named "Class Artist." Allen Konigsberg lived at Avenue K and East Tenth Street, a half block from me but on the opposite side of Avenue K, the dividing line between the lower middle class and the middle middle class, and was one grade ahead at both Midwood and P.S. 99. Hardly anyone paid much attention to the funny-looking, skinny, little red-haired kid with big glasses. Just see *Stardust Memories* and you will get his take on our school days.

Midwood had about four thousand students, and the student body was overwhelmingly Jewish. I had figured out by then that Jews were probably not a majority in other places. To find out a bit more about the outside world, I decided to go to Trinity College in Hartford, Connecticut.

At Trinity, I did indeed discover what it was like when Jews were a minority—big-time. When I entered in 1954, Trinity had a total enrollment of 836, exclusively male. There were only two Jews in my class, and one of them was "passing" as a gentile. Chapel was compulsory, every morning at 7:30. And it definitely was not ecumenical as it is now, but Orthodox High Episcopalian.

I had no sooner gotten settled in my dorm than I made the ritual pilgrimage to East Hartford to a store called the English Shop so I could be accoutered as a proper young WASP. The next week I went home for the Jewish High Holy Days, an event that was never ignored in my household because it gave my mother an opportunity to show off her latest wardrobe. Being my mother's son, I was eager to show off as Joe College, so I wore my newly acquired navy blue Trinity blazer. As we walked to our seats, the rabbi, who had bar mitzvahed me five years earlier, was staring at me as a vampire would regard the True Cross. In fact, that is exactly what he was regarding. It hadn't dawned on me that the Trinity crest consisted of the cross on a background of the papal crook and the bishop's miter.

I have rarely been as consistently miserable as I was at Trinity. This was my first encounter with overt anti-Semitism. All the social activities were conducted by the fraternities, and all the fraternities were restricted, meaning no Jews. Consequently, I was barred from all the social occasions that make up so much of college life. I was also referred to as a "kike" well within my earshot.

To put the icing on the cake, I discovered that although Midwood had given me a wonderful education, I was not completely prepared for college academics. In high school when we wrote a book report, it was about our understanding of the book's meaning and its style, done very informally, almost stream of consciousness. I had no idea what *ibid.* meant, had never been required to create footnotes, and could not grasp such structured methods. In French class at Trinity, I was having trouble understanding the nuances of conjugations, subjunctives, and the like. Even though I had spent the previous summer bumming through France, becoming reasonably familiar with the language, and was the only one in my class who could actually speak French, I came close to flunking the course, winding up with a D, based on an A in the lab portion and an F in the course work.

By the end of the first year I was on four, count 'em, four probations: academic probation; chapel probation (I had missed several mornings); social probation (I preferred to stay snuggled up with Shelly on Sunday nights and often came back late on Monday); and gym probation (I was lousy at sports and these guys took all that stuff so seriously!).

My sophomore year, my parents moved to Miami Beach and gave me their car with the proviso that I drive it down to them at the end of the year. Showing up on campus in 1955 in a three-year-old Oldsmobile convertible (aquamarine and white with a red leather interior—my mother had gotten a bargain on it) immediately caused my prestige to soar. Such was the value system in an era when very few college students had cars and those who did generally drove eight-year-old Chevys or Fords. I started getting invited as a "guest" to functions and dances. I loaned the car a lot. I was no doubt at least as popular as that fat kid, Flounder, who got to use a family car in *Animal House,* to the delight of his fraternity brothers.

By the end of my sophomore year in June 1956, I had proved my point and was off all the probations. I decided to quit while I was ahead. Halfway through my undergraduate program, I decided to take off for a year to live in Manhattan and work as a draftsman, so I could see whether I liked the profession of architecture. My writing at the time was focusing more and more on architecture and its significance. If I really had an aptitude for architecture, I felt I would rather do it than write about it. Besides, being in the city, I could spend a lot more time with Shelly, who was going to Pratt Institute for a degree in commercial art.

I transferred to Columbia's School of General Studies, attending at night and working for Skidmore, Owings & Merrill as a junior draftsman/office boy during the day. The year 1956–57 was also momentous for me because I got my first apartment, a fourth-floor walkup studio in a crumbling old brownstone on 106th Street between West End Avenue and Riverside Drive. By the end of the year I was still unsettled and unsure, but I knew I had to take more time off to understand what I was about, and I also wanted to marry Shelly.

Shelly and I got married in June of 1957, three months before my twenty-first birthday. I was scheduled for induction into the army in September, and with my departure imminent, my parents no longer had any (financial) control of me—a prime reason for the whole army bit. Had it been 1967, I probably would have wound up in San Francisco wearing flowers in my hair. But this was 1957, so I joined the military. The army became my path for self-realization. I developed the self-confidence to be a man by doing my best to become the number one damn soldier in the entire Sixth Army.

I told my parents in April or May of 1957 that I was about to be drafted, neglecting to advise them that I had volunteered for the draft, and they were unaware that the draft was inactive at that time. I also informed them that Shelly and I planned to elope, so farewell, good-bye, it's been nice. My mother called several days later from Miami, where they were living, and, true to her flair for histrionics, informed me in a halting voice that she had just been to the doctor and had been diagnosed with heart disease, so it was doubtful that she was long for this earth. If we would *please* "elope" in Miami, she would arrange for us to be married in the rabbi's study, just the immediate family, and as a token of their remorse over having given us such a hard time over the years, they would pay for a wonderful honeymoon to the Virgin Islands. She declared that this might be her last chance to see me, as she probably would be gone when I returned from the army. Her last wish was to see her darling boy happily wed.

Being young and stupid, I bought it. With much trepidation, Shelly agreed. Her mother agreed to come, but her father, shamed by his inability to pay for any kind of a wedding for his daughter and humiliated that the Lapidus family was giving us largesse, refused to attend.

I bet you can write the script by now.

Shelly and I flew down to Miami and had a quiet little ceremony in the rabbi's study, just as my mother had promised—with only my parents, my brother, and Shelly's mother present. Afterward my mother suggested we go to the Algiers Hotel (which Morris had designed) for "a little brunch." We walked into the grand ballroom, where three hundred people, most of whom I had never seen before, were waiting. The band struck up "Here Comes the Bride." I thought Shelly would die on the spot. Her mother was mortified, and I felt like crawling into a hole in the ground. It was a less than auspicious start to a marriage.

The highlight of our marriage, from my mother's standpoint, came thirteen years later (yes, Bea was still very much alive then, despite her foretelling her imminent demise in 1957), after Shelly and I drifted apart and got divorced. My mother felt completely vindicated when we split up.

Later, when I married my second wife, Nancy, I decided we should go to Miami to introduce her to my family, who by this time were all living there. This included uncles, aunts, cousins, and my brother.

I had rented a private room for dinner in a nice restaurant. What to do about my parents, from whom I had become estranged because of many episodes over the years? I called my mother, who knew about my second marriage via Aunt Evelyn, and told her I was having a family dinner to introduce my wife to the family. Since she still qualified as "family"—just barely—she and my father were invited too.

My mother ordered us over to her apartment immediately. In no mood to go there and pay homage, I replied, "Come to the dinner or don't come," and hung up.

I later learned from Aunt Evelyn that Bea called to ask for advice—which was interesting in and of itself because my parents loathed Evelyn and Sol. In fact, when Uncle Sol retired, and he was the last living relative my father had, Sol and Ev moved to Miami. My mother was furious, and she said (her exact words), "They think they can move to Florida and enter our social circle. Well, they have another thing coming—they are not of our class!"

Now, with my second marriage a fait accompli, my mother kvetched to Aunt Ev, "They got married without inviting us, he married some shiksa, and now he wants us to meet her. What do you think I should do?" (As was the norm on family matters, Morris was willing to go along with whatever Beatrice decided.)

Evelyn: "Fold them both into your arms and shower them with gifts!"

Bea: "THAT'S NOT WHAT I HAD IN MIND!"

But they did appear at my banquet; the loss of face would have been too great if they hadn't showed up. Of course they behaved with their usual frosty hauteur.

My mother's sole comment to me was, "Well, she's a nurse. When you get sick, maybe she'll take care of you."

Now I'm married to my soul mate Caroline. Both my parents died several years before my romance with Caroline began, so Caroline never met them. I consider it a good omen.

3

You're in the Air Force/
Marines/Army Now

I had joined the air force ROTC unit at Trinity, figuring that since I loved flying, I could become an air force pilot and thus get free of my mother. I was planning to continue at Columbia architecture school, but they dropped ROTC, barring me from transferring to that program in Morningside Heights. Instead, I joined the Marine Corps reserve.

That earned me a new uniform, my second. We drilled on weekday evenings and weekends. I was literally and personally horrified by the marines' battle strategy, a remnant of their success ousting the Japanese from island hellholes like Guadalcanal and Iwo Jima in the South Pacific not much more than a decade earlier: "Fuck all this fancy flanking strategy and shit. You guys just go charging right up to the pillbox, and one of youse will probably live long enough to throw a grenade—just like we done at Iwo." Even though we were not particularly mad at anyone at the time, this was not a thrilling prospect. I was also getting tired of being hit on the helmet and called a "Yid." I will say that in the Marine Corps they at least called me a "kike" to my face, instead of snickering behind my back the way some fellow students had at Trinity. And slugging a guy who said something like that to me was considered a desirable marine reaction, while it probably would have gotten me expelled from college.

I finally realized I had sort of messed things up and not made the cleverest of decisions when I joined the marines. Yes, the uniform sure was spiffy, and when I hitchhiked back to New York from Hartford in uniform (in those days it was still safe to hitchhike), I always got a ride immediately. And if I went into a bar in my uniform (which I did only after drill sessions with the other marines), we were guaranteed to end up in a fight with a bunch of sailors. (The hatred between marines and sailors was in part because one of the duties of marines is to be the police force for the navy onboard ships.) But anti-Semitism was rife in the Marine Corps and the prospects for survival in the event of any international unpleasantness seemed dim, given that the DIs (drill instructors) appeared to salivate while talking about how many of their buddies were killed or mutilated, with an emphasis on all the gory details. I thought it might be a tad healthier to transfer to the navy; after all, it would be a lateral move, since the marines are officially a part of the navy. (I was somewhat naïve, like Private Benjamin, in this regard.) I found a nice naval reserve officer who said he would love to have me, but when I broached the subject to my marine commanding officer, he ordered me to drop down and give him twenty (push-ups, that is). He resolved that such traitorous thoughts on my part might best be addressed by putting me on active duty in some distant and unpleasant locale.

Thus it was that I went down to my friendly draft board and volunteered for the army. Of course there were no computers in 1957, so when I neglected to mention the fact that I was engaged to another (the marines), the army had no way of cross-checking. And so I became one of the precious few who have worn the uniform of the air force, the marines, and the army.

In the fall of 1957, I was inducted into the army and went off to Fort Dix, New Jersey, to learn how to be a warrior. My parents never once visited me. On the first weekend that we were permitted to have visitors, I was the only one with no guests. Shelly had no way of getting to Fort Dix, and my parents were, well, my parents.

When I enlisted in the army, the kindly sergeant who conducted my induction interview, where they determine what special skills you possess, swore that with my unique qualifications, I would be assigned to the MOS (military occupational specialty) for which I was suited. I had spent many summers and school vacations being an apprentice draftsman at my father's office, so he assured me that I would be sent to Fort Belvoir, Virginia, the army's drafting and engineering center.

How strange, then, that when I arrived at my duty station, Fort Leonard Wood, Missouri, it didn't look at all like Fort Belvoir, Virginia. It was a freezing late November day out there at this base in the Ozark Mountains. We new soldiers were greeted with a communication emblazoned on the company bulletin board: "WELCOME TO CAMP LEONARD WOOD. WHEN THE WORLD NEEDS AN ENEMA, THIS IS WHERE THEY STICK IT IN."

Even worse, my brand-new "specialty" was combat engineer. Another comforting message informed us that the motto of the combat engineers was, "The first ones in, the last ones out." It turned out that the combat engineers have always had a dubious distinction: the highest casualty rates in the entire U.S. Army. You can imagine how elated I was. If you didn't get killed or mangled in training (we had 12 percent casualties in training), just wait until you experienced actual combat with enemy forces.

Graduation day! We were lined up on a bitter-cold Saturday morning in February 1958, the gray skies pissing down snow and sleet, to await our orders for our permanent duty stations. The CO read out a name and an assignment. Every one was for "Eighth U.S. Army." Translation: Korea! The war had been over for five years, but the Chinese and North Koreans had seeded the country with thousands of mines made of plastic, which rendered them impossible to locate with metal detectors. The state of the art in mine detection at the time was to send out squads of combat engineers with hand probes. Consequently, there was a permanent and pressing need for replacements. I was terrified.

But when the commander reached my name, he uttered, "Sixth U.S. Army." Given my history with the armed forces, my immediate thought was, "What could *possibly* be worse than Korea?" Turns out God had finally decided to smile on me; the Sixth Army was based near the paradiselike setting of Carmel, California. How come the only two guys in my company who got sent to California instead of Korea were an Oklahoma farm boy named Richard Crusinberry and me? Maybe for me it was because the Jewish God noticed that the night before, while I was walking disconsolately around the base, not even realizing it was Friday evening, I heard the chants of Shabbat services emanating from the post's Jewish chapel—in which I had never set foot—and, in desperate need of some form of comfort, I stepped inside. In that familiar environment, reminiscent of so many peaceful times in the synagogue in

Brooklyn, I managed to calm down enough to actually get some sleep that night.

The Sixth Army was based at Fort Ord, California—not only near the resorts of Carmel and Monterey but also not all that far from San Francisco in one direction and Hearst Castle at San Simeon (which I first viewed from the turret of an M-59 tank) in the other. If the army had its own version of the Club Fed brand of "hospitality" in the U.S. prison system, this was it. Before long I was assigned to the Fifty-ninth Engineer Company, attached to the Seventh Cavalry at Camp Roberts in Paso Robles, California, where attendance was mandatory at the Thursday evening showing of *They Died with Their Boots On* (the story of Custer's last stand; he was commander of J Company of the Seventh Cav).

So far, so good, for the most part. Unfortunately, the marines had finally come to realize that I wasn't still wedded to "the Corps." Before long a letter from "USMC headquarters" was forwarded to me in California. It notified me that I was being called up for three years of active duty. Being an incurable wiseass, I responded in a letter stating: "I would love to accept your kind invitation but I am otherwise engaged." (Signed) "Alan H. Lapidus, Spec. 4, U.S. Army US51407977."

For some reason, my communication enraged the Marine Corps. I became the subject of a tug-of-war between two commanding generals who represented competing branches of Uncle Sam's fightin' corps. The marines argued that since I had signed on with them first and omitted to tell the army some rather crucial information when I joined up, my army enlistment was invalid. The army's answer was that possession is nine-tenths of the law and they habeased my corpus, meaning my body was theirs. I dreaded to think what would become of me if I had to go back to the marines, although I suspected that if that happened, I wouldn't be in misery (or this world) for long. But through sheer good luck, my army outfit was engaged in top secret work—among other things, testing handheld atomic weapons. The big bang was no "theory" to me. And, yes, that is probably why I no longer have a thyroid gland.

Thanks to my having a security clearance and being such an invaluable trooper, the army emerged victorious in this army-marine game. I breathed a sigh of relief. Make that about a thousand sighs of relief.

4

At Columbia (and Almost Prematurely Ejected)

For a brand-new student of architecture, merely walking onto Columbia's campus and viewing Avery Hall, which housed the School of Architecture, was awe inspiring. Much of the campus had been designed in the late nineteenth century by the renowned classical firm of McKim, Mead & White. The White who was a named partner was the immortal Stanford White. Well, not quite immortal. He was slain in 1906 at the age of fifty-two by Harry K. Thaw, a railroad heir from Pittsburgh. Thaw, a mentally unbalanced and often violent man, was married to Evelyn Nesbit, the infamous teenage showgirl on the red velvet swing whom White had seduced when she was but sixteen.

In addition to the Columbia campus, the White firm designed the Washington Square Arch, the Chicago World's Columbian Exposition of 1893, and just about every other prestigious building in New York around the turn of the twentieth century, including the original Madison Square Garden, where Thaw shot White to death in the arena's rooftop theater.

As architects whose job was to design a school of architecture, members of the firm felt compelled to do their best work. The entire floor system was suspended from the roof of Avery Hall, eliminating the need for columns and giving the studio a light and airy feel. They also provided large windows and skylights for maximum brightness. The building had a studio on each end, with a library separating the two. First- and fourth-year classes were held in the south studio, second and third in the north. The building was filled with warm and collegial spaces that contained drawing paper, drafting tools, and assorted paints, brushes, and inks strewn around in "artistic" disorder. While giving a lecture at the school about ten years ago, I asked the dean to let me revisit the studios. Not a drawing board anywhere. No paints, inks, or paper. Only neat little carrels with CAD (computer-aided design) machines. Stanford White would have been appalled.

The study of architecture generally defied academic categorization when I attended Columbia from 1959 to 1963. The school's identity crisis was representative of the profession as a whole. You had to have had at least two years at a liberal arts college before you could be admitted to a four-year course of study that led to nothing more than a bachelor's degree. That's right: In the same time frame that sane people require to earn a master's degree and start on a Ph.D., or finish college and almost earn a law degree, or go two-thirds of the way through medical school, the hapless architectural student ends up with nothing more than a bachelor's degree.

To put this situation in perspective: In the mid-1970s, *The New York Times* reported that the only architects likely to earn more than $100,000 per year were partners in major firms. And that's after starting fresh out of graduate architecture school with a salary of perhaps $25,000 to $35,000 a year. Meanwhile, young lawyers from top law schools were starting at $75,000 to $85,000 a year—and the disparity only increases with time, then as now. So much for Paul Newman's cinematic helicopter and penthouse office.

My three dozen classmates were an eclectic bunch. Not one of us really understood what an architect actually did. About a third dropped out over the next four years. My best friend at Columbia, Harry Parnass, was the son of German Jews who had fled Berlin in 1938. Harry admitted that when he entered architectural school, he knew the names of only two architects—Frank Lloyd Wright and Morris Lapidus. Our class also included a couple of preppies (Bob Scheadel and Stewart White), a tough Irish working-class kid named O'Connor, and a Greek immigrant, Gus Economou.

The international style was all the rage, and our gods were Mies van der Rohe, Le Corbusier, and Louis Kahn. It was only after several years of education that we came to realize that architects don't change the world after all. At best, they can build structures to reflect and accommodate a changed and changing world.

A typical day in architecture school might begin with life drawing at 9 o'clock. As you dragged your barely conscious bones to your first class, you were confronted by the vision of a totally nude middle-aged, somewhat saggy model, sitting on a stool slurping a cup of coffee. For two hours. The majority of models were female. Which was fortunate, because the sight of naked men at that hour usually put me off my feed. I was awake and alert enough, though, to wonder why the women were completely naked, but the men always wore jockstraps.

Of course life drawing was much more than an exercise in voyeurism of a sort. Architects in that age, when God was in his heaven and computers had not yet usurped humans, were required to be able to sketch. The best way to polish your skills as an artist is to draw the nude female, preferably with many folds. Producing quick sketches of a complex human form (the usual exercises were one-minute and five-minute poses) while the models changed poses forced you to quickly organize the drawing and practice shading and shadow work. As a general rule, if you can draw a complex form quickly, sketching buildings is a snap.

Only three members of our class were married. Shelly and I were wed in 1957, but we spent much of our first year of marital life apart while she completed her final year at Pratt Institute and the U.S. Army was teaching me how to be a ferocious warrior. After she graduated in June 1958, she came out to Paso Robles, where I was stationed, and the following year we moved back to Manhattan when I entered Columbia. We found a $75-a-month studio apartment in a beautiful old building on Riverside Drive at 117th Street, two blocks from Columbia. Our place was on the first floor in the back, with a spectacular view of an air shaft—we had to listen to the radio to find out what we should wear when we went out.

Shelly was more or less the den mother of my class. She was a working commercial artist (at *Scholastic Magazine*, where she was an assistant art director), so she already knew how to draw, paint, and render, while we architecture students were trying to learn those skills. Shelly would come to the drafting room after work and help anyone who was having problems with a project. The studio at the School of Architecture was the best place for her to find me. School was an all-encompassing experience that occupied my entire existence. Since the boards we worked on were too large and fragile to transport out of the building, everyone worked in the studio until the small hours of the morning. In those days, the way to spot the School of Architecture at any university was to look for a building with all the lights on at 3 o'clock in the morning. Since our class was small and we spent as much as eighteen hours a day together (there were no electives, so we went to classes en masse), we pretty much bonded as a group. One of my classmates, with whom I had dinner about eight years ago, remarked that all the guys in the class (meaning nearly the entire class, since it included a total of one woman) had been in love with Shelly.

After a couple hours as artistes, we washed the charcoal or Conté Crayon off our hands and walked across campus to the engineering building. There we would pour concrete and place steel reinforcing bars, or rebars, in the concrete, or go to a class that enlightened us on the wonders of plumbing, heating, ventilating, and electrical engineering. At least our mechanical engineering professor had a wry sense of humor. One lecture concerned the path of wastewater from the toilet bowl after you flushed it—and this was our last class before lunch! Professor Wright would try to explain the function of plumbing pipes. We could understand such concepts as cold water supply, hot water supply, and wastewater return, but something called a vent pipe generated looks of incomprehension. "Water displaces air as it goes through a conduit, so it must be vented to avoid a vacuum," the professor explained. Huh? "Let's put it this way—suppose that every toilet seat in the Empire State Building was occupied at the same time, and everyone flushed at the same moment. Without a vent pipe, no one would be able to get up from the seat until the guy on the top floor opened his mouth." Now, *he* was a teacher!

Our other courses contained a mishmash of art, science, technology, architectural history, and city planning. One of the rules we gradually became aware of was that an architect should never give a simple description or explanation if an obscure or pretentious one was available.

Verbal obfuscation was essential for imbuing heroic significance to what were essentially arbitrary design decisions.

One class introduced us to the various types of historical structures. Our pompous and pretentious professor, John Haskins was his name, announced one day that we would study a primitive, portable, demountable, organic tension structure. A tepee! He also liked to propound such overintellectualized bullshit as: Since a building normally has four sides, and since the sun is on a trajectory from southeast to southwest, a structure should have four different façades to deal with the varying positions of the sun. No windows on the southwest, small windows on the southeast, slit windows on the south, and picture windows on the north. Blessedly, I don't remember much else from his rants.

Each afternoon was devoted to design studio. The design class was what had brought us to the graduate school in the first place. We sat in the lofty studios on the fourth and top floor of Avery Hall, where the aesthetic god of the moment would try to imbue us with the true light of deathless architecture. On my first day, I sat nervously at my drafting table, which was a board two feet wide and three feet long, freshly covered in green laminene (a plasticized cardboard universally used to cover drafting and drawing boards so as to provide a smooth surface on which to draw). There I was, ready and eager to receive wisdom and guidance. Our instructor, an effete German in his late forties named Gerhard Kallmann, was both a slavish disciple of the Bauhaus and a founder of the blessedly short-lived style known as the New Brutalism. According to this school of thought, raw concrete was the ideal finish for practically any building. The concrete should be so coarse that even the marks made by the form boards (the wooden patterns into which concrete is poured) would not be ground off but left as the only decoration. Kallmann won the competition to design a new Boston City Hall—thankfully, one of the few extant specimens of this style. Practically all the good citizens of Boston hate the building.

About five foot eight, slender, and immaculately dressed in his European-cut suits, Kallmann was given to uttering nonsense such as, "A true architect should be able to go to the building site and draw exquisite sketches of the building in the dirt with the tip of his umbrella." Once, after he failed to show up for class on a beautiful spring day, Kallmann explained, "In the springtime one should dress in one's finery and promenade down Fifth Avenue like a true gentleman." Kallmann spent the year trying to inflict upon us a love of stark, unadorned concrete and steel, along with total disdain for any ornaments or decoration.

Once Kallmann told us to bring in "an aesthetic object" the next day and place it on our boards, to help him gain insight into what we each considered to be good design. The next day, the budding aesthetes who were my classmates produced an assortment of vases, sculptures, flatware, jewelry, and the like. Fresh out of the army, I placed an MK-II hand grenade in the corner of my board.

Just so he and I understood each other.

In actual point of fact, the grenade was not live but one I had had to defuse as part of my combat engineer training—stand in a concrete block bunker, pull the pin, release the "spoon" (which means it will explode in three to five seconds), and, while it is hissing in your hand, calmly unscrew the fuse mechanism and toss the mechanism over the wall. I felt I had earned the right to "appropriate" it for my hope chest. Kallmann took one look at my trophy, again rolled his eyes up toward the deities, and did not even stop to say a word.

Thankfully, the likes of Kallmann and Haskins were counterbalanced by faculty heroes such as Eugene Raskin. He was in every classical sense of the word a Teacher with a capital "T" who schooled us in the sociology of architecture. Raskin also taught us that being a human being was a vital part of being an architect. There was a vast difference, he explained, between what we should do as architects and what pure technicians like engineers wanted to do. Raskin introduced us to the work of engineers and our interaction with them as architects. As with all vital life lessons, I remember what he said practically verbatim:

"Engineers got their job titles because in ancient times these were the guys that designed the engines of war, such as catapults, battering rams, and the like. But even in the best-run societies, there are these unfortunate interludes of peace, when the rulers had to think of something else to keep these guys employed. So they started by having them design battlements and fortifications, and then had them turn their attention to building for the church (which often was financing the wars) and the nobility.

"Now, these engineers think in terms of efficiency, and efficiency is their sole objective. Therefore, if you are designing a high-rise urban hotel [which I would have occasion to do] and you want to enrich the experience of the guests [as I would], you might want to put the swimming pool on the roof, where the guests could have a magnificent view of the city, enjoy the cooling breeze, and be far from the urban noise and dirt. This, of course, will horrify the structural engineer. He will think you are nuts, since putting such a heavy load of water at the top of the building will require extra reinforcing all the way to the ground. Not to mention that the mechanical engineer will be horrified by the thought of pumping that much water up to the roof. So from the engineer's point of view, the only really logical place to put the pool is in the lowest level of the cellar — no additional load and right next to the water supply.

"In short, if an architect designed a building without an engineer, it would probably fall down. If an engineer designed a building without an architect, they would have to tear it down."

About thirty years later, when I designed the Crowne Plaza Times Square at Broadway and Forty-eighth Street, I placed the swimming pool on the roof. Although it's on the lower roof (fifteenth floor), it has proved so popular that the pool and adjacent health club have been expanded drastically and opened to outside members. The outside memberships have been a huge source of revenue, enough to pay for the additional structural and mechanical costs.

My mentor, Gene Raskin, who had his own successful architectural practice, decided at one point to close his office and buy a sailboat, and he and his wife, Francesca, spent the next year sailing around the world. Many of his friends and colleagues inquired with shock and horror why he would shut down a lucrative practice. His answer was one of the precepts I've lived by: "If I don't enjoy my life, who will?" He also spoke against compromising one's principles as an architect: "When I look at myself in the mirror each morning, I want to feel only aesthetic disgust (as opposed to moral disgust)."

The two main reasons I wanted to go to Columbia were that my father had gone there and Gene was there. Gene was also a well-known folksinger, and I, too, was a folkie with ambitions of doing it for a living. While I was at Columbia, I played at several local coffeehouses, including the First Born at Amsterdam and 104th. One of my steady fans was a geeky Columbia College student who had short, curly blond hair and usually wore a shirt and tie. He didn't look at all like "the type," as we folkies liked to think of it. He planned to become an architect and even married one, but ultimately changed careers, exactly the opposite of my dream of becoming a professional folksinger and winding up as an architect. My fan's name was Artie Garfunkel. Art, who received a master's in mathematics, was math tutor for the son of Leo Komarin, my father's chief draftsman and the man who would teach me how to be a draftsman. Years later, 1975, to be exact, I went to see the film *Barry Lyndon*, which had just opened at the Ziegfeld Theater, and Art was sitting in front of me. We started chatting, and I said to him, "Well, you gave up architecture for folk music and I gave up folk music for architecture, and the world is a better place." He laughed.

As a folksinger, I was very much aware of Gene Raskin and his wife's wonderful folk recordings for Elektra Records. They spent many of their summer vacations touring, mainly in Europe, as "Gene and Francesca." Gene wrote the smash hit "Those Were the Days." I ended up singing with them at their regular Thursday evening "hoot" at their apartment on Riverside Drive, ten blocks downtown from my own place on Riverside. These sessions included icons like Theo Bikel, Glen Yarbrough, the Limelighters, and other Upper West Side folkies.

During my training as a combat engineer I had learned how to blow up bridges, buildings, people, and any other being or item the army wanted to terminate with extreme prejudice. It seems that in order to blow up buildings and bridges, it was important to know what kind of loads were carried by every structural element. We were taught this by means of diagrams that demonstrated, in a simple form, stresses in structural frames and whether the stress was in tension or compression. Compression is a force that bears down, while tension is a force that wants to pull apart. The towers of a suspension bridge are in compression, but the strands of wire from which the roadway hangs are in tension. Tension members are best blown by charges on opposite sides, slightly offset from each other to create a shearing blast. Compression members can be blown with the charge on one side, a "kicker."

Our first structures class in architecture school had virtually the same diagrams, except that the forces were quantified in kips (thousands of pounds per square foot) instead of quaint army terms like "little pissant tension" or "big mother of a compression load." Cleaning up my terminology, I became the prodigy of my class in Structures 101.

After four years at Columbia, we had learned how to render in pencil, ink, charcoal, watercolor, and tempera (an opaque paint thicker than pure watercolors and not quite as delicate to work with); how to analyze structural frames; how to determine the strength of welds and rivets; the yield strengths of steel; the bending moments of columns (meaning the forces that make long, slender columns prone to buckling, just as if you were to place a long, slender drinking straw on a table and then put your hand on top and squeeze down; you have to either make the column thick enough to resist this tendency or else build braces into it); and the history of architecture, from the nomads' yerts to high-rise megastructures. We had been made familiar with heat exchangers, Scotch boilers, passive and active solar energy, fluid mechanics, electrical conductivity, and the theory of city planning. For pure aesthetic orgasmic delight, we were taught, you just couldn't beat an unadorned glass box. Little wonder that my father had avoided the Columbia School of Architecture (from which he had graduated in 1926) as the devil would the True Cross.

We had, in short, learned all sorts of skills, except the one that was essential for employment: how to draw construction documents. These are what are still erroneously called "blueprints," a term for the white on blue printing method that was obsolete by the 1960s. None of the architectural firms were hiring architectural graduates to design lofty buildings or plan cities in emerging countries. That would be akin to a recent graduate of journalism school applying to *The New York Times* and asking for a job writing the editorials.

The real meat of the architectural profession is producing the reams of drawings from which buildings are actually built. This work is not glamorous, it is not theoretical, it is not open to debate or philosophy. It is a craft. That secret was never taught to us, for the simple reason that precious few of our teachers, and certainly none of our design professors, had ever actually engaged in this mainstay of the profession. This was why they were teaching.

Buildings are not fashioned from romantically rendered pictures. The drawing must show *exactly* how the bricks fit together, how the windows are made, how they are installed, flashed, waterproofed, and secured. It must show how the plumbing fits with the structural elements, how the telephone lines are placed, how the electric power is distributed, where every electrical outlet is to be, as well as every door hinge, light, air-conditioning duct, bathroom tile, toilet. Anything that is not in the architects' drawings is not destined to be in the finished structure. And once you finish drawing all the details, you get to write about all of it in a voluminous book called "the specifications." The drawings will show a graphic representation of a door and the dimension lines will show its exact size, but the specifications will describe the grade of wood or steel and its fire rating, with cross-referencing to the hardware schedule that describes each and every hinge, closure, striker plate, lock set, keying system, and more. The specs do not stand for "spectacular"; they are not romantic; they won't get Faye Dunaway into the sack. But specs and working drawings do comprise perhaps 98 percent of what architects actually do. And we never learned any of this in school!

When I entered architectural school, we were still in the great conformist Eisenhower era. When John Kennedy was elected the following year, many of my contemporaries and I were galvanized by his charm and wit. Eisenhower was all about our parents; JFK was all about *us*. With our new sense of idealism, we began feeling like we could change the world.

Columbia's campus seemed like a good place to begin our "revolution"—tame though it was by the standards of just a few years later. And I almost became the fall guy.

In my third year at Columbia, I was elected president of the student organization at the School of Architecture. (My close friend Harry Parnass was voted vice president.) My duties included representing both the school at various functions such as those put on by the American Institute of Architects and the student body in its relations with the faculty and school administration. The Columbia campus as it had been designed by McKim, Mead & White was still unspoiled. In 1961, the school received a $2.5 million gift from the megabuilder Uris Corporation toward the

$7 million cost of a new building to house the School of Business Administration. Modestly named Uris Hall, it was to replace a never-finished McKim building called University Hall. Uris had attached one string: Uris itself must be retained to oversee designing and building the new structure. This edifice is an ugly box that was devised to be cheap and quick to erect, featuring a hideous glass curtain wall and mill finish aluminum as its exterior. The whole mess was ghastly, even by the standards of that period, when many of the structures being built in New York ran the gamut from glass curtain walls to glass curtain walls. It certainly *is* possible to create beautiful structures at a university; it was during that era that the Yale campus was greatly enhanced by Eli Saarinen's design for Stiles and Morse colleges and Louis Kahn's design of a new library. Uris and the architect who designed Columbia's business school, Robert S. Hutchins of the Moore & Hutchins firm, decidedly did *not* add to the beauty of the Columbia campus, though. Moreover, the new business school happened to be situated right next to our School of Architecture.

April 17, 1962, the day for groundbreaking ceremonies at the site of this glass turd, arrived. There was a big-time turnout of university officials such as president Grayson Kirk and Business School dean Courtney C. Brown, trustees and other officials, and the university's benefactors, the Uris brothers themselves, as well as the press. Watching from our fourth-floor studio windows as the powerful, the great, and the near-great and near-powerful assembled to honor and glorify the despoliation of a classic campus design—crass commercialism disguised as largesse—all of us architect hopefuls were filled with disgust. An architectural school design studio is stocked, of course, with an abundance of such useful items as poster board, Magic Markers, paints, and brushes. As if by spontaneous combustion, we agreed that this celebration of dross should not take place without us having a say. In short order, we created posters and banners, nailed them to pieces of wood, and then marched down to the gala celebration and stood at the back of the crowd with our signs. Mine read, "NO MORE UGLIES!" Others were equally expressive, and since we were all well trained in graphic design, they were colorful. We neither said anything nor caused any kind of disturbance. We merely stood there looking innocent. But remember—this was in 1963, and protests of this sort had not yet matured into the full-fledged riots of the years to come. One of the speakers tripped over her speech when she saw us, but other than that nothing much happened. However, the reporter from *The Times*, obviously bored at having to louse up a fine spring day by listening to a bunch of rich, pompous windbags talk about how wonderful they were, was enchanted. He wrote several stories, reporting that "fifteen students, all from the Columbia School of Architecture, . . . had approached quietly from the rear" while "those on the dais stared at the signs as they were raised, but offered no comment," and that one "Allan" Lapidus critiqued such additions to our fair campus as "unbelievable hunk[s]" that amounted to "just . . . storage house[s] for students . . . [that are] shoved into the campus like a cork."

Among those present and of the opinion that Uris Hall was a monument to all that was beautiful was Charles Colbert, dean of our own school and also a member of the university's Advisory Committee on Architecture and Planning. Colbert's take on our little rally was along the lines of Queen Victoria's "We are not amused."

Colbert, who became dean after I. M. Pei and other distinguished architects had turned down the post, summoned me to his office before long and accused me, as student president, of having inspired and led the besmirching of the university. Colbert informed me that I had "disgraced the university" and my graduation, still a year away, was in jeopardy. I informed *him* that the demonstration had been spontaneous and that we had every right to protest the despoliation of the campus. We were both snarling when I departed, and I knew that I was not only on his shit list but right at the top of it.

After taking over as dean the previous September, Colbert had decreed that the drafting room be painted stark white and that our drawing boards be covered with white, rather than standard green laminene. Most laminene is a light shade of green, a neutral color that is easy on the eyes. White, on the other hand, is a glaring and not at all friendly background color. Colbert had also mandated that no work was to be left on the boards overnight and that we had to clean the studio every night. Who did he think he was, a prototype of the Felix Unger character in *The Odd Couple*? Slovenliness is a distinguishing attribute of architecture students, more or less a badge of honor.

Even worse, Colbert had set about firing or trying to fire many of our most beloved professors, including my role model and the smartest and wisest of them all, Eugene Raskin, and Alexander Kouzmanoff, another widely admired faculty member, who helped design the UN headquarters. Kouzmanoff, the most inspirational design professor at the school, was a true Teacher who would spend hours with each of us, working out our design problems with intelligence, wit, and empathy. He was so enthusiastically dedicated that in one legendary incident he was drawing suggestions on a student's project with such gusto that he broke the point of his pencil, and then, instead of taking time to sharpen the pencil, he continued drawing with the nail of his index finger! Colbert took steps to rid himself of these stars so he could hire all his old buddies from Louisiana. Colbert tried to completely overhaul the undergraduate curriculum and then moved to deemphasize the undergraduate school and turn the School of Architecture into primarily a graduate school. He gave lecturer status to various developers who could then say, "I may be a sleazy schmuck, but I want you to know I am faculty at Columbia University." Moreover, we lowly (and tuition-paying) pupils were forced to listen to these self-important blowhards talk about how they made millions.

To put it mildly, Colbert was not loved by the student body.

Furious at what Colbert was doing to our school and acting as student president, in the spring of 1963, not long before graduation, I sent him a letter, signed by every member of the graduating class as well as a number of lowerclassmen, requesting that he meet with me and other student leaders to discuss our grievances. Instead of bothering to answer my letter, he forwarded it to the illustrious Jacques Barzun, a French-born and internationally renowned cultural historian, who was university provost. Colbert cited my letter as proof that the professors who had put me up to it (none had; this was strictly a student operation) and I were "troublemakers" trying to undermine his authority. Tipped off by a friendly secretary, I wrote Barzun that, "I understand that a petition to Dean Colbert, never intended for your eyes, has been sent to you. I would appreciate the opportunity to meet with you and discuss its contents."

Colbert, naturally, learned about my letter to Barzun and called me in before I could meet with Barzun. Functioning not only as prosecutor but also as judge and jury, Dean Colbert informed me that I was expelled forthwith and would not graduate. At that point, having nothing whatsoever to lose (it would have been difficult if not impossible for me to get into another school of architecture after being booted out by Columbia) and in a cold fury, I was able to secure an appointment with Barzun. I told Barzun not only about my own case; I also outlined the rape of the school, the destruction of student morale, and the loss or threatened loss of valued professors.

Barzun was appalled by the image of the students having to clean up an art studio every night. He allowed as how he had started out to become an architect and in the past had loved visiting the drafting studios. He was also troubled by my account of my expulsion. He offered me a proposition: He would mount a full-scale university investigation, and if everything I had told him was true, I would be reinstated and appropriate action would be taken against Colbert. On the other hand, if what I charged was not true, Barzun said he would see to it that I never entered another American university. Or, he said, I could walk out of his office now, and our conversation had never occurred. Having little choice and being in no mood to compromise, I put all my chips on an all-inclusive probe of Colbert.

Three weeks later Barzun called me back to his office. In somewhat shocked tones, he told me his inquiries had confirmed my account; it was actually worse than anyone had expected. Colbert resigned, effective June 30, 1963, but in fact left the campus almost immediately.

Barzun ended his conversation with me by apologizing on behalf of the entire university. I was back in good standing!

Not only did I graduate in 1963 as scheduled (several months after our son Adam was born), but I also was awarded the Alpha Rho Chi medal of the Architectural Honor Society for showing talent, sensitivity, and leadership. I didn't win the medal for academic achievement. In design, for example, my marks fluctuated between A and D, depending on how much the professor hated my father.

Regardless, I was now a graduated, educated, certified *architect*.

5

The Son Also Wants to Rise

I had a decided advantage over most of my architecture school class-mates, because I had spent many summers in my father's office under the tutelage of his chief draftsman, Leo Komarin. Leo was an extraordinary person and a major influence on my life and career, especially compared to my father, who rarely if ever showed me how to do anything.

Leo was a Czech-born Jew who spoke German, Russian, Polish, Czech, and English. He and his family escaped the Nazis in 1938 and came to America. He started drafting school as a teenager, and when the United States entered the war he enlisted on day one. Making use of his linguistic skills, he served in Europe and was with the first troops into Buchenwald. His stories about that experience would tear my heart out.

When I first met Leo, in the early 1950s, I was about fifteen. My father's office was at 249 East Forty-ninth Street, between Second and Third avenues. The Second Avenue el had been torn down shortly after the war, but that part of the East Side was still decidedly unfashionable into the 1950s, partly because the unsightly el had been there and in part because it was the area where the workforce that serviced the Fifth and Park Avenue households lived. My father bought a brownstone for $17,000 and converted it into his office. It was pretty snazzy looking, with a T square for a door pull. He had a framelike border built around the perimeter of the street façade, and the building's front was rippled translucent glass. The main drafting room was on the first floor, the offices were on the second floor, and he rented out the third and fourth floors. The blueprint and storage areas were in the basement.

As a European craftsman, Leo was very meticulous, and he taught me the basics of very classical architectural line work, such as how to draw a line with a pencil resting lightly on the edge of the straightedge while simultaneously rolling the pencil as you drew, so that the point did not flatten out and yield a fatter line. In those days you used leads that were either in a special holder or came in pencils with the annotation of their hardness. The hardest leads (4H) were used for very fine lines like dimension lines or very thin materials such as window glass, while the softest leads (5B) were used for sketching or filling in (blackening) between other lines to indicate dense material (concrete or steel members). Just looking at a line weight would tell you what type of material was being indicated. It was a very fine craft. A beautifully drawn set of construction documents ("blueprints") was a joy to behold. Architectural lettering was also a finely developed art. Thickening downstrokes of letters while lightly drawing the curved forms, pressing down at the end of a letter for emphasis, the proper spacing of the letters (a bigger space for vertical lines and a smaller space between curved letters), and all the individual curves and flourishes were the mark of a fine craftsman. It was Leo who instilled in me a love of this craft and showed me its fundamentals.

In those days, architects first learned to be draftsmen. They actually drew construction documents. They did not design utopian cities or research how to uplift the souls of the masses with glass curtain walls; they learned how to produce drawings that showed a builder how to put a building together.

Those skills Leo Komarin taught me are, unfortunately, for the most part a lost art in the architecture profession. Architects nowadays rely on CAD machines. CAD has virtually replaced drawing boards, pencils, pens, and tracing paper. These electronic devices enable a person with good computer skills and little or no architectural ability to become an architect. The traditional way to judge an architect's proficiency was simply to look at his or her mechanical drawings. In my father's office and later in my own, we customarily did our "working drawings" or construction documents on sheets of paper (later Mylar) that were thirty-six by forty-eight inches. In the course of producing a job, more than one person would work on each sheet. Typically, if one person was great at detailing window flashing, he would do those drawings; if another was a whiz at detailing wall sections, he would produce those. As many as four different draftspersons might work on a single sheet. Just by looking at the work, I could tell who had done what, because I could recognize their "hand." This was a point of pride among professionals.

With CAD machines, on the other hand, all the work looks identical. Therefore, as an employer, I have no way of judging anyone's skill. Worse, there is no way of verifying whether a given jobseeker has even done the drawings in his or her portfolio. It is the natural inclination for many candidates to exaggerate, if not out-and-out lie. With hand drafting, an architect's work is unique to that person and immediately tells you the level of his or her skill and experience.

These CADs do allow one person to turn out the work that would have previously taken four to six people to do, so they certainly are cost-effective, and they permit changes that otherwise would be difficult and time-consuming to be made rapidly. But they cause an erosion of craft, placing more distance between an architect and his work. About ten years ago the dean of Columbia's School of Architecture told me the "kids" are often more in love with the process than the product. They would draw a simple rectangle and be able to put it in three-point perspective, rotate it, and view it from different angles. This fascination with animation, the dean said, had become more interesting to many pupils than whatever it was they were twirling about on their machines. When you created this work by hand, you had to constantly go over what you had designed; in the process of graphics you could more thoroughly, and in more depth, have time to study, examine, and reexamine what you had designed. Loading vectors into a computer removes you from the intimate association of designer and object designed. Take a look at the classically designed and rendered buildings of the past and the convoluted crap done by some of today's "leading lights," and I think you will see what I mean.

I learned the intricacies of construction literally from the ground up, working as an on-site laborer for several summers and pouring concrete at the Eden Roc Hotel my father was designing in Miami Beach. I recall one time as I was schlepping and *shvitsing* at the Eden Roc, the foreman came around and told us the architect was coming to inspect the site. When Morris arrived, nattily dressed in his bow tie despite the heat, we didn't acknowledge each other; the last thing I wanted was for my fellow workmen to know who I was.

A few years later I did similar work at the DiLido Hotel site on the beach—now, after a $200 million restoration finished in 2003, a Ritz-Carlton, complete with the new Lapidus Lounge on the mezzanine, overlooking the ocean and the swimming pool. All things considered, I enjoyed construction work in Miami. The workday started at 7 in the morning and ended at 3 o'clock. Since I was already on the beach, I could go jump in the surf and lie on the sand in the afternoon. Besides, there was something "manly" about working clad in just construction boots and a pair of ragged (not for effect but for real) jeans. In those pre-OSHA days, there were no construction helmets or safety rails. I remember wheeling a wheelbarrow filled with concrete over a twelve-inch-wide plank, atop a three-story-high space, with rebars sticking out of the floor, no less. This was labor for a man's man!

In addition to pouring concrete, I carried wood, pried apart forms after the concrete had set, nailed forms together, and hosed down freshly poured concrete, a task that was necessary so the pour did not dry out too fast, which would cause shrinkage cracks to appear. Later, when I was in architectural school, during the summer between my junior and senior years, I was an architectural superintendent on another Morris project, the Summit Hotel in Manhattan (now the Metropolitan), where I had worked the previous summer doing construction. When I was a superintendent, the building was in its final or "fit out" stage, and all the interiors were being installed. I was responsible for making sure the right furniture got installed in the right rooms, and then I was supposed to give the front desk a list of rentable rooms at the end of each day; the hotel had opened with less than a third of its rooms fully furnished. Each morning I picked up a list of the status of each room and checked each one out to see what was still required. I remember going up to one of the penthouse suites listed as "Not Ready" and letting myself in with my passkey, only to find a bleary rotund man stumbling around and a naked woman lying on the bed. The john complained that he was paying "a hundred bucks a day for the room, and a hundred bucks for the broad, and not getting a hell of a lot of use out of either one." Oops! After that I always knocked, even if the official list said the room was not occupied. (The penthouse suites' furnishings were very expensive, and the head housekeepers—often Irish ladies of a certain age—used to yell when examining a recently vacated suite: "Oh the di-i-irty pigs, they didn't even bother to take the silk bedspread off!")

Working construction in New York City was a journey that taught me a lot that would be useful as the years passed. The unions dictated how many bricks a bricklayer could lay in one day. ("Why are bricks red?" went one joke. "You'd be red too if you were laid in public!") The old craftsmen had a rhythm they had learned early, during preunion days, and they could not slow down, so you would see the old-timers sitting around, bullshitting and smoking, by about 1 o'clock in the afternoon, because they had already laid their union-mandated limit of bricks. During the construction phase I was often and intentionally mistaken for some young kid getting started in the construction field. So at lunchtime I would sit on the edge of a raw concrete slab, my feet dangling down over Lexington Avenue with the rest of the guys, eating a huge meatball hero and with the obligatory quart of Schaefer beer in my hand, commenting on all the lovely secretaries walking by. Another little drama well worth watching took place on payday, as the cops from the precinct across the street got in line with the rest of us for their payoffs.

My hands-on construction experience was a liability to some extent when I entered architectural school. My designs were hobbled by my obstinate insistence on designing buildings that could actually be built. While my classmates were drawing structures soaring into the heavens, supported by one elegant column, I brutishly persisted in making designs that would not collapse on the hapless populace. Although my "rebellion" earned me some of those dismal design grades, my portfolio helped me later with actually becoming gainfully employed.

Reluctant to reprise my home life by placing myself under my father's despotic authority, I applied for and was given a job at the prestigious superfirm of Skidmore, Owings & Merrill. Morris was incredulous! The idea that I wouldn't enter his domain as a professional had never occurred to him. He had gone so far as to lecture me that I was not to expect preferential treatment in his office, and he stipulated a starting salary that was actually below the minimum wage, then $1.25 or so per hour. Skidmore offered me a wage that was not only legal but also above the poverty level.

Although Skidmore's chief draftsman recognized my name when he hired me, he sympathized with my situation, so I was introduced around the firm by my first name only. In truth, most entry-level hires were addressed by first name only. We were of little or no concern to the upper echelons who possessed actual last names.

Thus did I enter the world of high WASP corporate architecture. Skidmore was swamped with work. It was in the mid-1950s, the heyday of the march of the glass boxes up Park Avenue and down Sixth Avenue. The corporate world loved the glass box, but not for any reason that Ludwig Mies van der Rohe ever imagined. First, this type of "design," as it were, eliminated the need to have someone around who had any sort of aesthetic sensibility. It doesn't require much creativity to make a glass box, for heaven's sake. The monumental creative decisions had to do with what color glass—the big choice usually was between light gray and light green—and what type of corners to put on the structure's façades. Corporations usually hate having to make decisions based on aesthetics, but gray or green was a problem that, given the proper models, renderings, and historic studies, a special executive committee, after several months of meetings, field trips, and historic summaries, could usually come to grips with.

The second reason this type of edifice was popular was that it was really, *really* cheap to build. That is the real reason developers the world over embraced what the Bauhaus called the International Style—a "style" that could be built in a relatively short time. Time is money—ergo, really, *really* cheap! To prove the point, *Life* magazine once documented the erection of the entire façade of a high-rise office building on Forty-second Street in a single day. Rome wasn't built in a day, but the Sunoco building was!

Skidmore was perfectly positioned for the postwar building bonanza. Until shortly before I was hired, the firm had employed WASPs and

WASPs only. The current design genius of the firm was a talented young man named Gordon Bunshaft. He did some truly innovative work in the *real* International Style, most notably the Lever House on Park Avenue. Its open spaces and slender tower were the result of Lever Brothers opting to sacrifice lucrative allowable buildable area for looks, and this was a wonderfully innovative structure. This was because the president of Lever, Charles Luckman, was an extremely inventive architect—he helped design the latest incarnation of Madison Square Garden, Los Angeles International Airport, the Prudential Center in Boston, and the Cape Canaveral Space Center (now known as the John F. Kennedy Space Center).

As the accolades for Lever House and other buildings poured in, Bunshaft became the hero of the profession and the superstar of Skidmore. It was about then that he took off for Yom Kippur. Surprise! By the time I went to work there, the place had a few Jewish architects, an Asian, and—I am not making this up—a woman! The old-timers may have grumbled a bit, yet Skidmore nevertheless remained a bastion of white corporate ethos. The dress code mandated a white shirt and a muted tie. Shoes had to look sharp and spiffy; thus, a shoeshine boy (that's what the elderly black man was called) made rounds with his box so that the gentlemen could receive a proper shine while seated at their drafting tables.

I quickly learned that as the humblest of employees, it was my duty to relieve the office boy when he went on break. Moreover, I was not permitted to speak to the designers. These luminaries sat at boards with little hand sinks, behind a glass partition, making weighty decisions about gray or green glass.

To complete the scene, a receptionist sat at a glass desk with no front panel, in front of a glass wall behind which was a crimson velvet curtain. The firm selected this lady's clothes (which ran the gamut from black knee-length dresses to black knee-length dresses) as well as her jewelry, decreed the crimson shade of her lipstick (to match the backdrop, of course), and even paid to have her hair dyed jet-black, the better to match her wardrobe, no doubt. She would mutter that she exacted her revenge by wearing pink panties.

Morris had not received news of my new job with great enthusiasm.

"How did you get a job with Skidmore?"

"I applied."

"But why did they hire *you*?"

"I guess they liked my portfolio."

"You have a portfolio?"

My father had *never*, during my four years at his alma mater, asked to see my work.

"And I think they were mildly impressed that at graduation I was awarded the Medal of the Architectural Honor Society."

Looking more confused than I had ever seen him, he blurted out, "Why did they award you the honor society medal?"

"Well, Dad, for the same reason the honor society awarded you the medal when you graduated in 1926—I guess they thought I deserved it."

When I had told my father about winning the award, his response was, "Yeah, kid, I won that same award myself." I was proud that I had received the identical honor he had, but as the years passed I began to wonder why he never mentioned it again, in his memoir, *Too Much Is Never Enough*, or any other time. The whole thing became curiouser and curiouser to me. Eventually I decided to look into this mystery. The answer came in a 2006 e-mail to me from a top official of Alpha Rho Chi, the national professional fraternity for architecture:

"Mr. Lapidus,

"Your father would not have received the Alpha Rho Chi medal in 1926. Alpha Rho Chi did not start awarding medals until 1931."

In other words, Morris couldn't simply congratulate me for winning this medal; he needed to try to one-up me by claiming that he, too, had received it—four years before the prize was first given!

Meanwhile, back at the comparatively disreputable headquarters of Morris Lapidus in the aforementioned renovated brownstone off Second Avenue, my father's longtime partner, Leo Kornblath, left the firm in early 1961, taking with him several clients.

Leo was a gregarious fellow who glad-handed the clients and was terrific at drumming up business, an activity my father disdained. Morris always blithely told me that clients "just called him." I think he actually believed it. In fact, Leo was the rainmaker. Many years later, in his memoir, Morris gave Kornblath a backhanded compliment as a business getter, describing him as "a persuasive salesman but a lousy designer." Morris was an egocentric tyrant who believed that anyone who worked for him owed him undying loyalty. He viewed the world solely as it related to him. Example: At one time in the Florida office there was an architect who was the "job captain" of a sizable project. The title referred to the person who ran the venture and was in charge of all the coordination and making sure that the construction documents were done accurately and on time. This man, whose name I have forgotten, was extremely competent. One weekend he was riding his motorcycle and got into a terrible accident, ending up in the hospital on life support. My father's reaction was, "Bad for him, but terrible for me."

Leo's departure from the Morris Lapidus firm was prompted by his poaching a major client (one whom, in fact, Leo had brought in) and moonlighting a hotel design for him. When financing was secured for that project, Leo immediately jumped ship and established his own firm.

My father was an explosive man, and the situation between him and Kornblath quickly degenerated into a war, with the accountants and lawyers battling to the death over how much Leo was owed at the dissolution of the Lapidus-Kornblath firm. At one point during the negotiations (with my mother, whose position was, "Give nothing," coaching my father), my father screamed at Leo, "What do you want from me?" Leo's answer: "Your blood, if I can get it."

My father wound up having the last laugh. Leo later started doing business with a nice Jewish girl named, at least at her birth in Holland, Xaviera DeVries. Later in New York she was better known by her adopted name: Xaviera Hollander—aka "the Happy Hooker," the city's most prominent madam. It turned out that Leo was laundering money and evading some of his income taxes by paying monthly fees to Hollander, ostensibly for her "interior design services." She kicked the money back to him, but the arrangement gave Hollander, a resident alien, a supposedly legitimate source of income to help her convince the U.S. Immigration and Naturalization Service that the government should let her stay in this country. When all the dust had settled, Leo pleaded guilty to tax evasion charges in 1977 and was sentenced to prison. "After Leo's release, I do not know what became of the junior draftsman I had hired straight out of New York University and pushed into a position where I finally made him a partner. I certainly had not been a good judge of character," Morris crowed.

I had previously met Xaviera, quite coincidentally, when my father and I employed a public relations man, Frank Farrell, a former reporter and editor at the *New York World-Telegram*. Ada Louise Huxtable had taken to using the word "Lapidus" as a pejorative to denote a gross building. The final straw was when she was instrumental in killing an office tower project on Park Avenue that we were working on with Aristotle Onassis. Farrell was to broker a deal with *The Times* under which we would not sue the paper for defamation if she would stop using us as her personal punching bag. (Which was about the time she finally inspected the Bedford-Stuyvesant swimming pool we had designed for the city— see Chapter 6—and gave me and my work, but not Dad and his work, a rave review.)

Farrell, a large, broad-shouldered, personable man in his late fifties, was an incredible character who had been an Allied spy during World War II and knew everyone from Douglas MacArthur to Walter Winchell and Lowell Thomas to Roy Cohn to Joan Crawford and Bette Davis to Ginger Rogers and Ethel Merman. He was in our office at Lexington Avenue and Fifty-fourth Street one day talking to me about the case. When we finished, he asked if I wanted to see New York's most elegant "hook shop," as his next appointment was there and it was just one block away, at Fifty-third and Lex. Considering myself a manly stud, I was horrified at the idea of "paying for it." Farrell, a man with an eye for feminine beauty to the extent that he had served as a judge at the Miss America Pageant for several years, said we weren't going there to get laid, just to check out the operation. He had been asked by his buddy, the famous author Robin Moore, who was coauthoring Hollander's book *The Happy Hooker*, to intercede and persuade Xaviera that if she used customers' real names, she was dead meat. Out of curiosity, I accompanied Frank and met the most amazing assortment of characters. Xaviera greeted us at the door, looked at me, touched my nose, and said, "Aha, a landsman," or fellow Jew. Then I noticed the menorah on a shelf behind her.

She explained that back home in Holland, where her father was a respected surgeon, she had won a national contest as a multilingual translator and gotten a job at the UN. While she was working there she started dating Robert Feldman, coincidentally, again, my always-on-the-prowl attorney. Bob told me she was the only woman who wore him out so much that *he* had to fake being asleep, so he advised her that she should do this sort of thing for a living.

Before Xaviera and Farrell began their little talk about the book-publishing business, she introduced me to one of her ladies, whom she called "the professor." Xaviera said that as an architect, I might enjoy talking to this woman. My brand-new acquaintance was a stunning lady in her early thirties, clad in a black one-piece "cat suit" with a zipper down the front, unzipped to reveal the curves of her breasts. *Sure, I thought, I, Alan, the Kid, winner of the big honor at Columbia, son of and partner of the legendary Morris Lapidus, yeah, right, I'm going to have an architectural talk with this muffin.* She started by asking about my favorite architectural period. The Egyptian era, I told her. Within five minutes I was so out of my depth that I felt like a schoolboy. She was naming ancient structures with dates, places, and details that were totally beyond me.

When Farrell and Xaviera finished talking, we made our farewells. That would have been that, except that my life doesn't seem to work that way. Thomas Hoving, the city's parks commissioner under Mayor Lindsay, had moved on to be director of the Metropolitan Museum of Art. He called to invite me to attend the opening of a major show he curated: A King's Book of Kings—3,000 years of the Persian Empire. As Tom and I were passing through the reception line, he introduced me to a university professor, a gorgeous woman who also worked part-time at the Met. This time, no cat suit! Seeing my stunned expression, she took me by the arm and led me to a quiet corner, explaining to a mystified Hoving, "Oh, Alan and I are old friends." When we were alone, she confessed that this was the first time her vastly separate existences had collided, since she usually worked in the Met's back offices and didn't come into contact with the public. I asked the obvious: Why did she live a double life? Her answer, elegant in its simplicity: "I get turned on by being sold."

In the wake of Leo Kornblath's departure from my father's firm, it came to pass that at one of my family's dreadful dinners, my father unexpectedly asked to see my portfolio. I was so surprised at his acknowledgment of my existence that I presented it to him.

This was to be the first and last time in my life that I actually saw tears fill his eyes.

Morris asked me if I would work *with* him (not *for* him). By that time I had gained a real love for designing buildings, but I was terrified at the thought of working for such a forbidding eminence, and equally terrified of going into practice and actually competing against him.

Now he had made the decision easy for me. I completed my three-year apprenticeship at the office of Morris Lapidus, Architect.

6

Eye of the Beholder

At the time Morris Lapidus was given the job of designing the Fontainebleau in the early 1950s, his only instruction was to make it "drop-dead gorgeous." The background of his client, Ben Novack, was in retail stores. After World War II, Novack realized that Americans had money for the first time since the Depression, that the DC-3 could fly tourists from New York down to Miami Beach in just seven and a half hours (as opposed to the *Orange Blossom Special*, which required passengers to ride the rails for twenty-three hours), and that no new hotels had been built in Miami Beach since the 1930s. Besides, Novack was bored, and New York winters were cold. He and his partners first bought into some small hotel projects. They were successful, and the group sold them for big profits, then decided to go for the big time and really make their mark. They bought the huge and sprawling Firestone Estate, at the far end of Miami Beach.

When Novack made the grand announcement that he was going to build America's greatest hotel, the press asked who the architect was. Novack, who had not thought that far ahead, knew the name of just one architect, the guy who had designed his stores.

Thus was born a career.

Like many of the individuals I encountered on my own or through my father over the years, Ben Novack, who put my father, and thus me, on the map as a hotel designer, was quite a piece of work. I remember Novack

as a greasy, thin little guy with one of those pencil mustaches often associated with gigolos or movie villains. Morris used to tell stories about
Novack, including one that involved the death of Novack's mother in
Miami Beach while Ben Novack was in Europe on his honeymoon with
the soon-to-be next ex–Mrs. Ben Novack. Concerned that his brother
might try to grab the maternal finances, Ben did what came naturally to
him: He called one of his wholly owned subsidiaries, who happened to
be the Miami Beach chief of police, and had him lock up the brother
until Ben could return and screw him in the proper fashion. In keeping
with his history, Ben Senior was involved in a dispute over his own
money with his son, Ben Junior, who was trying to have the old man declared incompetent, when Senior passed away of heart and lung failure
in 1985. Senior was seventy-eight at the time but entirely competent to
manage his affairs, according to Senior's companion of five years when
he died, one Juana M. Rodriguez, a thirty-year-old bombshell who had
once been Miss Uruguay.

A particular habit of Ben Novack Sr.'s that drove my father crazy was
his penchant for informing people that it was *he* who had designed the
Fontainebleau, along with his assertion that he had hired Morris simply
to "draw the plans"—a claim that Ben Junior repeated decades later in a
newspaper interview, which also enraged my father. One contribution
Novack Senior did make was the name of the establishment, in a fit of
cultural pretension on the part of the principal owner. The name itself
offers a lot of insight into the type of megalomaniac barbarian Novack
was. During a trip with his wife of the moment, Novack had chanced by
Fontainebleau, the largest and most ornate chateâu used by French
kings, queens, and emperors. He liked the name and thought it would
add a bit of "French Provincial" class to his place in Miami Beach. Not
that Novack ever set foot inside the hotel's namesake; he was later quoted
in a news story, "We didn't stop to look at it. I don't go for those foreign
chateâux." The Fontainebleau Hotel would turn out to be the first example of what would later become known as Postmodernism, about as
"French Provincial" as is the Taj Mahal. Novack, of course, had no clue.

My father learned he was to be a hotel architect by reading about his
commission for the Fontainebleau in *The New York Times*. This relatively short article would prove to be almost singular among the many

The Times published about him, in that it did not contain any snide remarks.

Up until then, Morris had never designed a hotel. In fact, he had never designed a building of any type. His career had been exclusively in retail stores, most of them renovations of existing buildings. Actually, there's a story behind that, too. Morris publicly claimed that before the Fontainebleau he had been the architect for such Miami Beach hostelries as the Sans Souci, Biltmore Terrace, Algiers, and DiLido, as well as several other hotels and office buildings elsewhere. He had, in fact, simply been a design consultant or secondary architect on every one of those projects. The architects who had had the lead role on those buildings complained to the American Institute of Architects about Morris taking credit he wasn't entitled to, and the AIA summarily kicked him out. Other times, when it suited his purposes better, he often bragged that he had never been primary architect for a high-rise hotel or any other building.

Ben Novack Sr. and his partners bought the Sans Souci project that was being designed by the Miami Beach architect Henry Hohauser. Novack looked at the typical stucco-covered box that Hohauser was designing and decided to call in Morris (because Novack felt my father had a "flair") to do the interiors and jazz up the exterior. Ditto with all the other Miami pre-Fountainebleau hotels. Morris was chafing about being referred to as the "hotel doctor" when Novack blurted out Morris's name to *The Times* after he was asked who the architect for the Fontainebleau was to be. When Novack told my father that he was just going to let Morris do what he had done with all the other Miami Beach projects, and he was going to get a "real" architect to do the building and let Morris "jazz it up," my father accepted the ludicrously low fee that Novack made him take for the chance to do the whole thing himself.

Never having designed an entire hotel prior to the Fontainebleau project hardly was a handicap for Morris. Since his clients knew nothing about the hotel business, why should their architect have to? After all, he designed one hell of a store. This turned out to be sound logic, both simplistic and accurate. During the 1930s and 1940s, there was not a great sense of fashion in the design or presentation of retail shops targeting the middle class. The brand consciousness that drives today's society, to the extent that preadolescents won't go to school unless their togs have the proper brand names emblazoned on them, was still far in the future. One pair of women's black sensible shoes was virtually identical to another. Conformity was comfortable. Given that most retail goods looked the same, that similar items were in the same price range, and that such stores tended to be clustered in the same general locale, the variable that could lure a customer into one store rather than another was the design of the premises.

My father had started in store layout because, in those days, designing small stores was beneath the dignity of a respectable architect. Architects (with a capital A) designed banks, public buildings, and elegant estates. Even planning office buildings was considered to be on the fringes of the profession.

Morris got into this area of design out of love. Not love for building storefront establishments but love for Beatrice Perlman. When they began dating in the late 1920s, Bea, being the sensible Jewish girl she was, told Morris she would not consider marrying any man who was earning less than $100 a week. That was an impossible sum for a young architect in those days. So instead of continuing with the prestigious architectural firm he was working for, he went to work for a contractor who built stores and restaurants.

In that era, if you wanted to build a small retail shop, you hired a contractor to do the work. Design was not an issue worth talking about. These outfits always had some guy in the back who turned out a sketch that the contractor then built. Since no respectable architect would sully himself with this, Morris Lapidus began his career being not quite respectable. But he earned $100 a week.

My father had started out to become an actor. While attending NYU, he joined the Washington Square Players, which later became the Theatre Guild. Eventually he won a one-line role ("The baron has shot himself!") in the early 1920s Broadway production of *He Who Gets Slapped* (later a Lon Chaney movie). But in that era, you weren't just an actor. You also kept the books or swept up or did something else useful. Having innate artistic talent, Morris designed the stage sets. By his own admission, he was a pretty lousy actor, but he was fascinated by lighting, set design, color, and how a certain blend of these factors could sway the emotions of an audience. Although bored with acting, he loved creating fantasy environments for the productions, which eventually led him to decide on a career in this field. He enrolled in Columbia's architectural school to improve his set design, since this subject was not taught as an autonomous discipline.

After Morris became an architect and started designing stores, he began to refine all he had learned and observed when he was designing stage sets in the theater. He had the supreme advantage that no one gave a damn what he did, as long as customers came into the store—no "client input." He also told me that it generally took two or three months to do a store, so he could quickly see what worked and what didn't. His greatest freedom was the knowledge that most of the stores would last just a few years, so if he screwed up, it didn't matter much in the overall scheme of things. So he experimented with manipulating people's emotional responses to space, colors, forms, lighting, and decoration. This wasn't theoretical philosophy; if they chose one of his stores rather than the competitor, he knew he had employed the correct set of stimuli to elicit a desired reaction.

Hey! That sounds just like "form following function." All the architectural purists are excused now, so they can become ill.

The hotel industry in Miami Beach was much the same in the early 1950s as the retail store business in New York City had been a decade or two earlier. There was a row of hotels, on the same beach, with the same prices, the same food, and the same service. So what might distinguish one from another?

Morris Lapidus—because he had "a flair." When he started to design the Fontainebleau, he had twenty-five years of successful behavioral design behind him. He knew how to push people's buttons. *And* he was very smart.

Morris was not interested in "style" or any of the other concerns that so motivate the current crop of aesthetes. His only concern was to blow the socks off the people who would be paying hard-earned money to enjoy the vacation of their lives. But first, he asked himself the most intelligent of questions.

Ben Novack had asked him to design the most "elegant" hotel in the country.

The intelligent question: Whose idea of elegance?

My father thought to ask himself who these future guests would be.

In an epiphany, he realized that they would be people like him.

This was five years or so after the end of World War II. A generation of immigrants and the children of those immigrants had worked hard, had survived the Depression, had gotten through the perils and shortages of the war, and now, for the first time in their lives, they had the time and money to enjoy themselves.

Next question: What signified "elegance" to this group of Americans? They would feel horribly out of place at the Biltmore or the Breakers. In point of fact these rather unimaginatively designed places were "restricted," meaning gentiles only. The concept of faux European elegance signified to middle-class Jew and gentile alike that Jews weren't "good enough" for such surroundings.

So where did they get their concept of elegance?

Morris's epiphany number two: At the movies! Specifically, in the escapist movies of the 1930s; more specifically, in the films of Busby Berkeley.

Take a look at the Fontainebleau, the Eden Roc, the Americana, and then go to the video store and rent *Gold Diggers of 1935*. Voilà! The best piece of architectural advice that Morris Lapidus gave his architect son: "Always design for your client's clients." Everything else is commentary. Commentary is often written by media commentators, who, to drastically understate the truth, never took a single course in architecture or design.

The sum of my father's background by 1952 was nearly his financial undoing. And a lesson to which his son should have paid more attention. Morris was dying to do the hotel and Ben Novack took full advantage of the situation. He told Morris that he could have the job but only at a ruinous fee. Like so many architects before and since, Morris was in effect being forced to pay for the privilege of working in the profession he loved.

Novack offered $80,000 for doing all the architectural work and all the interior design, in addition to designing the chinaware, the cutlery, and even the staff uniforms. With the Fontainebleau budgeted at $12 million, the architect's standard fee of 4 percent should have been $480,000. Even in 1952 dollars, $80,000 amounted to highway robbery.

Morris, feeling he had no choice, agreed to Novack's terms. He did not want to remain a store designer; he wanted to show the world that he could shape a building as well as make the insides pretty. Reason was not a factor in his decision making. He wanted to realize himself as an architect.

It didn't take too long for Morris to understand the enormity of his mistake. Before the project was half completed, he had spent his entire fee. He went to Novack and told him he would have to abandon the project unless he was paid an additional $75,000. Novack, realizing that Lapidus was coming up with an awe-inspiring design, replied that if Morris would finance the rest of the work himself, *and* if Mr. Novack's partners liked the building, he would arrange to pay my father the additional money. But this would happen *only* when the building was complete, and *only* if his partners loved it.

Morris was faced with Hobson's choice. If he abandoned the project, he would still be financially devastated: He would lose the building, and his reputation would be ruined. In for a dime, in for a dollar—he decided to go all the way. Without telling my mother, he invaded the nest egg the two of them had saved up over the years, took out a series of personal loans, and went on with the work. When the hotel was nearly completed, Novack took his partners on a tour of the complex. My father waited anxiously as the group wandered around. When they were heading back, he approached Novack and asked if the group had liked the hotel. Novack said that they loved it. Like an eager puppy, my father asked if the partners had approved the additional $75,000. Novack, with a look of puzzlement, turned to my father and said: "What are you talking about, Morris? What $75,000?"

In what became an oft-told tale in my household, Morris went nuts. I mean, he totally lost it. In an instant he realized that Novack had lied to him, had never intended to pay him, and that he would be ruined professionally and become a bankrupt.

And that was the least of it.

When my mother found out what he had done, she would not stop at divorce. No, she would break any pieces of him that the Fontainebleau disaster hadn't managed to break. Icy terror had to have gripped Morris's heart.

All Morris remembered after Novack gave him the brush-off was lying flat on his back and being revived by a group of very worried looking Fontainebleau partners. He had snapped, grabbed a piece of lumber, and, with a murderous howl, tried to kill Ben Novack. It had taken many people to bring him down and subdue him. As they poured water from the swimming pool over his head, he blurted out his story.

It was even worse than he thought. Novack had told his partners that the architect's fee was $250,000 and had been pocketing the difference.

Thanks to Novack's partners, my father got his $75,000, plus a bonus. He even told my mother the full story. But not until a decade later.

Morris had knowingly gambled. And he won.

One footnote: After Morris tried to attack Ben Novack, Novack demanded that *Morris* apologize to *him* before Novack would agree to pay my father the additional money he was due. Novack's partners, who had taken Morris's side after hearing all the facts, nevertheless urged Morris to apologize: "Don't let pride stop you," counseled one. Apologize and get your money. Morris finally agreed to apologize, whereupon Novack added insult to injury, scolding Morris, "You should be sorry. Why didn't you talk louder? I never said I wasn't going to pay you." A lie, of course. "I didn't know what you were screaming about. You were whispering, and you know that I don't hear well."

7

A Swimming Pool Grows in Brooklyn

The election of John V. Lindsay as mayor in 1966 conveyed a sense to many New Yorkers that a mini-Camelot was upon us. Like JFK (the two men were born just four years apart), Lindsay, a former congressman and navy combat veteran from World War II, was movie star handsome, photogenic, born to wealth and privilege, and fast with a quip. True, he was a Republican, but a liberal one. He announced grandiose plans for new and innovative recreational facilities for all of us beleaguered urbanites. Implementing these schemes fell to Mayor Lindsay's appointed parks and recreation commissioner, the aforementioned Tom Hoving. Tom was a New York Brahmin, son of the chairman of Tiffany's, and a renowned scholar. He also had a wicked sense of humor that was perfectly in sync with Lindsay's.

One day a few months after Lindsay took office, my secretary buzzed me to announce that the mayor of New York was on the phone, asking to speak to my father. The firm had two offices, one in New York, the other in Miami Beach, where my father spent most of his time. Not wanting to inconvenience His Honor, and curious as hell, I took the call. Both Lindsay and Hoving were on the other end. I introduced myself as Lapidus Light.

After the requisite pleasantries, Lindsay and Hoving revealed what was on their minds. Since our firm had designed many a waterside retreat for the rich, the mayor asked if we would be willing to turn a 2.3-acre city block on Kosciusko Street into a pool and recreation center for the residents of Brooklyn's Bedford-Stuyvesant ghetto. But there was enough money in the budget for only the no-frills pool and usual municipal brick bathhouse. The facility was to be immense, with a pool capacity of three thousand swimmers, but the amount set aside for an architect's fees was minuscule. Lindsay and Hoving appealed to our civic responsibility as native New Yorkers, calling on us to help the city show that youth, enthusiasm, and creativity could upgrade the lives of the humblest city residents. I answered that their proposal sounded wonderful, not to worry about the small fee (the firm was doing quite well), although I would have to consult with my father. We set a lunch meeting at Tavern on the Green in Central Park for the following week when both my father and I could attend.

I was self-consciously delighted at the heady company at that luncheon. My father was engrossed in examining the location of the proposed project. He wistfully revealed that from about age twelve he had lived in Brooklyn and had grown up two blocks from the pool site and attended the neighborhood Brooklyn Boys High School. He recounted how his only opportunity for escaping the city's heat had been to dive off the wharves into the East River.

"I came from yesterday's ghettos. Of course we will do this project. I owe it to this city and to myself," Morris declared.

I have never had more love and respect for my father than I did at that moment.

Those sentimental feelings quickly died down. After lunch Morris left town, went back to Miami, never to be involved again, and dumped the entire project in my lap.

I viewed this pool project as an opportunity to improvise and quite possibly create something innovative and marvelous. But dealing with both a tight budget and the municipal bureaucracy might be beyond anyone's abilities. At a meeting soon after the agreement that we would design the pool, and after I had time to study everything that would be involved, I made a devil's arrangement with the mayor. I would design a facility that would fulfill everyone's desires for a fabulous urban recreational experience, but I wanted the mayor to handle any problems I might have with approvals from New York's medieval Building Department. Perhaps Lindsay, new to office, didn't know the department's reputation. In any event, he agreed.

After numerous meetings with local leaders and various community groups, I came up with a scheme that buried the enormous bathhouse half below grade, with the roof accessible by a flight of broad, monumental platform steps. The roof would become a spacious playground, furnished with various adventure settings that would be built from "found" or industrial objects.

A huge fountain through which people could wade and splash would be constructed from surplus plumbing pipes twisted in a sculptural form. I made the model from bent soldering wire, and the plumbing contractor, fulfilling a hidden desire to be an artist, fabricated it brilliantly. More discarded pipes were joined in fanciful ways and painted in primary colors to become an enormous jungle gym. One way to go from the top level to the deck below was to leap off the edge into a cargo net. Since Brooklyn was a major seaport, I was able to find many inexpensive, exotic, and useful items in local ships' chandleries.

I loved talking to the community groups and having the authority to transform their requests and wishes into tangible form. I was beginning to feel like a real architect. But my euphoria wasn't to last long. After many meetings with the personnel at the Parks Department, I had accumulated enough horror stories to be properly cowed.

Vandalism was a major problem. Whatever I designed would have to resemble the pillboxes that the Germans built along the Normandy beaches—yet look friendly and inviting. My design called for a reinforced concrete structure, but in angular and fanciful forms, painted in primary colors and heavily textured, with inset colored circles and other geometric forms. The half-submerged building was all angles, generated by circulation and sight lines, to kill any hint of municipal rectilinearity, a government entity's propensity to erect boring rectangular buildings and nothing but boring rectangular buildings.

Another issue was how to light the complex for nighttime use. The standard method was stadium lighting, but that had two drawbacks. A flood of light could easily blind someone glancing up from the three-meter diving platform. Moreover, I had to take into account the propensity of high-spirited kids (my pun is *not* unintentional) to take potshots and destroy the lights. The solution was a new form of lighting pole that was just being introduced along the nation's interstate highways. These poles were two hundred feet high, the tallest in the world, causing them to be referred to as "the twin towers": Because of their high angle, each individual light among the forty-eight 1,000-watt bulbs in the cluster at the top of the pole could illuminate a specific piece of ground. (Each bulb actually gave off four times the equivalent power of its wattage, or 4,000 watts apiece.) The principle was known as spotlighting, rather than floodlighting. Anyone looking up would see only one light, yet the entire area was lit bright enough to read a newspaper. A radiantly yellow service car could be attached to a slot in the pole to bring a maintenance crew up on an eight-and-a-half minute ride to relamp. The lightbulbs were out of range of small arms fire, another essential consideration.

However, the regulations of the City of New York do not permit the inclusion of any construction item that cannot be competitively bid. The light towers were proprietary, meaning they were patented and could be obtained only from the inventor and manufacturer in Red Wing, Minnesota.

I called City Hall.

The light towers went on the drawings.

When the project was ready to go to bid, we scheduled what is called a prebid conference. That's where contractors interested in bidding the job are given an overview by the architect and have an opportunity to ask questions. I made a big deal of stating that this project had a proprietary item, the huge light poles that had been approved by the City of New York, and no substitutions or alternates would be allowed. I held up a sheet of drawings and showed them to all the electrical contractors in the room.

A word about the bidding game: Contractors analyze the drawings, read the specifications, take the quantity of materials, figure out their cost, add a price for their time, calculate a profit margin and overhead costs, and submit a fixed-price bid. If theirs is the successful bid, that's the amount they get paid. If they estimate too low, they can get hurt financially; if their bid is high and somehow they are still the low bidder (meaning the other bidders were *really* pigs), they stand to make a great deal of money. But if they bid a fair price on the contract and then are able to substitute cheaper materials, they can clean up enormously. Of course, using less expensive materials can have its drawbacks. (Getting back to the film *The Towering Inferno*, for example, the fire that consumes Paul Newman's high-rise was caused by a sleazy contractor [his father-in-law] substituting cheaper wiring than the noble architect had specified.)

Once contracts are awarded for a project, the contractors, prior to actually building the work, must submit "shop drawings." These are sketches, based on the architect's construction documents, which show each specific object and how the contractor will erect it. They absolutely must conform to the architect's drawings. Ed, the electrical contractor who had submitted the low bid for the light towers at the Bed-Stuy pool, dutifully presented his shop drawings for the lighting. They showed—believe it or not—stadium floodlighting, instead of the spotlighting my construction documents specifically mandated! Unwilling to trust my powers of speech, I sent a certified letter to Ed and informed him that his substitution was totally unacceptable. I reminded him that he had been at the prebid conference and I was bloody well aware that stadium lights cost less than half of what I had specified, and his little game was not going to work. The budget allowed for the high poles, and that was what we expected to get.

But Ed was an old hand at city work.

New York City has the most archaic and unworkable rules governing municipal construction since Pharaoh built the Great Pyramid. And city functionaries administer these dictates with all the competence of Lucille Ball on the chocolate factory assembly line. The city wasn't messed up over simply applying rules; there was also a problem with paying contractors. It was routine for more than a year to elapse between completion of a job and payment. As a result, there was only a tiny pool of contractors willing to work for the municipality. But this small group had developed an extremely efficient method of enriching themselves. They used the system brilliantly.

As for me, I had never done any work for any municipality. In other words, I was the equivalent of blood in the water at the Great Barrier Reef.

Ed the electrical contractor sent a certified letter of his own to me, with copies to the parks commissioner, the mayor, the city councilman from his district, and the *Daily News*. Ed, I must say, was a masterful letter writer. Ed explained how good old Ed had conscientiously inspected the site and observed a public school across the street. If these monstrously huge poles were to collapse—say, in the next major hurricane or earthquake to strike the city (the towers, by the way, had been engineered to survive the next eruption of Krakatoa, which Ed somehow neglected to mention)—they would crash into the building where all these defenseless little moppets were studying. Ed could not bear the thought of all those mangled little bodies on his conscience. So, humanitarian that he was, he would build something that would protect them in their academic cocoon, despite the demands and the ego lust of a ruthlessly reckless architect. Just about the only detail Ed left out of his letter was an offer to reduce the price of his contract as a means of reflecting his humanitarianism.

Needless to say, no public official in her or his right mind is going to go on record as ordering the installation of anything that, in the event of the unthinkable, will result in bloody fingers being pointed his or her way. That's just the way it is.

Nonetheless, there were also some very smart people at the Parks Department who had had years of experience playing the same game. One, whom I will call Barry because I have forgotten his name, called for a meeting with good old Ed and me at the Armory, the department's headquarters. This venerable old building is located in Central Park, at Fifth Avenue and Sixty-second Street, near the entrance to Central Park Zoo.

I arrived first, as Barry was speaking to a subordinate. "Here's what we do," Barry said. "You take the fox out of its cage, and slip it into the roosters' cage. Tomorrow, before dawn. And damn it, be quiet about it. I don't want the *New York Post* calling me the 'Jack the Ripper of the Poultry World'!"

Shuffling some papers, Barry winked at me. "Some of the more influential citizens of this city live on Fifth Avenue and are likely to be displeased about loud crowing at 4 A.M."

At that moment, Ed walked in, looking very much like someone who viewed himself as the fox, not a rooster.

Before Ed could launch into his savior-of-the-kiddies speech, Barry held up a sheaf of official-looking papers.

"Ed, how much does the city owe you for past work?"

Faster than a speeding bullet, Ed mentioned a very big number.

"Ed, you've been waiting for that for what, a little over a year, right?"

"You know I have, Barry, and most of it should be processed in the next two months."

"We're not paying it."

Stunned silence.

"WHAT DO YOU MEAN YOU'RE 'NOT PAYING IT'? You *got* to pay it!"

"Well, Ed, you know how understaffed we are around here, and we just hired a bunch of summer interns, and stuff gets misfiled, and lost, and paperwork can get screwed up, sometimes we just can't find stuff. Could take years."

"I'LL SUE YOUR ASS!"

"Sue the City of New York? That would take, oh, let's see, two, three years to get to court. We've got lots of friends at the corporation counsel's office, they lose stuff too. Damn shame, really."

We got the light poles.

Welcome to government work!

As the drawings were completed, the Building Department filings started. The rejections also started, in predictable but amusing fashion. The first was from the Plumbing Department. I had joined surplus plumbing pipe to create a climbing playground. The department rejected this with the note that "two 90-degree angle bends cannot be used within two feet of each other," and my drawings showed them within 15 inches. REJECTED!

Mayor Lindsay had promised to help me solve problems with the city bureaucracy, but not wanting to have to ask him daily to make trips to the Building Department, I tried reason. That's how naïve I was. An unsmiling inspector listened as I explained that no water would be coursing through these red- and yellow-painted pipes. They were for climbing, recreation—you know, play! His expression never changed. "You are not permitted to use two ninety-degree angles in less than twenty-four inches. The regulation don't say nothing about whether they got water in them. That's the regs, that's final."

Still REJECTED.

I was back the next day, accompanied by Mayor Lindsay.

"I want these drawings approved," ordered the mayor.

"They ain't according to the code. I ain't approving nothing that violates code."

"I am the mayor of the City of New York, and I say that you approve these plans!"

"Hey, I voted for you, but I ain't approving plans that violate the Building Code."

The plumbing plans were approved by the mayor himself. Probably a first.

The next crisis occurred when the Plumbing Department spotted the adventure fountain I had created with a bent piece of solder, a large twisted metal tube from which water shpritzed. This water experience descended six feet from the top of the half-buried bathhouse to the pool level. The drop was by means of broad-angled, step platforms that had a sheet of water cascading down. Kids could sit in the water and play under the fountain. The department advised me in the rejection notice that this in fact was a stairway. A stairway had to conform to something called the "tread-riser ratio." Translation: The length of the flat part of a step in relation to the rise of the step was not in conformity with code. Undoubtedly not, inasmuch as the treads (the flat part) were usually two feet to five feet instead of a legal ten inches, and the riser, instead of being six inches to eight inches, was four inches. And each one was different. And wet. The mayor sent his man to the Plumbing Department.

The Building Department was equally confused over how to categorize a building that is half underground. If a space in a building is half underground, it is legally classified as a basement. If it is more than half underground, it is termed a cellar. So what I was building was a basement, but one without a first floor. Not to mention that the roof was actually a playground, and the exposed pipes didn't have water in them, and the stairs were a fountain.

All of which fell into conflict with the omnipresent sign in other city parks stating, "No One Allowed in Fountain." Of course, I designed it that way because once upon a time I had been a New York kid myself, and I always climbed in the fountains (when the cops weren't around). Try explaining that to a Building Department inspector.

Eventually, a miracle occurred. All the documents were approved and signed off on by an amazing cast of characters.

Time for construction to start.

Guess again!

Before completion of the construction documents, the city had acquired the site and demolished the dilapidated buildings on it. One fine day I received an official notice from the city to the effect that the demolition had been conducted illegally: The water, electric, sewer, and gas lines had not been disconnected, and therefore this leaking, stinking, sparking, inflammable mess was in violation of every demolition regulation since Joshua did his trumpet bit. And they were holding me, as the architect, responsible. How could I have hired such an incompetent and reckless demolition crew?

I spent several weeks striving to explain to the city that it was the city itself that had violated its own rules and savaged the site. I had never even been informed when the demolition had taken place.

Even the mayor's man was avoiding my calls by then.

Nevertheless, this crisis, too, did pass. It got solved and we actually began construction.

That's when the fun really began.

On a normal construction project (if there is such a thing), the general contractor, construction manager, or whatever the title du jour is, hires all the subcontractors and is responsible for the orderly progress of the work. That requires coordination, to make sure that each trade does its work in the proper sequence, without harming the work of the subcontractors that preceded them. Foundations, structural frame, plumbing, electric, exterior walls, interior walls, finishing—all have to be done in the proper order. Sounds logical, doesn't it? Not for government work!

New York City operates under the Wickes Law. This draconian gem was put in place during the 1920s for reasons obscure to most modern-day architects and contractors. Wickes provides that on a government job, no general contractor may have authority over the other trades. In short, no one has authority to coordinate anything. This explains why the city has never built anything on time or on budget. And, as long as this law is on the books, it never will.

Over the next several weeks, I observed an interesting little dance. The plumber laid out all his underground pipes. The next day the concrete subcontractor poured concrete over it, and in the process broke all the pipe. When water didn't flow, the concrete guy got paid extra to dig up all his concrete, the plumber got paid extra to replace the broken pipe, and then the concrete guy got paid extra to repour the concrete. Repeat.

This idiocy was brought into sharp focus in the 1980s after the city had been trying for eight years to rebuild the Wollman Skating Rink in Central Park. After all those years, and after expending God knows how much of the city's money, city officials still couldn't get the rink up and functioning. The funny thing was, they would lay out all the refrigerant piping, pour the concrete, and, wouldn't you know it, there would be leaks and they would have to do it all again. Enter The Donald. In righteous civic wrath, Trump took Mayor Koch to task and offered to build the damn thing himself. Having no other choice, hizzoner took him up on the offer. There are those, to be sure, who would quibble that this grand civic gesture on the part of my friend Donald Trump may have been motivated in part by an opportunity to generate favorable publicity and in part because his three prime properties, Trump Tower, Trump Parc, and the Plaza Hotel, all were known for their splendid park views, and having a raw construction site dead center in the vista added little to the scenery. Never you mind; Donald, unencumbered by the Wickes Law because he's in the private sector, got the job done in nine months and substantially under budget. He used real, as opposed to city, contractors, instilling in them the fear of disgrace (or at least never working for him again) if the work was not done reasonably, quickly, and faultlessly.

The real irony is that, even while everyone lauded his efforts, no one took the trouble to learn anything about how incompetently the municipality goes about its construction projects. Donald, regardless of what you think of his style, is a good builder, but *any* competent builder can do a lot better than the city.

As work progressed in Bed-Stuy, it quickly stopped progressing. This was about the time the electrical wiring and plumbing pipes (the kind with *real* water) were being installed. All this valuable wiring and copper piping was being stolen every night. The next day would be spent repairing the damage and reinstalling all the expensive material. Repeat step one. Although there was a night watchman on the site, he wisely locked himself inside his barred and fortified trailer office as soon as he came on duty, emerging only with the rising sun. Sort of a reverse Dracula. But if you knew this neighborhood, you wouldn't blame him. I asked my contact at Parks to provide guard dogs. I got a call back from the official in charge of community relations, informing me that the presence of guard dogs would offend the sensibility of the local community. I informed her that I lived next to Riverside Park, and that Parks was doing some work there. Big signs on the construction fence at Riverside Park stated, "Guard Dogs on Duty From Dusk to Dawn—No Trespassing." And no one on my block was offended.

I realized I was talking into a dead telephone.

At my next meeting with the community leaders, Almira Coursey, the neighborhood's spokesperson, asked why progress was so slow. I recounted the story of potentially wounded feelings.

"And just *who* said that to you?"

I gave Almira the name and number of the thoughtful parks official.

Almira got on the phone. The project got the dogs. The job got going. And ultimately got completed. The guard dogs didn't fare as well; all of them were poisoned.

After taking twice as long and costing three times as much as it should have, the recreation center finally opened in 1971. When I looked at what I had created, it was payment without equal. Only when I looked at the face of my newborn son have I felt a greater joy. Tom Hoving was equally proud. I vividly remember him patting me on the shoulder with excitement during the ceremony when we first tested the facility's nonregulation lights in November 1971 and they came on in all their magnificence.

In August 1972, after the Bedford-Stuyvesant Community Recreation Center opened, Tom Hoving called the architectural critic of *The New York Times* and invited her to review his, and Lindsay's, first completed project. It was to be their *only* completed project, in part because in

March 1967, after just one year in the Lindsay administration, Hoving moved over to the Metropolitan Museum. Because the Bed-Stuy pool complex was his major achievement as parks commissioner, Hoving stayed on top of it even after he moved to the Met. Hoving's 1972 call was to the fearsome Ada Louise Huxtable, who had been commentating on architecture since 1963 and won a Pulitzer Prize for criticism in 1970. As previously mentioned, she loathed the work of Morris Lapidus so much that she had started using "Lapidus" as a pejorative in her reviews. She politely informed Hoving that she was not inclined to punish her delicate sensibilities by reviewing whatever it was that the designer of the Fontainebleau had excreted upon Brooklyn.

Hoving later told me that pressure was brought to bear on Huxtable and *The Times*, although he never revealed the specifics of that pressure. In any event, Huxtable ultimately condescended to take a look at the Bed-Stuy project, and Hoving asked me to meet Huxtable at the pool and escort her through our masterwork. On a fine summer Saturday she showed up, dressed in a smart pantsuit, upswept hair, and high heels. Very much the patrician on a jaunt through the baddest, blackest ghetto in New York. She and I did not quite blend in seamlessly with the crowd.

I suggested that she look in the women's locker room, where I had placed several graphic designs using different colors of glazed concrete block. As she walked elegantly down the ramp, I overheard two black teenagers, shaking their heads as they watched: "I don't know, man, maybe she be Porto Rican!"

As we walked through the complex the *Times*woman suddenly stopped and faced me. "Alan," she declared, "this is *not* the work of Morris Lapidus!"

"Ms. Huxtable, the work of the firm is always credited to the principal of the firm, Morris Lapidus."

"Alan, no one tells the architecture editor of *The New York Times* how to write her reviews."

The following Sunday, *The Times* devoted a half page to a review that both elated and horrified me. Huxtable praised the final product as "a handsome new municipal swimming pool." She went on to state that although Morris had "conceived" the plan for the site, "with the entry into the firm of Morris's son, Alan, (the script should probably be changed here to Son of Lapidus) a new design philosophy appeared. . . . Something good, and appropriate," was the result. "There is a small irony involved in the design," she added, "in that Hoving wanted an architect who would produce the jazziest pool possible for the grim environs of Bed-Stuy, and he had the Lapidus Fontainebleau fantasies firmly in mind. What he got was not glitter, but a serious, sophisticated solution. He caught the Lapidus firm in mid-image."

I never mentioned the review to my father, but of course he read it. And he never mentioned it to me. He had been waiting all his life to get a favorable review in *The Times*.

The Times was not alone in finally praising a Lapidus project. Morris's design for the Fontainebleau so incensed editors at *The Architectural Record* that they vowed never again to refer to him or his firm. They broke that pledge to favorably review the Bed-Stuy Recreation Center. To the best of my knowledge, this was the first time in sixteen years that the firm had merited mention in that publication—for a design that was mine. That became another very sore point between my father and me.

Morris had never won a major architectural prize, either. One of the most prestigious architectural awards was bestowed by the City Club of New York. The Albert S. Bard Awards for Excellence in Architecture and Urban Design were presented only when projects of particular merit warranted it.

In June 1973, I received a call that we had won a Bard Award for the Bed-Stuy Community Pool. I took a deep breath and placed a call to Florida.

"Dad, we won the Bard Award."

"Really? For which project?"

"Bed-Stuy. The presentation is going to be in three weeks."

Long silence.

"I can't make it."

Click.

He and I never spoke of Bed-Stuy again.

Because I was very conscious of the fact that Morris had never won a design award, I told him "we" had won the Bard prize, even though he had had almost nothing to do with designing Bed-Stuy. It was a gift of love to him from his son. In typical Morris Lapidus fashion, he threw it right back into my face, possibly because he didn't want to be involved with an award for a project he knew in his heart of hearts he hadn't worked on.

Shortly after Morris published a coffee-table memoir, *Too Much Is Never Enough*, in 1996, I opened my copy and immediately saw at the front of the book two large color photos of the pool he had taken credit for "designing." Unable to swallow his claim, I put the book down without reading any more, not to open it again for ten years, five years after Morris died in 2001 at the age of ninety-eight.

The whole Bed-Stuy affair qualifies as a father-son tragedy. I would have given anything to work closely with my father on a project, any project, but particularly one that had such meaning to our family on account of where it was located. Instead of working closely together, Morris and I worked separately on separate designs—whichever one was occupying his time then, plus Bed-Stuy, my baby—separated by a distance of thirteen hundred miles.

It just wasn't meant to be.

8

Go Tell It on the Mountain

I spent the summer of 1954, when I was seventeen, living and working with a family in Cuba. In those days the island was ruled by the dictator Fulgencio Batista. As the summer began, I was in Miami, as I was every summer, working as a junior draftsman in my father's office. At that time my father was finishing his second (and I still think his best) Miami Beach megahotel, the Eden Roc. He was having the flamboyant and gargantuan bronze lighting fixtures fabricated by a Cuban company. It was a huge contract, and the owner of the Cuban firm, Lamparas Quesada, invited our family down to Havana as a thank-you and as an opportunity for Morris to see the progress of the work. The Quesada family included a son who was exactly my age, and we took to each other. The Quesadas suggested to my father that I spend the summer living with them, working at their factory (shades of my grandfather, the metalsmith), and learning Spanish, as it might prove useful one day.

I was to return to Cuba some forty-five years later, when an intelligence agency of the U.S. government had need of an architect with a known reputation who was not of Latin descent, who spoke Spanish, and who was familiar with Havana. (More about that in Chapter 15.)

Meanwhile, I had the opportunity to put my Spanish to good use, starting in 1965, when our firm received a commission to redesign and refurbish a tired old resort in Puerto Rico. Our client, Lou Puro, a principal in Purofied Products, which manufactured down comforters, pillows, and the like, had decided to build a brand-new resort at Fajardo on the undeveloped eastern end of the island, some thirty-three miles from San Juan. Where an 89-room inn, with the rather pretentious name of El Conquistador (The Conqueror) stood, he would build a spectacular 388-room hotel, complete with casino, health club, convention facilities, marina, and golf course. The project would have to be designed in the New York office, since that was Puro's primary residence. I would initiate the design, but my father was to have all the client contact.

This job, which would consume three years, posed many daunting design problems. The locale was the entire side of a mountain overlooking the water, at the exact point where the Caribbean Sea meets the Atlantic Ocean. The view was the stuff of a travel agent's fantasy. The mountain was both an awesome sight and an awesome site. In short, Puro wanted to erect a high-rise on top of the mountain. Rule One of architecture, we had learned at Columbia, is: Never build on the top of a mountain. In those days, I still tried to play by the rules. And this particular mountain was composed of a nightmare mix of unstable volcanic rock, shale, and sand, littered with huge boulders that occasionally were loosened by our work and went rolling downhill, sometimes striking workers or damaging construction we had already done down below.

Complicated enough, but what to do in the event of rain? And here in the tropics, there was plenty of rain. For this reason, I devised a series of concrete walks that served as both decor and pedestrian transport in dry weather and became sluices that carried rainwater into an ornamental pool from which excess water flowed into a drain line that ran under the hotel and down the hill.

Blithely ignoring Morris's instruction to give the client what he wanted, putting the hotel on top, I built a model of the mountain and started sculpting a sweeping curve growing out of a fold of the slope. One day while I was in the midst of this design, Lou Puro asked Morris for a tour of the New York office. As Morris and Puro swept by, Puro glanced down at the huge architectural model, the *macquette*, that I was working on. He recognized his site. He saw what I was doing. Morris had never acknowledged that anyone other than he was working on the design, but now the cat was out of the bag.

Even more remarkable about that day, my father actually introduced me to our client—using my first *and* last names! From then on, the Conquistador was my baby.

One always bears a special love for a firstborn, and the Conquistador was my first hotel. I still love it, even though it has grown old and ugly with many new additions of mixed styles that overshadow the simple purity of its first incarnation. Others say it is still a terrific resort, but I remember her as she first was.

A myriad of elements had to be melded into a cohesive whole, without screwing up the site, which, after all, was the reason for building the resort in that location. My solution was to arrange the components in a gentle cascade of structures, descending the slope.

At the top of the hill were the original eighty-nine rooms; these I joined to a V-shaped structure wrapping around the mountain, below the crest. The center of the V would have the mountain going up through it, as an interior wild garden. Each and every room would face out to sea. Halfway down the slope was a gentle fold in the hillside. Into that, I nestled a soaring curved building that descended with the terrain. Each level stepped out from the one above it to echo the fall of the land. The top two levels had rooms, below that was the pool deck and a bar/restaurant, and below that another room floor. At the base of the hill was the ocean, which in fact had been placed by Mother Nature, not by yours truly. Cabanas and a snack bar were at beach level.

A nice concept, I felt, except for yet *another* major problem: How to transport people, food, cleaning and service supplies, and garbage up and down and to and from these facilities. Since it was a mountain, the only solution I could think of was ski lifts, for which there had not been a huge demand in Puerto Rico. Until now.

By coincidence, I had recently seen a television newscast about a company in New England that had come up with a plan to use a helicopter to install ski lift towers. I had been impressed with the elegant simplicity of the solution. The trouble with helicopter installation had been how to stabilize the ski lift tower as it dangled beneath the helicopter. There were eight steel bolts sticking out of the concrete foundation that had to be threaded into eight holes in the base of this very large tower that would be swinging beneath a none too steady whirlybird. Trying to winch down these massive structures would invariably set up an oscillation that precluded threading this particular needle. A New Hampshire manufacturer named O. D. Hopkins devised the solution. As the helicopter lowered the tower to within two feet of the base, O.D. had eight burly Hampshiremen reach up and pull the helicopter itself down. With the chopper in a neutral hover, it was not a major effort, and it enabled the crew to precisely line up the bolts with the holes. A classic example of "If you can't raise the bridge, lower the river."

This was exactly the type of original thinking I needed.

I placed a call to New Hampshire.

O. D. Hopkins was both an American original and one of the smartest individuals I have ever met. After an initial lengthy telephone conversation, in the course of which I started laying out my problem, O.D., in what I was subsequently to discover was a "Down East" twang, suggested that I drive up to Contoocook, New Hampshire, so he and I could sit down and see whether we might be able to "doodle" a solution. As it was winter, and his wife, Jane, was a member of the Ascutney Ski Patrol, he suggested that I could get in some skiing if I wanted. Our meeting turned into a weekend trip so that he and I could spend some uninterrupted time together, and my wife was invited to come along. Shelly and I would leave New York after work on Friday and arrive in New Hampshire about 11 o'clock that night. O.D. allowed as how folks in his part of the world were sound asleep by then, but he said Shelly and I should just come on up and let ourselves in, and we would meet for breakfast the next morning. He gave me directions to his large old farmhouse. How, I asked him, would we find our way to our room in a large house where we were strangers?

"Won't be difficult," was his reply.

Filled with confidence that this person, whom I had never met, was a man of his word, we set out for the world of the Yankee. Arriving late that night, we found ourselves gazing at a house that could have been the poster child for *Down East* magazine. An outside light was on, and we could see some lights indoors. Hesitantly, I opened the door and discovered a trail of toilet paper leading from the door, around the corner, up the stairs, and into our room.

I knew I had found the right man.

O.D. was a big, robust man, probably in his late forties. He had gone to a good boarding school that his family had endowed, at least in part, but he had little or no college education, not that it mattered. He wore clothes typical of a New Hampshire backwoodsman—plaid flannel shirts, canvas work pants or bib overalls, engineer's boots, wool plaid earflap hats. Once he came riding by on his ancient Farmall tractor, looked down at me, the city slicker, and called out, "Hey, Alan, don't I look bucolic as all hell?" Jane, a real knockout, was also a country girl. But underestimate them, especially O.D., at your own risk. O.D. was one of the sharpest people I've ever met. If it was mechanical, he could build it, fix it, or invent it.

His family's history was truly fascinating. In the 1800s, his ancestors made a fortune harvesting ice from the nearby lakes, storing it in big icehouses that he showed me on his land, and then shipping it to India for the big bucks, or, if they wanted some fast money, down the coast to Georgia so the planters could have ice in their drinks. He said his kids were still going to school on that money.

O.D. also had a business building and operating carnival rides. He would go on the state fair circuit every summer and haul in the money. Another of his talents, along with Jane's, was making a Kahlua-type beverage, their standard Christmas gift to all their friends and family. It was as good as the best you could buy in a store. O.D. once told me their secret: They boiled up a huge vat of strong coffee, mixed it with vodka, put in a heaping pile of vanilla beans, cooked it some more, and then strained it through a pair of Jane's panties. (No, I never asked the obvious question.) You've got to love American ingenuity and knowhow like that.

My weekend with O.D. produced an elegant solution to Conquistador, a new friend, and an appreciation of the type of individual who made this country great.

The answer to the vertical transportation issue at Conquistador was straightforward and ingenious. It was a glass-sided car running down the mountain, on a set of tracks, lowered by gravity and hauled up by a ski lift engine. The car could have a freight car attached to it to handle all the service needs. O.D. and I designed it to be both functional and a fun ride. The views from the tram, over the Caribbean Sea, were spectacular.

When the resort opened, an immediately popular excursion was to drive out to Conquistador and ride the tramway down to the poolside restaurant for lunch.

While the freight-moving system was being installed, I started having some worries for my friend's financial well-being. Becoming wiser in the ways of clients, I had begun to realize that the final payment for services was often a "sometimes" thing. Many clients seem to feel that once you have delivered the goods, paying you is simply an unjust imposition on their generosity. After all, they had given you all this work; it was kind of pushy for you to expect full payment as well.

"O.D.," I told him, "I'm a little concerned. I know you come from a world where people keep to their word and pay fair money for good service. But this place and these people can be something else. You've got a pretty hefty final payment coming to you after the system is running, and these guys . . ."

"Alan, let me tell you a story about my great granddaddy Jethro."

I knew when to shut up and listen.

"Now, Grandpa Jethro was a fine mason, built the finest fireplaces in Contoocook. One day the banker asks him to build the fireplace in his new house. That banker had a pretty skinflinty reputation, and folks took to warning Jethro about doing business with 'im. But Grandpa built him a fine fireplace. When it was finished, the banker spent all kinds of time inspecting his work and even peered up the chimney to make sure he could see the sky and there were no blockages. He was satisfied and told Grandpa that he would get around to payin' him soon enough. Grandpa allowed as how they had spoken about getting paid when the job was done. The banker got short with him and said that he would pay when it suited him. Grandpa went home, sort of smiling. The banker builds himself a big fire in his fine new fireplace and the place fills with smoke. Everything in the house is covered with soot. Banker, well, he comes pounding on Grandpa's door, screaming and cussin' something fierce.

" 'Of course the fireplace don't work. You didn't pay me.'

"After some more cussin' and sputterin', Mr. Banker finally pays Grandpa, who goes over to the house and drops a rock down the chimney, breaking the pane of glass that he had mortared into it.

"Alan, there's a drive wheel in that machine that won't last but two or three months. If I get my money on time, I'll call and tell 'em where it is. If not . . ."

After a lot of cussin' and sputterin' from our client, O.D. got his payment and the tramway worked fine.

Conquistador was my introduction to working in the Caribbean, and working for the types of people who built the resorts in those days. Nowadays it is practically all corporate—staid megacompanies building prepackaged joy for tour groups. But in the midsixties this was a business for the individual entrepreneur, who had a lot of faith, money, and vision. These guys were wildmen. Many had absolutely no experience in the hospitality field, but they had the foresight to realize that the jet plane had made accessible the entire Caribbean. The islands were busily building runways that could accommodate the new Boeing jets, and every man's fantasy of a romantic Caribbean getaway could be a reality. Since the Lapidus firm had become synonymous with beach resorts, we ended up building the first of the new wave of these vacation Meccas.

The upside was that we were the firstest with the mostest. The downside was that, since such large-scale construction was fairly new to the islands, there was no experienced workforce available. Not only was I busy learning how to design a vacation fantasy, I also had to teach the available work crew how to build it.

But first I had to figure out what the hell I was doing. I had just been handed the opportunity to design a resort for a new group of customers. But who were these people?

It must be emphasized how much the jet plane revolutionized the way Americans lived by the mid-1960s. The jet airliner was fast, making convenient destinations that had been too distant. The aircraft could fly above the storm clouds, so the distress caused by flying through bad weather was largely a thing of the past, and the new generation of planes had the range to make overwater flight safe and routine. And with all those new seats to fill, air travel was affordable. The Caribbean was no longer for the privileged few. It was accessible. And I was going to give them a destination.

I would design this for people like me.

Our parents' generation had weathered the first half of the twentieth century. They had sent their children to school so their offspring could do better in life than they had. My generation was remote enough from Ellis Island to talk like Middle America, yet we were close enough not to take for granted what had been achieved. But we wanted our own places to have fun, and no, it wasn't the Fontainebleau. We liked to think that we were a little more adventurous. Just as Busby Berkeley had epitomized glamour to my parents' generation, I sought a similar glamour icon for my contemporaries. What movies had given me and my generation our ideas of enchantment and sophistication?

Bond, James Bond!

Irony of ironies, the opening scenes of *Goldfinger* are set at the Fontaineblcau, designed by my father, and the closing sequence was filmed at my pride and joy, El Conquistador. But the actual realization of my scheme was to be my baptism by fire.

With resort hotels, "the season" is the most important survival factor. In the Caribbean, the big bucks start rolling in at Thanksgiving, and the major flow of cash ends by the time the snow melts back home. With the onset of spring, the high rollers and high livers are replaced by package-tour schleppers and low-spending Europeans. Any resort that opens in the low-dollar off-season will have a very hard time financially.

By the time Lou Puro gave me the green light, the time was impossibly short. This was an extremely complex set of structures, to be built into the side of a mountain in an all but inaccessible part of a remote island, and the structures were curved, angled, and cantilevered.

A reasonable time frame would allow six months for substantially complete construction documents, two months for bidding and negotiating, and a two-year construction period: thirty-two months. I had nineteen.

I tried to explain all these technicalities to Lou, who, like many of his ilk had never built a building. He had made his fortune manufacturing pillows—the original "feather merchant."

He dismissed my problems by saying in his best sinister snarl, "Hey, kid, you ain't up to the job, I'll give it to someone else."

I started to work.

From the beginning, I realized that there would be no time for competitive bidding. I would have to work with a contractor from the get-go. As each section was drawn, the contractor would have to start ordering the construction materials and mobilizing his construction forces. Instead of producing the drawings in a logical sequence, design for stages requiring components that took the longest to be manufactured would have to be done first. That meant I would have to order all the elevators before the placement and size of the shafts were finalized. All electrical equipment would be ordered by guessing what the actual electrical loads would end up being. You get the idea.

This was either a leap of faith or an act of stupidity. Or both. Later, this nutball improvisation came to be called "fast-track construction."

It's time to explain a little about what we architects do. An architect works with and is responsible for the work of a gaggle of engineers. Now, the only thing any of us learned from our engineering classes was how to talk, in a reasonably intelligent manner, with engineers. The architect has as his subcontractors structural, mechanical, electrical, and plumbing engineers. The last three disciplines, because of their close coordination, are, for the sake of the architect's sanity, usually in one firm—a so-called MEP firm. But only if anyone cares that the architect remain sane. In Puerto Rico, at that time, those specialties were all in separate firms, the members of which considered it unprofessional to talk to or in any manner coordinate with one another. There are also a number of other consultants and engineers on a major resort, but they are usually hired by the client and coordinated by the architect. Don't worry, it's confusing as hell to me, too. On this project, and for any other resort of this magnitude, the cast of characters, and I use the word advisedly, included, in addition to the above: kitchen designer, laundry designer, lighting designer (interior and exterior), interior designer, graphics consultant, elevator consultant, systems consultant, golf course architect, and hardware consultant.

Lou Puro hired a Puerto Rican contractor, Rexach Construction, that turned out to be terrific, and we set to work. Since only Puerto Rican–licensed architects are allowed to work in Puerto Rico, I was officially listed as "hotel consultant"; all my work was done through a local architect. That was José de la Torre, both very talented and a delight to work with. José, or "Pepe," had fled Castro's' Cuba and resettled in Puerto Rico. He was overjoyed that this "gringo" hotshot he was to work with not only spoke Spanish but also spoke it with a Cuban accent. And I knew all the great curse words.

At the time, the recently arrived Cuban influx was rapidly taking over and dominating the island's economy. While Puerto Ricans tend to be laid back, Cubans often are hyper. They have been called "the Jews of the Caribbean," an apt description. Displaced and driven out of their homeland, they established thriving businesses and successful practices throughout the Caribbean, most spectacularly in Miami and Puerto Rico.

The Puerto Ricans were not thrilled by this influx, and the ensuing tensions between the two groups made my life interesting. The electrical engineer was Puerto Rican, the mechanical was Cuban. This pair did not like communicating with each other, working with each other, or being in the same room with each other.

But working with Pepe was a pleasure. He was very careful to be sensitive to my Yankee peculiarities. On our first visit together to the site, he told me that he knew that "Americans" do not believe in the traditional three-hour Latin lunch. He was getting used to these new ways, he claimed, so for lunch we would go to a local bodega, a type of grocery store–cum–lunch counter. We would eat standing up, a mere snack, just like in the States.

The experience was as he described. At least as to eating standing up. We started with a beer, then had some empanadas, next came plates of broiled olives and sausage, followed by a *sandwich cubano* (a hero sandwich consisting of two types of pork, three types of cheese, and some pickles, toasted). All this was accompanied by black beans and white rice (*moros y cristianos*), along with *mafongo* (fried plantains). This was washed down with many glasses of a good rioja. For dessert there was flan and *pudin diplomatico*, some cheese, fresh fruit, and then a fine cigar and brandy.

But we never sat down. And lunch did take just two and a half hours. After which I couldn't see straight. Either José was rapidly learning how to be a Yankee, or else I was rapidly learning how to be a *Cubano*.

Pepe's office completed the production drawings for the rooms and infrastructure, and my office drew plans for the structures that contained the restaurants, ballrooms, kitchens, health club, and casino.

Ah, yes, the casino. By the time Conquistador was under construction, I had taken over the on-site supervision of the other Puerto Rico hotel our firm was doing for Lou Puro. Although it had been designed in the Lapidus office in Florida, my regular presence on the Island to keep Conquistador moving made it logical for me to look in on progress at El San Juan, where we were upgrading, renovating, and making additions to an older hotel originally named the San Juan InterContinental.

Pan American Airways had established the InterContinental hotel chain back in the 1940s when the airline specialized in flying to distant ports of call where the lodging facilities were either too "exotic" or nonexistent. In order to assure that its upscale clientele would always have access to accommodations that featured clean linens, hot water, soft toilet paper (actually, any kind of toilet paper), and friendly natives, Pan Am entered the hotel game.

InterCon hotels tended to resemble boxes with windows. Being the only game in town, Pan Am didn't have to work too hard to fill rooms. But when the jumbo jets started arriving, the old dowager hostelries had to be spruced up, sold, or shut down. The San Juan InterContinental had in fact closed and been bought by my client, Mr. Puro.

Our work evolved against the backdrop of the Caribbean becoming the new Miami Beach—even as Miami Beach had become the new Catskills. The difference was that gaming was legal offshore, albeit tightly regulated. The combination of sin, sex, and other forbidden delights has always been an indispensable recipe for a vacation paradise. Sun, sand, and clear waters helped, but in truth you could find all that in Boca Raton or San Diego. Until the end of 1958, Cuba had been the preferred destination for fun seekers from *el Norte*, but then a puritanical, bearded "anti-imperialist" strongman emerged from Cuba's mountains and targeted the casinos, their pleasures, and the good old boys who ran them. The good times abruptly stopped rolling. Thus did Puerto Rico replace Cuba as the island in the sun for American tourists. It was only logical that some of the same "connected" folks who had made a tidy sum by catering to some very primal urges in Cuba would look to do the same in this new venue.

There were, alas, major differences. The laws of the United States governed Puerto Rico, which was sufficient to spoil most of the fun. For starters, you could no longer comparison-shop for the most accommodating Latin politician. Plus, live sex shows involving farm animals were not encouraged. Most important, no doubt, slot machines were banned. And the airports were scrutinized to keep out known bad guys. Lou Puro, in fact, once asked me whether the waters just off El Conquistador were deep enough to accommodate "oceangoing yachts"—a sure sign that he was looking for ways to receive "guests" who would have been turned away at Puerto Rico's airports.

Puerto Rico, in short, might be a replacement, but it was also destined to be a poor substitute for the fun and games offered in Batista's Cuba.

In the course of my Puerto Rican sojourn, I was to learn that the Latinos had a somewhat Zen attitude toward construction that was lamentably lacking in their northern colleagues. In the land of the gringo, the entire focus is on getting the construction phase over with as quickly and efficiently as possible, so that the building can open and the money start flowing.

Previously, because of my fascination with Japan and all things Japanese, I had immersed myself in the Japanese culture. As part of this process, I had studied judo for five years. One day at the dojo, the sensei (teacher) gave us a demonstration of Zen archery. He would look at the target, close his eyes, and fire an arrow that invariably hit the target. Seeing our awestruck occidental faces, he would serenely state that instead of concentrating on hitting the target, one must concentrate on the flight of the arrow.

In the Caribbean, the construction process was like the flight of the arrow, a social event, an end in and of itself, to be savored and enjoyed. It was an opportunity for everyone to get together and discuss the day's horrendous technical problems, drink many cups of espresso, exchange the latest political gossip, and gradually arrive at a solution to the situation. Next would come many congratulations to everyone involved and a break for a meal and a good cigar, followed by a repeat of the entire process. After I stopped being hysterical about how nothing was being done systematically, I gradually began to remember how this attitude prevailed during my time living in Cuba, and I got with the program. I realized that the completion of the project represented the end of an amiable series of get-togethers. Yeah, the owners were happy, but our social agenda was shot to hell.

A lot of the problems that arose during the course of construction were self-inflicted, to be sure. As I had begun to realize in Puerto Rico, coordinating all the drawings was considered somehow unmanly. Coordination means that the architect is responsible for the review and synchronization of the drawings done by all those engineers and consultants I was talking about. It should be pointed out that under the laws of physics, two objects, such as a huge beam and a huge air-conditioning duct, cannot occupy the same space. So one of those items has to be moved or else transformed into a more compatible shape. It also means that the interior designer's drawings have to be scrutinized, and his or her soaring twelve-foot-high vaulted ceiling may have to be reconfigured to fit into a ten-foot-high room. Interior designers have a disconcerting habit of trying to make the interior of a building larger than the exterior. This rarely works.

If the architect fails to coordinate the drawings, all the engineers and consultants involved have to be gathered at the site, where they discuss the day's problems, like how does the really big duct coexist with the really big beam? After much more espresso and discussion of the latest political gossip, a solution emerges: How about taking the big duct and moving it to the *side* of the big beam?

My role in this process varied from project to project. In some instances, such as Conquistador, my firm and my associate architect produced as complete a set of construction documents as would be done for a stateside project. Other times and in other locales, my involvement ranged from a set of design drawings, to a preliminary set of construction documents, to a fairly complete drawing package. I usually had stateside engineers do at least a set of preliminary drawings, which were either completed by the local engineers or formed the basis of the contractor finishing the engineering with his own forces.

A word about what I mean when I say "design." This does not pertain just to the aesthetic qualities of the building. When you design a hotel, you are not designing only a building; you are designing a functioning business. The two main issues in the basic layout of a hotel are security and efficiency. South of the border, efficiency is regarded as a weird and esoteric Yankee invention. Democracy is too, but that's another story. Part of this attitude is due to a certain Latin love of chaos, but another reason is simple economics. Labor, the most expensive commodity in the United States, is the cheapest commodity in Latin America. I soon got up to speed on the basic economic realities of the region and adjusted my thinking accordingly.

After and as part of efficiency comes layout. If the layout is awkward, additional employees will be needed. At the present time, the average cost for an unskilled employee at a hotel in the urban United States, including all required and customary benefits, is about $40,000 per year. Hotels function on two and, in some cases, three shifts. If the design of the structure requires, say, ten additional employees because it duplicates facilities, or does not place them in the proper locations, and half of those positions are two-shift jobs, then you have just deducted $600,000 from the annual profit of the hotel.

For practical reasons, the foodstuffs have to be delivered to a loading dock, where they are manifested and checked and then routed to dry storage or refrigerated storage, which ideally is connected to the kitchen, which in turn should be right next to the restaurants. All this without an opportunity for food to take a little side trip to the cars of the employees.

That's why I usually cluster all the different restaurants around one central kitchen. What is commonly thought of as a "kitchen" is actually a cooking line, with its own prep area, stoves, ovens, reach-in ice boxes, Frialators, and salamanders (no, no—a salamander is a broiler, not an appetizer). But all the restaurants will draw from the same central commissary for all of their foodstuffs, coffee, ice, and in many cases desserts and salad ingredients. The various eateries should also share a common pot wash and dish wash to service each separate cooking line. If you have separate kitchens in different locations, you are, essentially, duplicating these jobs.

The same principles apply to the location of the laundry. Maids collect laundry from the rooms and take it to a service room on each floor. They dump the soiled linen into a laundry chute, which should empty directly into the laundry room. If it dumps into a remote collection room, additional personnel must then spend time retrieving it and carting it to the laundry room. Which also gives workers a wonderful opportunity to increase their home linen inventory. Employee pilferage of anything and everything—nailed down or not—has historically been a problem in the hospitality industry.

Hotels are chock-full of items that everyone would like to have in their home. There are all kinds of food items, linens, furniture, cleaning supplies, fancy soaps and shampoos, robes, and booze. Again, the layout of the facility determines how much of this goes missing. Of course, most of the people who work in hotels are the very paragons of virtue and would never, *never* be tempted to appropriate any of the above, but it's smart to make sure that temptation is not placed before them—for the benefit of those who might have the occasional moral lapse. If security is not properly dealt with in the design, the losses can be crippling, and in at least one case I know of, cause a hotel to go broke.

Although I would dearly love to believe that all my clients wanted to retain my services because I designed buildings of such breathtaking loveliness that they would cause the angels to sing, they also undoubtedly were aware of my reputation for designing hotels that actually turned a profit. Turning a profit is aesthetically pleasing to hotel owners.

Of course, if a hotel is ugly as sin, potential guests may not be tempted to stay in it. The object of the game is, after all, to put the "heads in the beds." As an architect, I really want to believe that aesthetics are the deciding factor—the Fontainebleau and the Conquistador sure proved that point. But I have seen some really ugly buildings succeed because the location was perfect, the price was right, and the building functioned efficiently and securely.

As a matter of fact, I have been the architect for several places that were at best bland, if not downright ugly. A case in point: the Churchill Hotel in London, a 476-room Loews facility our firm worked on during the late 1960s and early '70s. In order to use the name, Sir Winston's estate had to give approval, and between the overseers of the Churchill estate and the London City County, which at that point would not accept any building that had any individuality, the hotel's design took banal to new extremes.

Then there was the Aventura in North Miami Beach, a planned twenty-building monstrosity of high-rise condos. Our marching orders were to maintain a rock-bottom budget. The only "design statements" we could include were different hues of paint! Every other aspect had to be absolutely conventional, which equates with cheap. Rectangles, nothing fancy, no architectural flourishes, nada. We were a "working" architectural firm, meaning we welcomed jobs, especially big ones; if a client wanted cheap, we gave him cheap.

My background as a pilot was starting to come in handy during construction of Conquistador. From the air I got a wonderful perspective of progress on the main buildings up high, the restaurant, bar, and pool areas midway down the slope, and the beach and snack bar at the bottom, taking a few aerial snapshots to document the evolution of the project. All this would have taken an entire day on the ground, before the tramway was up and running.

On the ground itself, unfortunately, the situation was not quite that simple. One of the great cultural clashes took place when the tramway was being installed. O. D. Hopkins and all his merry men were solid, sober, straightforward "Hampshire" men. They arrived at the remote town of Fajardo to install our tramway, wearing solid work boots, plaid shirts, and serious expressions. They decidedly did not fit in with the local workforce.

The most critical phase of the installation was the proper alignment of the steel rails down which our hybrid vehicle would descend. This was a sensitive job, requiring extreme precision. A team would man theodolites, surveying tools that consisted of a powerful telescope, that would fix on a marker held by one of the other workers. The guy looking through the theodolite would note the angle and elevation of the marker. Since the mountain was steep and the terrain uneven, we would have five theodolites taking position fixes that would then be marked and coordinated.

It had taken two days to coordinate all the points down the mountain, and we were about to have all the survey instruments take the final fix, when a sailboat rounded the point just below the mountain. The sailboat had several topless beauties on deck. With a cry of "*Mira, chicas!*" every telescopic theodolite on the mountain swung away from the azimuths that it had taken days to plot, while our happy band of local surveyors screamed down to the boat's passengers, inviting them to come up to the mountain for various interesting forms of recreation.

This type of distraction was a continuing source of peril for my structures. Of course it has been the age-old prerogative, nay, the *obligation* of construction workers the world over to leer at comely ladies and make lewd comments on their endowments and the probable susceptibility to their manly charms. But the workforce in Puerto Rico tended to be dangerously liable to such distractions.

I began to realize how serious this was after the building collapsed. Well, actually, it was only *part* of the building.

Let's go back to structural-engineering concepts. I had decided to incorporate a huge balcony into the health club building so that all those happy vacationers could enjoy the spectacular views of the Caribbean. The balcony was a cantilever. A cantilever is a slab (usually concrete) that sticks out of a structure and is supported only where it is attached to the building. What makes this work is that the concrete has steel reinforcing bars known as rebars embedded within the slab to hold up the structure. Without these rebars, the concrete would be prone to bending downward if it could. But it can't—concrete doesn't bend, it breaks. You can imagine the consequences.

Calculating how many rebars are required, how big they should be, and what spacing they should be placed at is an extremely exact science. I know, because I flunked that course at Columbia and had to repeat it in summer school. Structural engineers are great at that kind of exactitude, and we had a truly great structural engineer. He had a Ph.D. from the Illinois Institute of Technology and was one of the sharpest guys I have ever worked with. Gregorio Hernandez was the kind of structural engineer you wanted to have on your team if you were going to try to design a fifteen-foot-deep, forty-foot-long cantilever. Therefore, I was somewhat mystified (mystified came a few minutes after terrified) when this formidable piece of engineering collapsed while I was standing about ten feet away from it, on the fine day when the support props were pulled. The concrete is left to harden in wooden forms for twenty-eight days, during which time it is setting and, supposedly, tightly bonding to all those carefully designed reinforcing bars. Four-by-four wooden props hold the whole thing up during this process. When the concrete has set, a steel cable is looped around these supports, and a tractor pulls them away. The aim is that what you've built will remain up in the air.

This time it didn't.

Brushing the concrete dust out of my eyes, I ran over to the tangled mass of concrete and shattered wood lying on the ground.

Guess what? There were no steel rebars.

We had just proved that concrete is really lousy in tension.

When I delicately asked the reason for this little omission, I was informed that the rebars had not been delivered to the site on the day that they were forming the balcony. Not wanting to leave that portion of the site to find the rebars (it had the ideal view of the many recreational vessels that sailed by with their many recreational women getting toasted without unsightly tan lines), the workmen had simply stayed at their posts and valiantly set out to see if they could make it stand up (the balcony, that is) by using a lot more concrete.

Concrete is a precise (that word again) mixture of portland cement, sand, gravel, and water. The proportions of each determine the strength of the concrete. Because of the steep slope of the site, it was not possible to use Redi-Mix trucks (the big ones with rotating drums). These trucks do keep the concrete mixed to exact specifications, which is why when you see them in traffic or parked outside a construction site, their drums are turning—to keep the mix just right. Timing is also of the essence; if too long a period elapses between the mixing and the pouring of the concrete, the entire load must be discarded. And my Puerto Rico workforce was not exactly known for its concern with time or details. Especially when there were bikini-clad *chicas* in the vicinity. Without these trucks, much of the concrete had to be mixed on the site, by precisely measuring the amount of water, sand, gravel, and cement. You know what's coming, don't you?

This time, in 1968, the Lanai Building, one of the structures that contained guest rooms, was located halfway down the mountain but didn't collapse. It didn't topple only because we had taken the precaution of taking a core sample of the concrete mix that had been poured. The concrete, which was supposed to have a strength of thirty-five hundred pounds per square foot, came up with a strength one-tenth of that number. I have no idea which of the many variables the workmen screwed up; all I know is that when core samples were taken, the concrete had approximately the compressive strength of a boiled strand of pasta. It was good only as a kind of a mold for pouring a second roof over the first roof.

The other item that caused me to learn some innovative inspection techniques was the pouring of the long columns that supported the entire building. Pouring concrete into long, narrow wooden forms filled with re-bars is an exacting procedure. The concrete has to be vibrated as it is poured, to make sure it flows down and through the cage of reinforcing steel and fills the forms without leaving any spaces or "voids," which would cause a structural discontinuity in the structure. Believe me, you don't want structural discontinuities in major supporting columns. And your in-surance company *really* doesn't want that sort of thing. The vibrating es-sential to this operation is accomplished by four-foot-long cylindrical pneumatic vibrators that look just like King Kong's manhood. Needless to say, performing this physically arduous job is the subject of many a laugh and cheer by one's fellow workers. And in the macho-soaked environment of a Latino construction site, it is not a job to be coveted. A job that is not to be coveted is a job that is unfailingly done badly.

I took to wandering the construction site with a five-pound maul. When I inspected newly poured columns, I learned to look for portions of concrete that were darker than the surrounding area. When the wooden forms were removed from the fresh poured columns, I often found large voids caused by inadequate vibration of the concrete as it was being formed. Lugging a fifteen-pound replica of the big monkey's nether parts through wet and solidifying concrete while your fellow workers make colorful remarks concerning the reason for your popular-ity with the ladies can cause a man to hurry through his job. In order to cover this little gaffe, the workers would take some wet cement and plas-ter over these holes. This made the columns appear to be fine and dandy. Except they weren't quite the same color as the rest of the con-crete. When I gave these dark spots a bash with my maul, the plaster would disintegrate, revealing a large hole with exposed naked reinforc-ing bars. After I made the contractor cut out a few of these monsters and repour them, a long and expensive operation, he began to oversee these operations with a new vigor.

I had also taken over the task of supervising the construction of El San Juan. While I was designing a stand-alone Chinese restaurant there called Back Street Hong Kong, I got to know Chef Kwan, the main man. After the restaurant opened, I would go in there at the end of the day, after I had finished architecting, whenever I was working in Puerto Rico over the course of two years. I would report to the kitchen to man the cook line, where Kwan taught me the proper techniques and ingredients for Chinese cooking, which I have put in practice both as a cook and as part of my "foodie" persona, which had me contributing to Gael Greene's "Insatiable Gourmet" reviews in *New York Magazine*. I became pretty good at translating orders from Spanish-speaking Puerto Rican waiters into Cantonese. My skills came in very handy one day on the Upper West Side of Manhattan, which is blessed with many Cuban-Chinese restaurants. These emporiums were started by Chinese refugees who had originally fled Mao's China but were not allowed in the US of A, so they settled in Cuba. Then when Castro took over, they had to flee once more, but this time they made it to the United States. Only Puerto Ricans can completely understand Puerto Rican Spanish, so problems can arise. One evening I was happily slurping down some noodles in La Caridad Cuban-Chinese restaurant, when a Puerto Rican came in and tried to order shrimp with bean sprouts. In Spanish that's *camarones con frijolitos*; in Puerto Rican it's *camroescon filits*. The befuddled counterman could not figure out what this customer was saying until I leaned over and said "*gaCHOY ha*," the name of the dish in Cantonese. They both shot me an astounded look. It was one of my finer moments, and the customer got his dish.

The most memorable moment at El San Juan was the near collapse of the entire building. And this one was caused by a gringo, just to prove that this was an equal opportunity project for the mentally challenged. The project was being furnished by a wonderful, whimsical interior designer named Al Lanigan, a New Yorker with great taste, which extended to his wardrobe, best described as New York chic (at least as affected by a particular segment of New York society) and always perfectly tailored to Lanigan's frame of six foot one or so. Lanigan later attracted attention for creations such as his opulent motif for La Prima Donna restaurant in the Theater District. Back when we were working on the Conquistador, however, Al seemed to possess no knowledge whatsoever of how buildings are constructed. But he had endeared himself to and become the special friend of my client, who was willing to let Lanigan do practically whatever he wanted to do, as long as the results looked marvelous.

This project had been designed by my father, who devised an esoteric form known as a shell structure for the hotel's new coffee shop. Shell structures derive their strength from the shape of the structure itself. It is the same principle that dictates that if equal pressure is applied over the entire surface of an egg, the egg will be indestructible. An easy way to visualize this is to take an ordinary sheet of eight-and-a-half-by-eleven paper and hold it up by the bottom edge; it will flop over. If, however, you fold a crease down the paper and then hold it up, it will stand, and support a weight in addition to itself. This is also sometimes known as folded plate construction. If you've ever seen the Sheraton Hotel in New York (originally the Americana), you have seen this concept in action. The building, designed by Morris, is a sixty-story structure. A standard hotel, by definition, is sixty-five feet wide, consisting of a six-foot-wide corridor, on either side of which are twenty-eight-foot-deep rooms, plus a couple of feet for the thickness of the walls. There it is, now the secret is out, and you can design your own hotel. So the most efficiently shaped hotel is in increments of sixty-five feet in width, by whatever length you and the fire code will allow, by as high as you want to make it. The Sheraton, which has two thousand rooms, is four hundred feet long, sixty-five feet wide, and more than six hundred feet tall. The net effect is a building that is long, tall, and *very* narrow. It is, in fact, like a sail—a shape that the wind would have an easy time blowing down. Not an option! You can avoid this risk by either reinforcing the living hell out of the structure to resist this wind force, a ferociously expensive procedure, or taking the predetermined shape of the building, which vaguely resembles a sheet of eight-and-a-half-by-eleven paper, and creasing it, which provides it with the rigidity to resist the wind, without spending an extra dime. That's what Morris did. As an added benefit, that form looks kind of cool. He was one smart dude.

He applied those principles to the coffee shop in El San Juan, which was a shell structure, shaped somewhat like an egg, a configuration that supported the structure, thus making interior columns unnecessary. The only downside to this type of building is that if the shell is in any way breached or deformed, it loses its structural integrity. In other words, it falls down and goes *boom*! We had poured a floor slab, on top of which was our curved and sinuous shell. Interior designer Al Lanigan had, however, commissioned a marvelous sculpture to sit in the center of the restaurant. Since the name of this café was the Yellow Bird the fiberglass sculpture was of, you guessed it, a jaundiced avian. I was apprehensive from the start about this as yet unseen sculpture, so I asked Lanigan about the weight of his whimsical form. He looked at me dismissively, replying that it was just a piece of fiberglass; I mean, it wasn't a Rodin, for pity's sake, he was saying. I cautioned Al that the floor slab was designed to hold the weight of people and bagels only, not monumental sculpture. Al shot me the contemptuous look that the true aesthete bestows upon a lowly philistine. Chastened, I left. The next day, while I was at Conquistador, Al decided that his sculpture needed an appropriate pedestal. Not one to procrastinate, he commandeered a Redi-Mix truck that was heading for one of the other buildings on site and instructed the crew to drop the entire load of concrete into a wood form he had just caused to be built in the middle of the floor. Obligingly, the men dumped several tons of concrete onto a slab designed to bear a couple of hundred pounds. Some hours later, one of the workers observed the roof of the building opening up and admitting the rays of the Puerto Rican sun. Correctly surmising that the building wasn't really intended to have a retractable roof as sports stadiums later would, the workman summoned his foreman, who summoned Al Lanigan, who summoned our client, Lou Puro, who summoned my man Gregorio Hernandez, our structural engineer. Gregorio was an imposing individual, due to his commanding presence, rotund build, olive complexion, and aristocratic bearing. He cut a sharp contrast to Lou Puro, a short, thin, white-haired little man with ice-blue eyes who came across as what I call Jewish dapper—white slacks, white patent leather loafers worn without socks, pale blue silk shirt open at the collar so as to display an oversized gold chain he wore around his neck. Gregorio Hernandez was also the president of the local Engineering Society. He did not suffer fools easily.

By now there was a considerable and growing outdoor seating area within the shell of the restaurant. Gregorio studied the cracking structure, then the huge mound of concrete in the center of the floor span, then Al, and then he fixed his gaze on Lou. In a deceptively calm voice he informed Lou that the floor slab was structurally connected to the main building, and that the shell structure was tied in to the floor slab, and that the shell structure was failing because of an unauthorized load that had been placed on it without consulting him. It was a domino effect, Gregorio explained. When the shell collapsed, as it was bound to in a few hours, it would also bring down the main structure, which was at present full of several hundred paying guests. Then he turned on his heel and started to leave.

A shocked Lou asked Gregorio what he should do. With a look of utter scorn, Gregorio informed Lou that he could do whatever he wanted, but that he, Gregorio Hernandez, was on his way to the government's building department, where he would have all the permits revoked and make sure that Lou was never allowed to build anything, ever again, anywhere on the island.

Lou groveled. Yes, my intimidating, tough New York developer client begged. Of course, having one's building collapsing around one's head can tend to inspire a ton of humility. Even in a New York developer of the well-connected variety.

After Lou performed the proper acts of contrition, the entire workforce was dragooned to bring every piece of wood and steel they could find, as a means of propping up the drastically weakened floor. As his concrete pedestal was hacked to pieces, Al Lanigan fell into a terminal sulk.

By then I was more than ready to go back to New York.

Throughout my association with Lou Puro, he made no bones about the fact that he was part of what you might euphemistically term the "in-crowd." While I was working on El Conquistador and El San Juan, he liked to have dinner with me, which was fine except when, as per his habit, he imbibed too much, which often transformed him into a mean drunk. One evening about 10 or 11 o'clock while we were eating at another casino he owned, he suddenly demanded that I show him the latest plans. We spread them out on a craps table that was closed and started looking over them. In the midst of this bizarre scene—a zaftig cocktail waitress hanging over the boss, boozy tourists wandering up to see what was happening, and all that, Lou squinted at me with his very light blue eyes and asked, "Alan, is this joint going to be open for the season?"— which, as mentioned, was all-important for financial considerations. Well, I explained, we had gotten a very late start, it was a bitch getting labor and materials out to the site, and I outlined several other very real reasons why I was worried about opening in time. Nevertheless, I assured him, I was doing my best. From his standpoint it was essential to be open before cold weather set in up north, and he snarled at me, "Alan, if this joint ain't open for the season, I'm gonna cut your heart out!" Standing directly behind me, his "guy" whispered in my ear, "Hey, Alan, that wasn't a figure of speech."

Lou and Al Lanigan, Lou's interior designer, had insisted that every inch of the lobby and public spaces be covered in pink marble, which they claimed was the only acceptable material for a place as classy as the one they were building. They also went on at great length about how they had gone to Italy and made "such a deal" to buy the marble on the cheap. *But*—some of the invoices intended for them were misdirected to my office, and I noticed that their alleged bargain price for the marble was almost double the usual cost. Obviously, my patron was ripping off his silent partners, who would not have liked that at all. Lou owed me about a quarter of a million bucks, and if his partners found out what was going on, he and the entire project, not to mention the money he owed me, would be in serious jeopardy. Moreover, as was customary when doing business with people like Lou, our contract was strictly oral and based upon a handshake.

At that point I asked Lou to pay my outstanding bill.

"Hey, Alan, what's up?" Lou said. "All of a sudden you don't trust me? We shook hands on the deal."

"I trust you with my life, Lou." How true! "But if, God forbid, anything should happen, like you get hit by a beer truck, nobody knows how much I am owed."

"Hey! I'm very careful when I cross the street."

End of discussion.

I knew Lou had a local attorney—the type commonly referred to as "consigliere"—so I went to talk to that individual. I laid out for him the invoices I had received by mistake. After he took one look at them, there was no need for me to elaborate.

"What do you intend to do with these?" he asked.

"I need to have my account brought up to date."

"Do you understand the implications of what you are saying?"

"I need to have my account brought up to date."

"Well, Mr. Lapidus, you are either very smart or very stupid. I can guarantee you that very shortly your account will be brought up to date, or else some misfortune may possibly befall you."

I thanked him and left.

My check for payment in full arrived within a week. And I was paid promptly for my remaining work.

I had relied on my ace in the hole: I knew I was a lot more valuable to Lou Puro alive than dead, since without me there was no chance the place would open in time. Which it did.

At the beginning of the job, Lou had promised me—also orally—that once the hotel opened, my wife, our son Adam, and I would be his guests for a week. True to the code that a promise and a handshake are absolutely binding on one's honor, the formal invitation soon arrived from the hotel's general manager, and we did in fact spend a wonderful week there. Adam actually had played a bit role in the design of the hotel, or at least its pool. While Conquistador was under construction, I wanted to be sure that he would be able to stand up in the pool, so I measured from his feet to his shoulders, and that became the depth of the shallow end of the pool. He liked to tell his friends that if they wanted to know how tall he was when he was five, they should check out the swimming pool there. Of course no one could foresee that he would grow up to be a six-foot-ten basketball center, known to his teammates as "T.J.," or "Tall Jew."

About thirty years passed. Then, in the mid-1990s and totally by chance, I ran into Lou one evening as he was exiting the Friars Club in New York City. Time had been kind to him. He still had all his hair, although it had turned snow-white, and those blue eyes were just as intense. With a big smile and a hearty handshake he introduced me to his cronies: "This is Alan Lapidus. A great architect, but he just doesn't take your word for things." After thirty years!

In architecture, if you manage to complete a given type of job once, you're an expert. If you do it twice, you become the world's authority. In the late '60s, a confluence of circumstances had plunged me into the wonderful world of Latin American hotel construction. I had designed the Conquistador and El San Juan; I spoke Spanish; the firm had served as architects for two hotels that our southern cousins revered, the Fontainebleau and the Eden Roc; and my personality was *muy simpático* with the *alma español* (the Spanish soul). In other words, I had the

demeanor of an amiable adolescent who could design a hotel that actually would remain standing (usually) and functional. Over the next few
decades, as a result, I found myself working in the jungles of El Salvador, the steamy swamps of Guayaquil, Ecuador, the rain forest of
Amazonia (see Chapter 16), and numerous emerging Caribbean islands.
Some of those islands were technically Dutch and some American, but
the Latin spirit and my grasp of it were all-encompassing—and all that
mattered.

9

What Happens in Vegas . . .

Atlantic City was opening for business, and I was doing my best to get in on the action. But there was one obstacle for me to overcome: Although I had designed half a dozen casinos in the Caribbean, I was new to the American gaming industry. If I was going to be designing casinos in Atlantic City, I had to know the domestic casino business inside and out, the objective being that my plans would serve my clients' needs. In 1978, early on in my Atlantic City career, Rocky Aoki, the head of the Benihana Steakhouse chain, retained me to draw up what was planned as the Benihana Hotel and Casino on the Boardwalk site of the legendary old Shelburne Hotel. Rocky sent me to Las Vegas for some postgraduate study, the kind of wisdom they sure don't teach you in architecture school. What I learned about casinos on this trip did in fact become very useful in my design philosophy.

Notwithstanding my background in gaming abroad, I had been to Las Vegas just twice before and was pretty much a stranger to the town. Clad in my eastern establishment uniform of blue blazer, gray flannel slacks, and Brooks Brothers button-down shirt, I appeared to be the only person *not* wearing garments made from chemicals. A uniformed driver, holding an ornate sign bearing my name, led me to a limousine that had obviously been on steroids. The interior was teak and white leather, and this rolling palace was equipped with a full bar, a stereo, a TV set with VHS player, mood lighting, and a couch seat. Slightly overwhelmed, I thanked the chauffeur for bringing my hotel room to me.

My last trip to Vegas had been in 1970, when my father and I were invited to talk to some moneymen about designing a new casino-hotel on the Strip. At the time he and I were heavily involved in the emerging world of Caribbean hotels and casinos. Morris's Fontainebleau Hotel in Miami Beach had evolved into the icon of the American dream resort, and our El Conquistador in Puerto Rico was becoming the in place for younger American fun seekers, so developers looking to create new, appealing vacation resorts were calling us frequently.

The Las Vegas people were planning the largest casino-hotel ever built, to be called the International. After a day or so of being tag-team interviewed by a variety of Vegas types, we were in a room when a middle-aged man of average height, quite slender, and with a long, pleasant face walked in. Clad in a yellow sport shirt and tan slacks, he could have been any midwestern tourist enjoying the sights, except that he gave his name as Kirk Kerkorian. At that time I knew nothing of the reclusive billionaire, which no doubt reveals how parochial I was. After discovering that he and I shared an interest in flying our own small planes, he took me aside for several hours and related his life story to me, including the fact that he didn't like to be photographed because he didn't want anyone to recognize him.

Kerkorian told me how he had tried to enlist in the Army Air Corps at the beginning of World War II but was rejected as a pilot because he didn't have the required minimum two years of college. Nor even a high school diploma. Instead, he got a job ferrying aircraft to England, which paid a good bit of money and inspired him to start buying surplus planes the U.S. government offered at outrageously low prices after the war. Because he had asthma, he wanted to live in a dry climate. That brought him to Las Vegas. One good investment led to another, and eventually he bought some cheap land on what would become the Strip. He had been a partner in several casino deals, but this was to be his big solo move.

Eventually he invited us to be his architects on the project. There was one proviso: One of us would have to move out to Las Vegas full-time. Neither Morris nor I had ever relocated permanently for any other project, and neither of us felt like moving to the desert, so we turned him down. Kerkorian went ahead with other architects. By the time the place opened, it had been renamed the Las Vegas Hilton. So much for intelligence and foresight on the part of Morris and Alan Lapidus.

My mentor in Vegas on the later 1978 trip, slated to run Rocky Aoki's Atlantic City venture, was a man named Jimmy Hill, then the casino boss of Caesars Palace, one of the justifiably fabled resorts on the Las Vegas Strip. I should make clear that when I describe Jimmy as "casino boss," that's the job I was told he had. Conforming with the custom in Vegas for people of importance, he carried no business card or anything else that bore his exact title. As Kirk Kerkorian explained to me when I asked for his business card, "I don't have business cards. No one knows what I look like, so anyone could have business cards made up with my name on them and pass himself off as me." In other words, if someone who seems to be a Las Vegas mover and shaker hands you a business card, it may well be phony.

Jimmy quickly took me under his wing and started teaching me exactly what kind of joint he and the Aoki investors wanted. My tutorial began the evening of my arrival, when I met him at the entrance to the casino. Jimmy was of an indeterminate age, probably somewhere between sixty and seventy-five. He was heavily tanned, his face shouting that he had spent much of his life in a sunny climate even before Vegas—Cuba, back in the day, the Bahamas, maybe the Riviera. He wore a gray silk suit, white-on-white shirt, and a pale blue tie, along with the obligatory pinkie ring. Plus sunglasses that shaded from an impenetrable dark brown to clear. When Jimmy aimed those steel-framed eyeglasses at you, you felt like he was looking right through you.

As Jimmy and I stood and gazed out at the sea of clanging, chiming, whooping slot machines and beyond to the brilliantly lit green felt of the tables that first night, I recognized that my life as an Upper West Side quasi intellectual was about to be forever altered.

Jimmy kept his hands in his pockets and gestured toward the gaming floor with his chin.

"What do you know about gaming?"

"Well, I've built some resorts in the Caribbean."

"I didn't ask what you built, I asked what you know."

"Oh, the psychology of it?"

Switching into my professorial mode, I launched into a display of my knowledge. (Come to think if it, my knowledge, or lack thereof, was why Rocky Aoki had paid for me to visit Jimmy.) "I think the whole objective of the casino business is participatory theater. We set the stage and let people act out their own fantasies about being high rollers. If the stage set—the casino hotel—is grand enough, if the materials bespeak luxury and affluence, then the building endows the people in it with the mindset that they are the rich and famous, and before they know it, they blow the egg money. In other words, what we are doing is designing a controlling environment that detaches the patron from the ordinary aspects of everyday reality so that he can . . ."

I noticed that Jimmy was eyeing me as if I were a fish that died about a week ago and somebody had laid the item on his plate.

"Did you just use the word 'bespeak'?" he barked. "Look, Al [I hate being called Al], what we are doing is giving the guy back his cock. The average guy busts his hump fifty weeks out of the year. He gets two lousy weeks off and comes to Vegas. He walks into the casino, and a chick with tits out to *here*, I mean, someone this guy would never have the balls to talk to, comes up to him with her goodies sticking out, and says, 'Sir, may I offer you a complimentary glass of champagne?' Hey, the guy's a stud. He can't wait to hit the tables."

Las Vegas casinos are laid out so that a guest has to cross the gaming floor to get to any other part of the hotel, including the bathroom. Especially the bathroom. In Atlantic City, by contrast, draconian design regulations mandate that guests must be able to reach any area of the hotel, from any other area, without entering the casino. The New Jersey rules—drawn up only a few years earlier—also require that the casino floor not be visible from the hotel entrance. Jimmy was horrified.

"Who's the asshole that thought that one up?"

"The Casino Control Commission."

"Any of them have gaming experience?"

"Not a bit."

"Hotel experience?"

"I think they may have stayed in a few."

"Who are these guys?"

"A former judge, a business guy who is from one of the politically connected money families, a black woman, and a politician."

"How long did they spend in Vegas?"

"As far as I know, they never visited Vegas."

"And they are in charge of starting a new gaming state?"

"Yep."

Reply unprintable.

As we took a slow walk around the gaming floor, Jimmy explained the logic of the layout. "It's sort of like a supermarket. The impulse items are the slots, the table games are the staples, and the baccarat pit is the fancy-food section. Slots surround the floor. You have to go through them when you come in or go out and when you cash out at the bank, plus they have their own pit, kind of like the junk-food section. The staples are in the center of the floor. That's why they come, so we draw 'em through the slots first. If they got any bucks left after they play, they feed the machines. Baccarat gets its own fancy pit. Basically it's an idiot's game. You have to be able to count all the way up to nine. With black-jack you got to get all the way up to twenty-one. But by making baccarat the big-money game, strictly for the high rollers, we create a prestige thing. The baccarat pit gets its own cocktail waitresses, the best-looking ones. The pit is fancier than the floor, and we put up a velvet rope to keep the riffraff out. The only reason it's got all this prestige is that you get to lose major bucks in a very elegant setting."

At that moment a shout emanated from one of the craps tables, where a crowd had started to form. We wandered over. A player on a roll had amassed an impressive pile of chips.

"Do you get concerned when a player is on a major winning streak?" I asked Jimmy.

"No. We love it. If the guy wins big, all the other players are going to get inspiration and blow it big-time. The law of averages is always work-ing for us. No matter how much this guy wins, eventually he's going to give it all back to us, with interest. Nothing inspires someone to lose like a big winning streak."

We continued walking and talking.

"Let's take a look at the bank," he suggested. He guided me over to an unmarked door with a ubiquitous small silver half dome above it. These little artifacts dotted the ceiling of the gaming floor. I knew that they contained small high-definition "pan-and-tilt" remote control cameras. Big Brother was definitely watching.

Jimmy slid a key card into a slot on the door, and we entered a small passageway at the end of which was an identical door, with an identical key slot. This was known as the "man trap," because the opposite door could not be opened until the first door had been shut and locked. This device prevented someone from breaking down the door and helping himself to all the goodies stored here. If he blew the first door, the second was enough of a delay for the Seventh Cavalry to arrive.

Together, Jimmy and I entered the "bank." I had a deliciously illicit feeling of being an insider as I looked out through the tellers' windows to the throngs who were lined up, eager to exchange their hard currency for the chips that were passports to the world of dreams and, hope against hope, wish fulfillment. The throngs were eager to be fleeced, to be more accurate. In the center of this large area was the vault. Its door stood open; on the floor was a large pile of what looked like white canvas mail sacks, secured by ordinary wire ties with six-figure numbers written on their cardboard tags. Following my gaze, Jimmy casually remarked, "The cash can get backed up when the count is slow."

Inside the vault was a large rack with flat trays. "These are the backup chips. If someone has counterfeited our chips or is running some kind of a scam, we can recall the chips on the floor and replace them with this second set. It's what the military calls a deterrent. The scammers know what we got, so they don't even try."

"Never?"

"It's not worth all the trouble if it's just a few chips. But, what the hell, it's the price of doing business. But then again, greed is what always trips these guys up. If they get away with a few chips, then they are going to want more. They always want more, until they get more than they bargained for. That's human nature, our ace in the hole."

Next, Jimmy led me to the "eye." Exiting the money store, we climbed a stairway in back, where a security guard sat outside yet another carefully secured door. When Jimmy opened it, I found myself in another surreal environment—an enormous dark space, roughly the same size as the gaming floor below.

I had landed in a world that technically did not exist, an area you won't find marked on any elevator panel or on any stair landing. When I subsequently produced construction drawings for casinos, my plans always referred to this sector as either a "mechanical floor" or "truss space." In the casino vocabulary of Las Vegas, it is called the "eye in the sky." In Atlantic City, it is called the "peek."

Although the eye did, in fact, have large steel trusses, and the space *was* crisscrossed with massive ducts that vented the smoke-filled casino air and resupplied it with fresh, chilled air, it also contained a vast network of carpeted catwalks. Laid out in orderly pathways, the catwalks paralleled long banks of angled windows that looked over the gaming tables, windows that appeared to be mirrors from below on the casino floor. The catwalks were carpeted to muffle the sound of the watchers walking upon them and illuminated by low-intensity lights lining the sides, much like a movie theater aisle. Low railings separated the catwalks from the windows a few feet below.

The only other light in this vast space was what leaked via the windows from the scene below. Through these windows, the bright green of the felt tabletops, the colors of the gamblers' clothing, the costumes of the employees, and the frantic goings-on below constituted a stark contrast to the gloom of the eye. Most incongruous of all was the overpowering quiet that pervaded the watchers' space. The overall effect was akin to watching a silent movie in a huge theater without seats.

After looking on silently for a few minutes, Jimmy and I moved along a stark and unadorned corridor into a scene that resembled nothing so much as Mission Control. We had entered what actually was the control room, the nerve center of the eye. Within this locked and guarded space was a wall of TV monitors. At a console in front of this bank of screens sat technicians, each surrounded by a cluster of small pedestal-mounted control sticks that remotely operated the "pan, zoom, and tilt" cameras located within the strategically placed mirrored bubbles that dotted the ceiling of the floor below. Also situated on the control pedestal were two large screens that could take over from any of the pictures displayed on the smaller screens. When the displays were switched from the small to the large screens, a time and location tape automatically played across the bottom.

The technology seemed amazingly sophisticated. One of the techs demonstrated the power of the zoom feature. He focused a camera on a credit slip at one of the pits, bringing the signature into clearly visible view. Next, he panned around the tables, zeroing in on one player picking his nose, another with a nervous tic, and other fascinating candid close-ups of the unsuspecting. Placing a hand on the shoulder of one of the camera operators, Jimmy casually asked whether the man had observed anything worth noting.

"Well, I got a chick in pit five, table three, seat two, that's wearing a dress that's so low and so loose that I can see that she is a natural blonde." It was an old Vegas joke, strictly for my benefit.

My guide and I descended the stairs and continued our tour of the "back of the house." In a hotel, anything that the public sees is the "front of the house" while the parts they don't see are considered the "back of the house." Except, that is, for my future client, the Disney Corporation, where the facilities are divided into "backstage" and "onstage."

But this was Vegas, a world away from Disney World, which became even more evident when we wandered down yet another faceless corridor and arrived at a jail cell. I was familiar with the gaming regulations that govern every aspect of the casinos in Atlantic City, so I was aware that New Jersey casinos had been granted quasi-police powers. If someone is suspected of cheating, the casino security forces have the right, or actually the obligation, to detain the suspect in a state-mandated jail cell that the regs describe as to size, shape, ventilation, even down to details as minute as the location of manacle attach points. New Jersey laws clearly have been inspired by similar regulations in Las Vegas.

Looking into the cell, I remarked nervously, "I guess this is where someone goes if he gets unlucky."

Jimmy's eyes narrowed. "Al, this is where he goes if he gets real *lucky*." It took me several beats to realize what he was saying—that cheaters were much better off in the hands of the law than at the mercy of those who lived outside the law. As Jimmy saw my expression change with dawning comprehension, he let out a small snicker. "Okay, kid, let's talk."

He pushed open the door to the cell and we sat down on the cot. That was Jimmy's idea of a joke.

"They used to do things in Vegas in a slightly different way before all this corporate shit started. Let me put it this way, in the old days this town was not run by the Little Sisters of Mercy. Times change, things change, but let me give you a little education. I know, from the beard, the tweeds, and the flannels that you're an eastern liberal kind of a guy, but let's reason this out.

"Some joker comes to Vegas on a convention, and he decides that he's a wise guy. He starts thumb-marking the cards. We spot him on the cameras and the guy in the eye verifies it visually. Now, we don't *suspect* that he's marking the cards, we've got him on camera from three different angles, plus verification from the eye, *and* we grab the cards.

"So we're doing it your way, the new way, by the book. We escort him to this nice air-conditioned cell that the regulations require us to have, and we call the Clark County cops off the street, where they are trying to stop *real* crime. They take him downtown to the slammer. They book him and he's tried according to the laws of God and man. We have a nice trial where we show the tapes and the cards with his marks and his prints, and the guy from the eye testifies. Not a big contest. Clark County doesn't take kindly to folks who try and mess up the game. He gets convicted and goes to the joint. He's a convicted felon. It costs the taxpayers twenty-five large or more a year to keep him locked up, his boss fires his ass, his old lady divorces the lowlife, his kids are ashamed that their old man is a con, and in prison he meets with all sorts of jailbirds who do disgusting things to his body. Plus, he learns all kinds of bad criminal shit. When he gets out, he has no job, no family, he has a record, and he becomes a menace to society.

"Now let's look at the way they used to do things. They spot the guy marking the deck. Instead of escorting him to this nice little jail cell, they escort him to the parking lot. There, they inform him that they are on to his game and are displeased. They then break his leg. Just one. They bring him back to his room and call the house doctor."

Jimmy noticed my look of surprise. "Hey, they're not animals. After his leg is set, he calls home and tells the little lady he had one too many and fell down some stairs. He comes home like a wounded hero. His boss, scared that the guy is going to sue because he was on a company convention, gives him all the time off he wants, with pay. Blue Cross picks up all the expenses, his family waits on the wounded warrior hand

and foot, he eventually goes back to work. And best of all, he's learned *never to do that stuff again*!

"Where were they wrong?"

I saw no need to disagree with Jimmy. And I was gaining real respect for the empirical understanding of human nature that guides the gaming world.

Our next stop was the "count" area where, well, the money gets counted. It is divided into the hard count, where the coins are weighed and mechanically sorted and tallied by machines, and the soft count where, in those days, the bills were hand-counted in an environment straight out of a bad science fiction movie. Since this room is supercritical, containing hundreds of thousands of dollars in unmarked, unsequenced used bills, it is the ideal place to steal.

To ensure that virtue prevails, there are rigid security measures. Among them, everyone has to get naked. Well, not both sexes together, but males and females strip to the buff in separate locker rooms and don house-issued coveralls *with no pockets*. Then they pass through a security screening to make sure there are no items on them that could be used to take the cash for a visit elsewhere. In the count room, they sit on opposite sides of a long, clear, Plexiglas table that has an opaque divider running its length. Above them, the pan-and-tilt cameras are twirling like ballerinas on speed. The Plexiglas ensures that the cameras can see that the counters' laps contain nothing but the counters' laps. A pile of money is handed to a counter who counts it. Then the sum is put on a piece of paper and the pile is handed to the counter on the other side of the divider, who also counts it and writes the amount. Both sums are compared, and if they agree, the pile is tagged and they move on to the next pile. If not, it is re-counted.

In my designs for casinos in Atlantic City, one perpetual and crucial issue has been security in the toilets for the count room. If the toilets are outside the count area, the counters have to go through the security procedures coming and going, which burns up a lot of time, especially for the ones with weak bladders. On the other hand, if the toilets are within the count area, the issue is whether it's appropriate to have ceiling cameras above the "throne." I was present at one heated discussion between the chief of security at the proposed Benihana Casino and the facility's director of human resources. The security chief viewed the world as a place inhabited by scammers, cheats, and thieves (imagine being a member of *his* immediate family!), while the human resources lady was horrified at the idea of cameras recording these most private human functions. The security chief was loudly pointing out that the toilet was the ideal place for a counter to deposit the company's cash into an individual's God-provided hidden carrying place.

The human resources lady was shocked, absolutely shocked. "And you propose putting cameras above the women's stalls?"

The security guy eyed her as if he had encountered someone without a brain. "For Christ's sake, they got *twice* as many places to stash it as the men!"

After our tour of the count room, Jimmy and I broke for dinner. The restaurant overlooked the gaming floor, thus providing another chance to analyze human behavioral modification. As we ate, I tried to tally what I had been observing. A definite philosophy governed this brave new world, which was not simply a happy-go-lucky place that serendipitously offered games of chance. The entire setup was the result of an ordered thought process, one that dealt with the *real* essence of human behavior. Human beings' actions and reactions are programmed by what I have since come to call signifier forms. Rectangles and right angles are no-nonsense shapes that bring out a rational response. It is not by happenstance that government buildings and office buildings take this form. Rounded corners, curves, and other sinuous shapes, by contrast, promise excitement and the unusual. My father had been right on target with his quarter-arc design of the Fontainebleau, which has become *the* image to signify fun, sun, and, perhaps, a little adventure. He had taken measure of the human animal and been able to tap into its most primal stimuli. And he had correctly analyzed the physical reactions of people to external physical stimuli, such as:

The moth theory—people gravitate to the most brightly lit area. This is a variation on the maxim in the theater that a seasoned actor can always "find the light," meaning he or she perpetually goes to the area of the stage where the light is brightest.

Curves and angles—people have a need to peer and go around corners to discover whatever is not readily apparent.

The woggle, the bean pole, and *the cheese hole*—since most folks live and work in rational rectilinear spaces, any space that has funny shapes, long poles, or holes in the wall (all of which were in Morris's signature design vocabulary) denotes fun, the unusual, play. In short, the good stuff.

Sitting amid the frenzied activity taking place all around me, I realized that this industry had gone Morris one better. Its founders and their successors had implemented a far more complex set of stimuli to influence the psychological motivations of human action and behavior.

That explains why, as is commonly known, time is not allowed to exist in a casino. There are no windows, no clocks, and no connection to the outside world. Everything in this insulated space is constant. The lighting level never varies, nor does the temperature or humidity. The restaurants and bars are always open, and everything is the same at 3 o'clock in the afternoon as it is at 3 o'clock in the morning. The whole environment is designed—successfully—to suppress the body's natural circadian rhythms.

In short, nothing by chance, everything by design.

Allow me a brief, Vegas-inspired aside. Just as a rock beneath the surface of a stream will cause the water to swirl and eventually create a new flow pattern (which is why rivers and streams usually are serpentine), certain visual stimuli and physical objects will cause people to move in predetermined paths. Lighting, color, sound (always have two different music venues at opposite ends of a long gaming floor) cause subliminal reactions which, if understood and controlled, will cause most people to react in a predictable way. In the case of casino design, for example, bet the rent money.

Before the casinos got so smart, architects (not today's crop, by any means) and dictators had traditionally been the control freaks of every civilization. It's no coincidence that there has always been a successful collaboration between the two. The despots, the absolute rulers, were the ones who had the lust to create remarkable structures. Not necessarily good or bad buildings, but *remarkable.* As in, "Look at *that* sumbitch!" Thus, the buildings endowed their creators with the aura of power.

Absolute rulers have long realized that people can be controlled by the constructed environment. Some of the most ancient structures in human history are monuments to influence human reactions. The Romans were the masters of this genre. They simply overscaled all their public buildings in order to convey the power of the state. A standard doorway is six feet eight inches tall. In many Roman civic structures, entry portals were at least fifteen feet tall. That made a human feel small and insignificant. The goal was not to create an entrance for people but rather to impress on the individual that he was entering the realm of the all powerful. When the Romans conquered a new territory, they built a road, an aqueduct, and a *thermae*, or bath. Although the road and the aqueduct were functional, they were also a sign to the defeated that the victors could transport people, commerce, armies, and water with surprising ease.

The *thermae* were built to knock their socks off. With their high vaults, hot and cold running water, and cavernous spaces, they were, in fact, silent lessons to the vanquished that one should not mess with these dudes.

The lesson was not lost on succeeding civilizations.

It is debatable whether the Catholic church could have had such a strong hold on medieval Europe had it not been for the Gothic cathedral. Consider your basic peasant, having a hard enough time trying to keep his family fed, alive, and unraped. He's told to tithe over a portion of his meager yearly crop for the adulation of a being who was not only God, but was actually three people, one of whom was a virgin mother, another was her son and a Jewish carpenter to boot, and a third was an ethereal being whom no one had seen but who had gotten the virgin pregnant. It is what I characterize as a hard sell.

Now deliver this same message in Chartres Cathedral. Said peasant lived in what can be quaintly described as a hovel, and the high-rise of the day would be the house of the local lord, which might be all of two stories. This was the most impressive structure in this guy's world. Now, arising on the flat landscape was this massive, gleaming stone structure. Once inside, the guy's head would snap back to take in the soaring masonry vaults with their pointed arches mysteriously shrouded in gloom, suffused with a purple radiance that filtered in through the stained glass (in and of itself, a mind-boggler). Behind him, the huge circular rose window overpowered his senses when, dazzled, he turned back to the entrance door.

What a rush! It was the fourteenth-century version of LSD.

From that point on, the guy was a true believer.

It was the architecture that had instilled faith. Without such structures, we would probably still believe in wood nymphs.

This lesson was not lost on succeeding civilizations, either. The fact is, architecture helps establish rules and laws, lure people into sensuous activities from gambling to drinking to sex, and even helps instill faith. The pharaohs, the Roman Empire, the religious faiths with their imposing churches and cathedrals never had much use for democracy. But they certainly had a great appreciation for the uses of architecture.

Winston Churchill once famously declared, "We shape our buildings and then our buildings shape us." That is a truism that can cut both ways. When I designed hotels for Disney (see Chapter 11), I learned that using a building's scale as a controlling medium could be just as effective in reverse. Children and adults love the Main Street USA attraction in the Disney theme parks. It features a mythical street in an idealized small town. The secret of the good feelings generated by this experience is that every building in this interactive stage set is *underscaled*. Every component of every building, up to and including the ceiling height, is just slightly and imperceptibly smaller, narrower, and shorter than normal. Kids feel taller, more empowered, when they enter this environment.

A carefully planned environment can influence and control human behavior. This is a lesson every successful architect must learn.

Over the course of four days in Las Vegas under Jimmy's tutelage, I learned more about the potential of architecture than I had in four years of architectural school. With him I saw thousands of supposedly rational people happily performing an act against self-interest: gaming. Most of the folks I was watching had worked hard for their money. In the business world, how many of them would have been seduced into a venture where the odds are so heavily stacked against them? In casino land, the best odds are at the craps table, but *only* if you have the type of mathematical mind that can calculate the changing odds with each throw of the dice. And even if you do, the odds are still against you. Depending on the game, the house has a 15 to 50 percent advantage. Yet in Las Vegas I watched hordes of humanity literally lined up to lose. As the head of the New Jersey Casino Control Board observed at one meeting I attended, "People do not build five-hundred-million-dollar casinos to offer even odds."

Jimmy was a natural-born teacher, and I was trying to be an apt pupil. I had observed the how, now I learned the why. There is an instinct in the human animal, particularly the male human animal, to picture oneself as heroic, capable of conquering heavy odds, triumphing or at least showing they have fought the good fight. We are also a breed of vicarious warriors. It's hardly surprising that ever since at least the Romans in the Coliseum, the masses have enjoyed sitting by and watching others do the fighting while they do the cheering. Ever watch a crowd at a sports bar during a hotly contested sporting event?

Gambling, on a primal level, is *la petite guerre*, the little war. Money substitutes for blood. If we win at the tables, we have valiantly triumphed over the odds, and if we lose, well, the odds were against us, but we fought the good fight. Gaming is rarely about money. It is about winning. Why else do zillionaires risk ruin by entering into more and different business schemes? It isn't to make them richer. These individuals already have more money than anyone can ever spend. Money is a way to keep score. You keep score to make sure that you are a winner.

Every aspect of the casino environment has evolved by recognizing what worked and then embellishing it. Since gaming is a macho thing, the organizers realized that profits could be enhanced by liberally sprinkling about an assortment of very good-looking women, dressed in costumes indicating some sort of servitude. Remember, in movie fantasies, slave girls are always flouncing around seminude, while the fully dressed lords and ladies disport themselves. What good is make-believe macho without a flock of adoring nymphets?

The art of designing the cocktail waitress costume is, in and of itself, an exercise in applied psychology, combined with a dose of architectural and/or engineering reality. (Howard Hughes, a genius at airplane design, among other things, attempted to pad the market for his 1943 movie *The Outlaw* with his design for a bra that enhanced the prominence of Jane Russell's top—already well-endowed by nature.) In the casino industry it is a given that breasts will be pushed up and out, legs will be wrapped in fishnet hose or other pseudohooker casings, and the outfit's overall theme will be erotic. Several casinos have gone a step further. Realizing that a good number of men actually find half-naked women somewhat intimidating ("Omigod, what if she actually wants to *do* something with me? I mean, it's okay to fantasize, but what if . . . !"), these psychologically savvy joints have provided all the women with the same head covering, often a harem girl's hat and veil, or else identical wigs, such as the ever-popular blond shoulder-length pageboy. This clever twist has the advantage of depersonalizing these "ladies" and making them appear identical—manufactured, such as Stepford babes—and therefore not really real. Therefore, they become food for fantasy without being personally intimidating.

Do the casino interests really think all this through in this manner? Absolutely! And this type of thinking pays off! The Las Vegas casino that has carried this thought process one step beyond most others is the Rio. When it first opened in 1996, I was there, carrying on my habitual informal survey of casino popularity. I asked every cabdriver I could find which casino was his personal favorite, and why. (Vegas cabdrivers are usually a savvy group of characters who love to share their views on everything pertaining to "the business.") The replies were consistent: The Rio was their playground of choice. When I asked why, to a man they winked and instructed me to check out the costumes the cocktail waitresses wear.

Acting on their advice, I learned by personal observation that American ingenuity had once again pushed the new frontier out further. The new frontier, was, in fact, *thongs!*

It's definitely worth noting here that this breakthrough occurred in the casino that was designed, built, and owned by an architect. After designing many other Las Vegas casinos, Tony Marnell asked himself the most important question that an architect can ever raise: "If I'm so damned smart, why aren't I rich?"

Tony Marnell is now both smart *and* rich. I learned a lot about him and the Rio because an old friend of mine, David Hanlon, was president and chief operating officer of the Rio when Marnell opened it. And the world of Las Vegas is enriched because Tony realized that while some females have fine bosoms, many more women have a lovely bottom.

Sexist? You bet, same as the entire gaming business and related operations. But also very real-world. And so very Las Vegas, so very much the gaming industry's mentality worldwide. In my experience, female high rollers are so rare as to be almost nonexistent. As a matter of fact, "high roller" itself is a term that's not used all that commonly in the gaming business. Big-time bettors are widely known within the industry as "whales," which originally meant people—men, that is—who could be counted on to risk at least $1 million in a single casino visit and has since been extended to include those who will bet at least several hundred thousand dollars per visit. The definition has been expanded in order to inflate the egos of more players in what is an intensely ego-driven business—a sop, again, to the *male* ego.

Sure, I know that the televised poker games of recent vintage often feature women, but don't forget they are *TV shows* that do not necessarily reflect reality, at least reality from the vantage point of the casino operators. All my casino designs have been commissioned by a male cult and for a male cult, featuring babes who put their assets on display while they serve drinks to the machos. In fact, the main concern of the management of every casino I've designed has been how to occupy the wife or girlfriend and keep her away from her man while he's losing the mortgage money. To this end I've designed ever more luxurious spas (heavier on facials, rubs, and body wraps than on exercise machines), as well as more and better shopping areas. This has reached its logical apogee in Las Vegas, where the new joints have more retail area, and very upscale retail at that, than gaming area. The gaming mavens have arrived at the realization that the time a guy spends at the tables is limited only by the depth of his pocket and his lady's propensity to distract him.

As mentioned before, I'm one of those eastern liberals, which means I believe in the dignity of and equal opportunity for women. Nevertheless, I can't ignore the realities of the casino universe, as epitomized by New Jersey Gaming Commission Chairman Joseph Lordi, always my touchstone of realpolitik. Lordi once was in the position of adjudicating a point of real contention: A men's group wanted the commission to force the casinos to hire men to serve cocktails. Quoting no known precedents on the subject, the chairman said with a smirk, "When the men have legs like these gals, that's when I will consider it."

Jimmy in Vegas was my third guru, the only one whose teachings dealt exclusively with the gaming business. My first mentor was my father. The second was John Hench, a famed story artist and animator at Disney. John, the institutional memory of the company, spent sixty-five years at Disney until his death in 2004 and was one of the last key figures there who had worked closely with Walt.

I started my own association with Hench in 1979, on my first design project for Disney, a resort called Mediterranean Village the company planned to build at Disney World in Florida. Hench was the artistic maven of the Disney domain, the "official portrait artist" for Mickey Mouse and the man Walt picked in 1945 to work with Salvador Dalí on an animated short called *Destino (Destiny)*, the story of a female dancer who glides through surreal scenes inspired by Dalí's paintings. (Because of financial problems at Disney, *Destino* was shelved soon after Hench and Dalí began their labors; eventually rediscovered in the firm's archives, it was released in 2003.) In his spare time Hench designed the torch for the 1960 Winter Olympics at Squaw Valley, California, that has been the model for Olympic torches ever since.

John was a tall, elegant septuagenarian, always impeccably dressed in a sport coat, open-collar shirt, ascot (he was one of the few people who could actually pull off wearing an ascot), and tailored slacks. When I got my first Disney job, John was the one who gave me my initial orientation and was the aesthetic boss I worked with. The initial canon he laid out for me was:

"Alan, a cartoon is seven minutes long. If we lose their attention for ten seconds, we've lost them. It is the same with three-dimensional design. If you lose people's interest or curiosity for the briefest of times, you lose them. Think of your designs from the eye level of a person going through and around them. The eye must *never* lose interest. There must always be something to make the customers happy or curious. They should always want to turn a corner to see what is happening there." After my experience with Disney, whenever I was teaching architectural design, I used John Hench's quote right after the definition of architecture as *"firmitas, utilitas, venustas"* (durable, useful, beautiful) by the first-century B.C. Roman architect Vitruvius—the truest description of architecture I've ever come across.

John Hench's dictum that "the eye must never lose interest" was essentially the same philosophy held by Jimmy and Morris.

When he planned a store, Morris had to figure out how to draw a person into it and all the way through. This he accomplished by recessing the entrance and leading patrons through an alley of display windows, until they were—almost magically, actually—inside the store. Once he had them in the store, he had to draw them way back into the facility, since most New York City stores were long and narrow. Morris made use of bright colors on the far walls, and also upped the intensity of the lighting at the rear of the establishment. He also employed curving walls that subtly caused patrons to follow the sinuous bends ever deeper into the retail space.

Hench and the Disney team achieved similar results by designing spaces that were tangential to other interesting forms, in a way that always had people eager to see what was around the corner—which was usually the unexpected. For example, they used topiary in the form of Disney characters scattered everywhere. Most people have never seen topiary, much less a tree in the shape of Goofy. I learned that another purpose of the shrubbery is to conceal bantam low-volume audio speakers that emit "It's a Small, Small World" and other Disney ditties. No, you are not just imagining that you hear music wherever you go. The Disney folks were the only ones outside of the casino industry to grasp the power of music early on. Employing various "dancing water" fountains that run in sync with the music provides visual as well as aural stimulation throughout the Disney cosmos.

From an architect's point of view, what really caught my attention was a collection of nuggets of wisdom (one in particular) that were written on index cards and pinned to the walls of the conference room in the Disney headquarters building in Glendale. The one I remember most vividly was uttered during one of the ongoing debates between the visual guys (architects, designers) and the music people. It said very simply, "Nobody leaves the Park whistling the architecture."

That amounted to Jimmy's saying that the purpose of the casino was to "give the guy back his cock." He meant that all of the sensory stimuli were aimed at endowing the patron with a sense of magnanimity and grandeur to get him in the proper mind-set to throw away his money.

What fascinated me about Jimmy's philosophy was that, without any background as an architect like Morris or in design like John Hench, Jimmy's teachings were the logical extension of their credos. Morris did this with the physical structures he built. Jimmy extended it to all the ancillary senses, except that his props were attractive women and their bodies, sound, textures, and a truly deep understanding of the male psyche.

The casinos have put into play all the tricks Morris and Disney used. They use music (always place a lounge with a music act within earshot, no matter how big the gaming floor), shape (employ unusual forms, especially the ceilings, since it's the main visual element that can be seen, because the horizontal sight plane usually is filled with people milling about), and texture (from the felt of the tables to smooth metal and luxurious fabrics for wall coverings and draperies; rich leather—usually faux—for seats and rails; and the color palette of royalty: reds, purples, gold, black, and stark white crystal chandeliers).

All three of my gurus were telling me essentially the same thing: Proper design is most definitely not a matter of cheap tricks or a vocabulary of forms and shapes; it is, rather, the ability to put oneself into the eyeballs of the beholder *at eye level.* Most architects pay attention only to the plane, looking straight down—the God's-eye view—or plan, meaning what the layout looks like from above. But the design mode that encourages people to spend money must incorporate all three dimensions.

I transformed this trio's examples into practice in all my buildings, most notably in my design for Trump Plaza (see Chapter 10), where I committed the almost revolutionary and sinful heresy of siting the gaming area on the second floor and including escalators enveloped in a crush of mirrors and mind-boggling lights that lured bettors on a magic carpet ride up and into the casino—which would be the final resting place, as far as most of them were concerned, of however much money they were prepared to lose.

In sum, none of my mentors gave me the same phrase book, but each was saying the same thing: Design spaces from the viewpoint and mindset of the person going into and through that space. What do you want them to think and do? How can the space I am designing facilitate the desired reaction?

All else is commentary.

All the work I have done designing casinos is ironic for one basic reason: I do not gamble. Which probably places me in a minority of the population.

Nevertheless, I do work for pay, and once I started specializing in building hotels and resorts, and gambling started proliferating outside of Nevada as well as in that state, my involvement was almost inevitable.

Casino gaming and, for that matter, most forms of gambling are a fact of life. Being against them is akin to trying to stop the tide. Wagering is an activity found in every culture and every civilization since the dawn of time. It is, after food and shelter, one of the primal interests of the human species.

In 1979, as casino gambling was gaining momentum in states other than Nevada, I attended a conference on gaming in Las Vegas, put together by Merrill Lynch. More than three thousand people attended, most of them from banking, the stock market, and other Wall Street–related industries. Jimmy wasn't invited. Gaming had just been legalized in New Jersey and the Indian casinos were still in their infancy, but the money boys knew that a whole new ball game was starting. The financial analysts who spoke said that, even back then, gambling (over 90 percent illegal) was the second largest component of the gross national product, and billions of dollars were being wagered annually on NFL games alone—repeat, even back then.

I'm well aware that many people have had their lives wrecked by compulsive betting. Of course the same is true of compulsive drinkers and substance abusers, eaters, sex addicts, and credit card abusers like the nice middle-class lady who was once my office manager and ultimately charged a quarter of a million dollars' worth of goods to my office and wound up with a misdemeanor conviction on her record. What has to be understood is that most gamblers would gamble with or without the presence of casinos. From what I have observed, it's also much better to be in hock to a casino than to Big Paulie, the leg breaker for your friendly neighborhood bookie. Do casinos increase the number of gamblers? Probably. But not by much, according to the Merrill Lynch people and others I've talked to over the years. The numbers speak for themselves: Casinos provide a legal venue for people to do what they would otherwise do illegally in "friendly" card games, office pools, and bets placed through unlicensed bookmakers. I was fascinated to read after Chief Justice William Rehnquist's death in 2005 that he loved to organize betting pools at the Court. Small-stakes pools? Yes. Illegal? Yes, indeed!

The upside is the billions of tax dollars now being legally generated in places like New Jersey. The enabling legislation in New Jersey provided that the tax revenues would be dedicated to education and services for the elderly. If gambling had not become legal there and in many other jurisdictions, vast amounts still would have been bet illegally—money that would have generated no taxes.

So even though I never gamble, I found a low-risk way of making money in the gaming industry.

In the classic 1995 film *The Usual Suspects*, Kevin Spacey's character, Verbal, avowed that "the greatest trick the devil ever pulled was convincing the world he didn't exist." The greatest trick the gaming industry has ever pulled is to consistently make losers believe they are winners.

Jimmy explained how this was accomplished. "In the old days [meaning the '50s and '60s], most of our customers came from L.A. In those days, fifty grand, say, was considered *real* money. Now suppose some guy with a fifty-grand line [of credit] is playing at the table and he's down, say, forty large. The pit bosses always know their big players. You never let a player go to his limit. The pit boss says to him, 'Hey, Mr. Smith, the dice are cold tonight, don't chase it, take a break. Why don't you go over to the showroom and catch the revue. Give the dice a chance to warm up.'

"He goes to the nightclub and the maître d' (who has been called by the pit boss) greets him like he is a god. 'Mr. Smith, so glad you could come here tonight, welcome to our show.' The maître d' ushers Mr. Smith to a ringside table, there's a bottle of Dom Perignon cooling in an ice bucket, a box of Havanas are sitting on the table, and a bunch of topless cuties are shaking it in his face. A little while later the maître d' asks which of them he'd like.

"He has a night to remember.

"Next morning he's checking out and the shift manager comes over and asks him how he enjoyed his stay, and should they deliver his new Cadillac convertible or would he like to drive it home? The guy cruises home driving his new short. He tells all his buddies about his adventures and how they love him at the casino. Not only is he eager to get back, but all of his drinking buddies can't wait to go with him.

"And what did it cost us? In those days we bought the Caddies by the truckload, so they cost us maybe four or five grand each, the booze and the broad, a couple of hundred, and *the guy just left us with forty large. And* he can't wait to do it again.

"If you make some john feel like he's somebody really special, if you shower him with tokens of your respect, he's yours forever."

Jimmy was not destined to put his vast body of wisdom to use in Atlantic City; although it got all of its permits, based on my plans, the casino Rocky Aoki intended for him to run never made it off the drawing boards. Even so, I was to see Jimmy's theories translated into reality time and again. I used to commute to my projects in Atlantic City in my own small plane. One evening I was riding a casino's limo back to the Atlantic City airport in the company of a couple of high rollers headed to their private jets. One was loudly holding forth, trying to impress his fellow passengers. He bragged how the pit boss recognized him and always made sure his favorite cognac was available. When this guy got hungry, he went on, there was a special table waiting for him in the most expensive restaurants. In general, he was treated like royalty. Each visit to Atlantic City left him glowing with excitement.

I asked him how he had done at the tables this time.

"Oh, I don't know, lost maybe ten, twelve grand."

This he voiced dismissively, a matter of trivial importance. It's worth mentioning that most gamblers routinely exaggerate their winnings and understate their losses, so the "maybe ten, twelve grand" the man copped to was simply the sum he *confessed* to dropping.

Here was a person who had just bought some good cognac and a mediocre meal for at least ten thousand dollars, and he felt like the biggest winner in the Western world.

I rest Jimmy's case.

10

Donald Down the Shore

From our earliest dealings, it became evident to me that part of Donald Trump's genius is that he knows what he doesn't know. He never admits that he doesn't know everything, but that is only his public persona. Donald hires very capable people. His organization when I first started working with him was tiny. At any given moment I never saw more than half a dozen people in his office, other than the administrative staff. But his executives were all very, very good at what they did. Later on, this thinness of staff was to come back and haunt him, following a helicopter crash that killed three of his top hotel operations people. There was no backup, and when his Taj Mahal Casino opened in Atlantic City, he paid dearly for not having an "in-depth" organization.

In real estate, having the ability, as Donald does, to predict what type of facility is needed or wanted in a particular location at a particular time is the type of intuition on which fortunes are made. In other words, all one needs to be a successful developer is the ability to see into the future. A major development often takes at least four years to transform from concept into finished product. If you can intuit the market conditions that far into the future, and if the economic conditions do not radically change during that period, and if no one else is a year ahead of you at the same time and place, and if the world doesn't go to hell in the interval, and if you can convince the money folks of the validity of your idea—if all these pieces fall into place, then you, too, can be a successful developer. Real estate is a field where you have to have the balls and the brawn and the intellect to get your idea past all the formidable obstacles and naysayers.

When the design for Trump Plaza was completed, I called Donald to set up an appointment. In those days, things were a tad lower key than they are now. He said he would come right over to my office. (Nowadays, of course, Donald does not go to an architect's office; we come to him.) Back then, though, he glanced quickly at the dozen or so different floor plans that had been meticulously developed and then went straight to the graphic depiction of what the building would look like. He stared at the elevations for about ten seconds and said, "That's it, Alan. Don't change anything."

And then he was gone.

To this day, Trump Plaza remains the only building I ever designed that went from first sketch to completed structure with absolutely no design changes or modifications. Practically every project I have ever worked on has undergone myriad changes. The Disney hotels in Orlando were probably the worst because of all the many and varied parties involved and everyone having input. When the construction documents were more than 50 percent complete, the bean counters at Tishman decided that the project was too expensive and that a lot of money could be saved by reducing the width of each of the twenty-five hundred rooms (which had been dictated by Sheraton and Westin, which would be operating the hotels) at the Swan and the Dolphin by six inches. To effect this change we had to essentially scrap the half million dollars of work that had been done and redraw the entire complex.

On the Crowne Plaza in Times Square, the entire building was designed to have an illuminated "crowne" (actually a circular projected cornice) at the highest point of the building with the signage gleaming down on Broadway, the architectural equivalent of having an orchestra build up to a crescendo (see Chapter 13). The bean counters on that project decided that since city zoning was not going to give us an illumination credit for the illuminated crown—because only lights on the bottom 120 feet would count for that purpose, they could save $120,000 by eliminating the crown. I never would have designed the façade the way I did without it. The building was also designed to be completely lit up at night. The surface textures were designed to reflect this light, since I wanted to bring back the "glitter" to Broadway. The lights were installed, but, in order to economize, they have never been turned on. Since then the building has been sold, and I don't believe the new owners even know that the lights exist.

I designed the transportation center for Caesars in Atlantic City with huge urns on top of the "pediments" and flames pouring out of these urns. The accountants deemed this arrangement too costly, so it never was installed. However, when I was last in Las Vegas, I noticed that Caesars had lifted these features from my Atlantic City plans and installed them out there. They look great! They're just twenty-five hundred miles to the west.

Hardly any of this cost cutting was necessary. Almost all of my buildings have been financially successful, but even in the case of buildings on budget, some joker was always trying to be a hero and show the boss what a hotshot he was by pulling money out of the project. Most of the savings were accomplished by cheapening elements—instead of beautifully detailed windows, use the cheapest available; in place of really good brick, use the lowest priced on the market; instead of using stone, use stucco; don't install a brick driveway when you can substitute pressed concrete with bricklike indentations and paint it. Usually nothing big, but God *is* in the details. It was like being pecked to death by ducks.

For all of Donald's reputation as an "economizer," I clearly remember meetings about Trump Plaza where contractors would try to convince him to make cuts such as eliminating "all those fuckin' angles. They cost a fuckin' fortune. I can save you a million bucks if we just straighten out the goddamn façade."

Trump: "Build it like it is drawn!"

Donald relied on gut instinct because he knew that that is what his future customers relied on. When you see a building, if you have any opinion about it at all, it is usually your first reaction that counts. Only architecture critics and architecture students worry over a building like a dog with a bone. In one of his most famous and most dead-on accurate sayings, Donald once expressed the opinion that "a building's financial success is directly inverse to Paul Goldberger's praise." (Goldberger was then the architecture critic of *The New York Times*.)

As the drawings for the casino proceeded, I launched into the usual round of meetings with the staffs of the various New Jersey agencies. I had long ago come to realize that by involving the regulators and securing their input at an early stage, I could better create a building that would gain approval.

While designing places in Atlantic City for Trump and others, I was struck by the difference among my various clients. The Japanese came from an authoritarian society, so they listened, listened very well, indeed, and were loath to offend. Bob Guccione of *Penthouse* magazine, by contrast, listened to no one but his inner muse, and he and his muse were quite content to believe that the world was theirs to command. Guccione thought his X-rated Roman epic *Caligula* would generate a fortune in box office receipts that he could pour into building the casino. But his cinematic masterpiece attracted paying customers by the hundreds if not thousands, instead of the tens of millions Guccione had expected (see Chapter 18).

Donald attended almost every meeting about his building with the state regulators, even the meetings with just the working staff of the agencies. Hell, *especially* the meetings with the staff. He understood that the commissioners usually acted on the recommendations of their staffs. All the staffers at the two big controlling units, CAFRA (the Coastal Area Facilities Review Agency) and the Casino Control Commission, were young, most within a couple of years of thirty, and quite dedicated and idealistic. Donald, or else his brother Robert, was there for every meeting. At these sessions, Donald toned down all the hyperbole and listened with laserlike attention. When he disagreed with something the state people wanted, he was (dare I say it?) downright diplomatic. The staff loved it. They were being accorded the rapt attention and respect of the famous man himself. The project was approved by CAFRA in record time. His appreciation of the importance of staff-level meetings was no small part of Donald's success.

Trump was also mindful of the fact that Atlantic City was (and still is) a small town. Anyone who understands the small town mind-set knows that the key to any undertaking in that type of venue is the local lawyers. So what did Donald do? He hired practically every attorney in town who specialized in projects like his. All of them were given a piece of the legal pie, as well as the bragging rights that they were Donald Trump's lawyers, not to mention a vested interest in seeing his project succeed. Moreover, there was the added benefit of making sure none of them could litigate *against* him.

To illustrate exactly how astute Donald is, compare and contrast his New Jersey strategy with the tactics of the mighty Hilton Hotel Corporation, which displayed such corporate arrogance and stupidity that it snatched a mind-boggling defeat from the jaws of almost certain victory. Hilton executives' big mistake was their failure to recognize that in New Jersey, the Casino Control Commission amounts to a lay version of the Catholic church. If you regularly fall to your knees, pay homage, and confess your sins, you are likely to be granted absolution. Then and only then can you enter the pearly gates—meaning, gain a license to open a casino.

Hilton had been courted to come to New Jersey by Governor Brendan Byrne. The governor thought it would be perfect to have a "hotel" company instead of gambling outfits like Caesars, Tropicana, and Resorts build and run casinos in Atlantic City. If he and his staff had done their homework, they would have discovered that nearly half the profits and one-third of the revenue for the entire Hilton Hotel Corporation were generated by just two properties—the Las Vegas casinos. With full overconfidence and incompetence, Hilton, captivated by a gala "welcome to New Jersey" event hosted by Governor Byrne himself, hired the wrong people in New Jersey, made all the bad moves, antagonized almost everyone connected with the state—and, surprise, was denied a gaming license. Having invested $350 million and hired and trained three thousand casino workers, Hilton was in sort of a bind. Faced with a one-shot lose-and-you're-out right of appeal and just thirty days to file the appeal, Hilton punted, searching frantically for a buyer.

And they found one: Ever since, the ill-fated or, more to the point, never-to-be Hilton casino has been known as the Trump Marina Hotel and Casino. That's correct: The Donald took the whole enterprise off of Hilton's hands—at a bargain basement, distress sale price, to be sure.

When the drawings for Trump Plaza were about 20 percent finished, Donald decided the time had come to start playing hardball with the state. He didn't want to spend over $1 million on architectural fees without assurance he could put my plans to use. Until then, in their haste to open, casino owners had obtained construction permits, built their buildings, opened with a temporary gaming license—and *then* found themselves at the mercy of the Casino Control Commission when they applied for a permanent license. Not only had the commissioners occasionally required modifications to already functioning hotels, they had also forced some major operators to replace top executives.

Donald was having none of that. In the same spirit that Governor Byrne had courted Hilton, state agencies had wooed Donald. He was the icon they were hoping for: a New York (read, local, given its proximity to New Jersey) developer with a squeaky-clean reputation and no ties to any other gaming venture. All this Donald knew, and he made the most of it.

Trump insisted that his gaming license be issued before he turned the first spade of dirt. Either the state would license the facility based on my plans, or else, he vowed, he would pack it in. He publicly stated that if the New Jersey powers that be wanted a developer as clean as the driven snow like him, they would have to play by developers' rules. And no rational developer, he insisted, would sink money into construction of a building without assurance that he could also operate it. His logic made sense—even in New Jersey.

A full hearing on Trump's license was held in 1982 in Lawrenceville, just outside Trenton, the state capital, and there were all the trappings for what was, to the best of my knowledge, the first such hearing ever convened for this purpose. The room itself was typical New Jersey quasi dignified, a mixture of cheap Sheetrock walls and faux wood paneling. The unique nature of the hearing, combined with its celebrity applicant, resulted in the room being packed. For this major media event, a battery of TV cameras lined the back of the room, most from local stations, but CBS and NBC were there too. The lights, of course, were hot and blinding.

Donald, resplendent in a blue suit and maroon tie, was well aware that he was the star of this show, and he adopted a manner of noblesse oblige, acting the part of reluctant debutante as he outlined how he would bring his golden touch to the sordid shores of New Jersey if state officials would just see the light of reason—*his* brand of reason. His brand of reason, it must be said, was absolutely correct.

I, meanwhile, wore my standard architect's costume, consisting of a black turtleneck sweater, brown tweed sport jacket, black flannels, and oxblood Bass Weejuns. I should add that the only times I wore a suit and tie were for meetings with bankers. And my father *never* in his life wore a regular tie, just those bow ties he considered part of his "architect's outfit."

As best as I can recall it, at the opening of the hearing Donald was asked, "Mr. Trump, why did you decide to build a casino in Atlantic City?"

Wearing a slightly bored expression, he replied, "I really didn't. As you know, my interests are, and always have been in New York real estate. But I have an old family friend, Alan Lapidus. Our fathers worked together, and Alan had done some plans for a project down here, and the guys stiffed him. So he called me up and asked me to take a look at it. If I took over the project, then he could get paid. It looked interesting, so I picked it up. Not my usual thing, but if I can do a favor for an old friend, I will. But I have to tell you, no developer in his right mind is going to put a shovel in the ground unless he gets all his permits and licenses first."

I was trying as hard as I could to keep a straight face. I had no idea that Donald was going to downplay his desire to get into the Atlantic City casino business and instead emphasize the favor he was doing me. I had to admire the guy. Donald had obviously realized that he stood a better chance of success by sounding almost disinterested instead of overly eager, and he managed to do that and still answer the question truthfully. It was pure Donald at his most ingenious.

Then it was my turn to be questioned. After stating my name I was asked, "Mr. Lapidus, you have heard Mr. Trump's statement?"

"Yes."

"Is that what happened?"

I said it was.

Afterward, when we were alone, I cornered Donald. "Donald, if you're going to lay it on me, at least clue me in beforehand!"

He eyed me and almost smiled.

"Hell, Alan, I had no idea what I was going to say until I said it."

Donald got his license. And who can complain? Trump Plaza has lured million of visitors to the south Jersey Shore, generated tens if not hundreds of millions in tax revenues over the years for the state, and employed thousands of workers.

During my Atlantic City period, unusual circumstances surrounded a hearing before another state agency I was involved in. To back up for a moment, in 1966 my father and I were designing the Paradise Island Hotel in Nassau for some "boys" with "interesting backgrounds." At one on-site conference with the principals, whose company later changed its name from the Mary Carter Paint Company to Resorts International, I noticed a nice little older Jewish man wander over and stand at the back of the group with his tiny white dog. The man was wearing white patent leather loafers, mustard-colored slacks, and an open white shirt called a guayabera, which had been standard wear in pre-Castro Cuba. (And still is among the Cuban expatriate community in Miami.) As the meeting broke up, my father made a point of shaking hands deferentially with the nice little older Jewish man, whom he introduced to me as "Mr. Lansky." As in Meyer Lansky, the financial genius for the Mob.

Flash-forward a few years, to when I was heavily involved in Atlantic City. I attended a meeting of the state Casino Control Commission, which was considering an application from Resorts to operate their casino in Atlantic City. The commissioners were attempting to link Resorts to organized crime as a means of denying them a license. During that hearing, one of the key figures who had owned interests in Paradise Island recognized me and walked over. With an evil eye, he asked me if I wasn't "Morris's kid." When I affirmed that I was, he asked me what I was doing there. I don't think the gun was quite out of the holster yet, so when I told him I was there just as an observer and was waiting for the commissioners to consider another project of mine, not to testify, he put his hand on my shoulder, said "Good!" and walked away. I don't think I *really* would have wanted to testify about the Resorts project that day, even if my name had been on the witness list.

I eventually finished my drawings and Donald got the permits he needed in order to build, but a major problem remained: He still didn't have all the money it would cost to build Trump Plaza. He knew that at worst, with the permits in hand, he could sell the project for a huge profit if he couldn't raise the money to build it himself. Donald had used his own (and his father's) funds to get to the point that he was ready to build once he secured full financing. Meanwhile he continued searching for an institution to lend him over $100 million to complete the job.

There were several meetings with large groups of possible bankrollers. I did my dog and pony show at these sessions, followed by his upbeat spiel. Nevertheless, to use an appropriate cliché: no dice.

All the financial institutions had the same objections. Donald had proposed that he would run the operation by himself. He would hire the best gaming managers in the business, pay them a fortune, and the project would thrive. All well and good, the bankers said, *but:* Although he was obviously very bright and his projects in Manhattan were notable, he had completed only three developments—Trump Tower, the Grand Hyatt Hotel, and Trump Plaza, New York—and not all of them by himself. Moreover, the money people added, Donald had no experience running a hotel or a casino, and he simply was asking for too much money for the bankers to take a chance on an unknown quantity in the dog-eat-dog universe of casino operations.

Work on the project continued, but I was growing concerned about how much longer Donald would be able to carry it. He had alerted me that he wouldn't be able to proceed if he was unable to obtain financing. I had made a foolish mistake at the outset, acceding to Donald's request that I not take on new jobs while I was working on Trump Plaza without asking him to grant me a premature termination clause that required him to pay me for my work if he was unable to complete the venture. Furthermore, the entire construction and casino industries were closely watching the development of Trump Plaza, given whose name was on it, so his failure would have been mine as well. Donald's casino had come to constitute 80 percent of my firm's entire workload, meaning that abandoning Trump Plaza would no doubt have had a more devastating effect on me than on Donald. I would have had to lay off most of my staff, and on a personal note, I had just proposed to Nancy, the woman who would become my second wife, in part because I was feeling financially secure, when Donald warned me that the entire deal might fall through.

Meanwhile, Donald purchased the old Barbizon Plaza Hotel, then a seedy residential hotel on Central Park South, and asked me to survey it to test its adaptability for being converted into a proper hotel. I saw no problems. Not long after, in mid-1982, Donald called and asked me to join him at a meeting with Mike Rose, the chief operating officer of the Holiday

Inn Corporation. It was common knowledge in the industry that Holiday was looking for an upscale location in Manhattan for a new facility. At the time the company operated its traditional inns but was also planning to introduce its upscale Crowne Plaza label. What Holiday needed was a prestigious location to launch that brand.

This meeting took place in Donald's office at the Crown Zellerbach building across the street from Trump Tower, then under construction. Donald's office was decorated in the style later echoed in his permanent headquarters: massive maroon marble desk, lots of gilt, lush carpeting. When I arrived, the only others present were Donald and Mike Rose. As usual at most Trump meetings, there was not the entourage typical of other businessmen; no lawyers, consultants, or flunkies. Donald flew solo; he was at his best "winging it." Much of the meeting was devoted to technical issues related to converting the Barbizon Plaza into a Holiday Inn Crowne Plaza. Donald later did spiff up the Barbizon, placing a gold dome on it (actually, gold-colored fiberglass), and making a modest renovation before stamping it with the Trump Parc imprint and offering it to the world as an upscale condo. Marla Maples would come to occupy one of Trump Parc's units.

At the time of our meeting, Holiday Inns also owned Harrah's Casinos, a fact I must confess that had not registered on me. But of course it definitely had registered on The Donald. I presented the plans for the Barbizon, explaining how, without any major structural renovation, it could be converted into a moneymaking hotel.

The opportunity to witness these two masters of the universe bullshit each other and try to get the upper hand was remarkable. As the conversation between Trump and the six-foot-seven Mike Rose drifted around between architectural and financial details, Donald eased the talk toward the Harrah's Casino in Atlantic City, then the most profitable gaming operation in town. Mike Rose laid out the latest "win" figures from Harrah's and then offhandedly mentioned that the company was looking for a Boardwalk location for a second facility. This was common knowledge to Donald and everyone else interested in Atlantic City.

Donald expressed sympathy for Holiday's search, then, every bit as casually, mentioned that as fate would have it he, of course, owned the best location on the Boardwalk, right next to Convention Hall and at the very

My bar mitzvah at the St. George Hotel in Brooklyn, New York.

I bought this de Havilland Tiger Moth aircraft in Vancouver, British Columbia, and flew it back to New York.

My father's masterpiece, the Fontainebleau. From its opening in 1954, it changed the way Americans thought about resorts. It is regarded as the beginning of post-modern architecture. GOTSCHO-SCHLEISNER

My father and I reviewing a preliminary sketch of El Conquistador, Farjardo, Puerto Rico, the closest I ever came to designing a Morris Lapidus–style hotel. It was my first hotel design and still my favorite. LAPIDUS

Me at the opening of the Bedford-Stuyvesant swimming pool with Mayor John Lindsay and Congresswoman Shirley Chisholm.

El Conquistador. The hotel "flows" down the steep hillside with all of the various levels connected by a uniquely designed funicular railroad.

My father's first job involved designing the toilets in the Atlantic City Convention Hall (top, left). I designed the Trump Plaza Hotel and Casino (top, right) BEATRICE LANDUS

Caesars Atlantic City, an example of "fantasy" architecture. This is actually the parking garage.

CAESARS WORLD CASINO, ATLANTIC CITY

The original design (left) for the Crowne Plaza in New York. On the right is the building after the bean counters got through with it. LAPIDUS

The never-built Marriott Hotel,
designed for William Zeckendorf Jr.,
which led to my bankruptcy. LAPIDUS

The never-built Olympic Building,
designed for Aristotle Onassis.
LOUIS CHECKMAN

Auxiliary police officer, Twenty-fourth Precinct, 2001.

PETER ANGELO SIMON

gateway to the entire city. Mike Rose, pretending he wasn't all that interested in Donald's site on the Boardwalk, replied matter-of-factly that he had heard Donald was having a hard time getting his place financed. Donald, maintaining the pretense that funding was not a problem for him, was dismissive: "Oh, hell no! I just got a commitment from Crocker Bank to take the lead and fund the whole thing. Wait, I'll show you."

His longtime assistant, Norma Foerderer, entered the room, bearing a document on the letterhead of Crocker Bank. I knew very well that all Donald had was a "best efforts" commitment, which stated that the bank would *try* to assemble a group of investors to finance the deal. As soon as Donald had waved the Crocker Bank piece of paper in front of Rose's face, just long enough for him to see the letterhead, the document was shuffled aside. At that point I left Donald alone with Rose; it looked to me like Donald was maneuvering Rose to where he wanted him.

Before long, an announcement was made that the development was to be called the Harrah's Boardwalk Hotel and Casino at Trump Plaza. The name may not have flowed smoothly off the tongue, but it got the deal financed.

From day one, Donald began plotting the departure of his new partner. The centerpiece of his scheme was the availability of a site for a parking garage. One of the principal reasons for Harrah's success at its original location, which was near the Marina and not on the Boardwalk, was that that site had enough land to build an attached parking garage, allowing gamblers to park and then cross a covered bridge directly into the casino. Most of the Boardwalk locations, however, were too land-locked to hold a separate garage, and generally they offered only scattered surface parking lots, which were inconvenient for customers. Something like 98 percent of Atlantic City's visitors arrived on rubber tires (buses or private vehicles), and no facility except Harrah's had made adequate provisions for them. The original master plan for Atlantic City, in keeping with this municipality's penchant for codifying the ridiculous, had called for huge "intercept garages" to be built on the roads leading into town. Every vehicle would park at these behemoths and passengers would transfer to shuttle buses. As if that would have worked.

When the Harrah's people initially raised the garage question with Donald, he assured them that he had acquired the land directly across the street for an enormous parking facility. Harrah's had projected how much the casino would earn under the company's stewardship. The profits never reached the anticipated figures, mainly because Donald did not build the parking garage. And since the casino didn't achieve the results Harrah's had projected—because Donald didn't build the garage upon which Harrah's figures were predicated—Donald was able to break their contract. It was truly a catch-22 situation for Harrah's and a brilliant gambit on Donald's part. Harrah's eventually sold its share back to Donald in 1986, two years after Trump Plaza's opening. By then he had all the financing he needed. After Donald regained sole ownership of the project, he built the garage (named Central Park, partly as a tribute to Manhattan) and began counting the money as revenues shot up.

In addition to my work as an architect, my personal relationships made me doubly valuable to Donald. By then I was between marriages, commuting back and forth between Manhattan and Atlantic City by plane and doing my best to meet eligible ladies and have a social life. Since I worked most of the time, the logical place for me to meet women was on the job. Two of those I dated in Atlantic City during this period happened to be in important positions with state agencies we had to deal with. While we were dating, one woman accepted a top post at the Casino Control Commission, which possessed ultimate power to grant or deny licensure. The other was a key executive with the New Jersey State Historical Preservation Office. Historical preservation was an important issue whenever a developer needed permission to convert an existing and venerable structure into a new use. As much of the original building as possible had to be preserved. The historical preservation lady was also the person I had dealt with several years earlier while drawing up renovation and conversion plans for the historic Shelburne Hotel on the Boardwalk for Rocky Aoki and his Benihana empire.

She was a very attractive debutante type in her late twenties, with piercing blue eyes and short-cropped brown hair shot through with premature gray—to devastating effect. She also was an über-WASP from a patrician, came-over-on-the-*Mayflower*, politically connected type of family; in fact, she had once been invited to help decorate the White House Christmas tree.

Her background was made all the more memorable on an evening she and I spent with several others at a local Italian eatery called Pals (I guess Goodfellas would have been too obvious a name). One of just two of the "acceptable" old-time Atlantic City restaurants remaining, along with the Knife and Fork, which was more of a tourist joint, Pals was just the sort of place the set designer for *The Godfather* might have created: Murals of old Napoli covered the walls, red sauce usually accompanied the dish of choice, great osso buco, all you'd expect. Everybody who was anybody on the A.C. development scene could be found there, scribbling deals on the backs of napkins. One night at Pals, as a little test, I remarked in a loud voice, "Did you hear that the Tisch Brothers are coming back to Atlantic City?" It was a rumor I had made up on the spur of the moment, but it was perfectly logical, given that the Tisches were filthy rich, had gotten their start in Atlantic City as owners of the wonderful old Traymore Hotel (now long gone), and had long been involved in gaming as owners of, among others, Loews Monte Carlo in Monaco — which my father had designed. The very next day over lunch at Pals, my local architecture associate repeated my story back to me and asked me to call Larry Tisch and see if we could get the job!

On the evening my girlfriend and I dined there, our tablemates included the tall, slender, sun-wrinkled septuagenarian Herman "Stumpy" Orman, owner of Atlantic City's Cosmopolitan Hotel, reputed Mob overseer of business in the seaside city, and, I was told, a former associate of Bugsy Siegel; and Orman's "guy," a gentleman who was known as "Reds," a squat, solidly built, broad-shouldered Kojak clone who sported a shoulder holster and had once been an NYPD detective. My lady, who looked and acted as if she had stepped straight out of *Vogue*, made quite a contrast to the rest of us.

While we were eating, my friend Sherman Kendis, a local barrister, came over to talk to Orman. Sherman was focused on explaining to Stumpy why Sherman's client Leonard Mercer was having some, um, problems repaying Mr. Orman some money he was owed. (Mercer later served time for fraud and perjury in connection with some Teamster Pension Fund assets he diverted to pay for a restaurant.) The crucial part of the Sherman-Stumpy conversation went down as follows:

Kendis: Mr. Orman, my client, Mr. Mercer, may have to default on a payment to you.

Stumpy: "Default?" That is a very nice legal term, Mr. Attorney. Well, if your client "defaults," then I may have to have my associate *cancel his contract.*

My lady: Oh, Mr. Reds, are you an attorney too?

My poor sweet girlfriend, in all her sublime innocence, was clueless that the subject of the seemingly casual dinner conversation had shifted to murder.

Meanwhile, Donald continued to make frequent visits to the construction site. One day while he and I were standing on the beach, looking back toward the rising casino, his brow furrowed, always a sign that something big was coming.

"Alan, the building doesn't have enough 'presence.' It just looks too narrow."

The structure was five stories tall by then.

"Donald," I pointed out, "the block is 150 feet wide, and the building is built the full width of the block."

"It's too narrow!"

"What do you suggest—that we build the casino over the public street?"

"Exactly!"

Still new to Donaldthink, I sputtered a few objections. "Donald, first of all, I don't think the city will be willing to let you appropriate the public domain for private use. And, second, just look at the place—it's already built up to five stories. Even if you could get the municipality to let you build out, we would have to tear down what we've already done."

Two months later I found myself standing in front of the Atlantic City planning agency's department of public works, outlining how Donald Trump, motivated solely by his concern for the public weal, proposed to build, at enormous personal expense, a cap over both adjoining side streets. Out of the goodness of his heart, I continued, Mr. Trump wanted to replace the dark and narrow street that flanked the Atlantic City Convention Hall with a brightly lit, handsomely decorated arcade that would make the approach to the beach a lively and upbeat experience for the public. He also proposed to place extensive downward beamed lighting in this "canopy," as well as finish it in brilliant reflective gold. The final product would not only improve appearances but also provide cover from the rain. (Luckily, no one thought to ask just who would be going to the beach in the rain.)

And the best part, I closed, was that Mr. Trump would build this public amenity at no cost whatsoever to the city! Permission was duly granted, although the municipality said it would have to charge Donald a fee in spite of his generosity.

In the end, the building was expanded from 150 feet wide to 250, but there was that fee the city charged Donald: He was required to pay Atlantic City one dollar a year!

And the topper: This entire transaction was conducted under the direction of jowly, serial cigar-smoking Commissioner Colanzi (as far as I could tell, his first name *was* Commissioner), whose desk featured a large bronze plaque that read: "WHEN YOU HAVE THEM BY THE BALLS, THEIR HEARTS AND MINDS WILL FOLLOW." He and his fellow commissioners were certainly entitled to believe whatever they wanted, especially as to who had whom by the balls.

Building this monster was quite a trick. Because it was within 150 feet of the shoreline, it had to stand on concrete piles. But the permitting process for driving piles that close to the shore could take a year or more. For a solution, Donald and I called upon my brilliant structural engineer and longtime friend, Vincent DeSimone. Vinny, I must say, was a perfect fit in Atlantic City. He came from a poor Italian family in Brooklyn, where his father was prominent in the longshoremen's union. As such, Vinny was not unfamiliar with the world of the Mob, since many of his contemporaries from the hood were made members. Although Vinny was the kid from the Italian ghetto who went straight and became an engineer, he never forgot his beginnings in the Mob-infested world of the Brooklyn waterfront. He didn't volunteer much about that part of his life, but he and I often traveled together on projects, and in late-night conversations, fueled by abundant quantities of booze, he would open up and tell tales that put movies like *Married to the Mob* to shame. By the way, the climactic scenes in that 1988 film, starring Michelle Pfeiffer and Alec Baldwin, were filmed at the Eden Roc Hotel in Miami Beach. Eden Roc was then the last surviving pure example of Morris's work, unmarred by "improvements" like those that were done at the Fontainebleau.

At one point, Vinny introduced me to some goombahs from South Philly and similar venues, whose plan was to buy the Mayflower Hotel site on the Boardwalk and turn it into a casino. Vinny told these "investors" that the only way they could pull it off was to hire me as their architect. I was invited to join about a dozen of the Boys at a Sinatra concert at Resorts in Atlantic City. When Frank strode on stage, all of them got to their feet, clapping and cheering and screaming. They hung on Sinatra's every tune and word as raptly as if they were in the presence of the pope himself. It was a black-tie event, and all of the guys wore their tuxes with the collars unbuttoned and their black bow ties hanging loose. One of their main topics of conversation was how "Frank's only mistake was to marry that piece of shit broad Mia Farrow." Sinatra was drunk, had no voice, and kept forgetting the lyrics, but the crowd kept screaming and howling like a pack of bobby-soxers from his early days.

Before and after the concert I outlined my ideas on how to transform the Mayflower. No one appreciated my thoughts more than the South Philly goombah who kept proclaiming, "My cock is hard! My cock is so hard!" Now that's what I call original architectural critique.

In case you're wondering what their names were, each and every one identified himself by first name only, immediately adding, "Howyadoin'?" The only time I ever learned a last name from anyone in those circles during the preliminaries was that prior occasion when my father introduced me to "Mr. Lansky." The Mayflower project itself, unfortunately, never came to fruition.

My question for Vinny on Trump's Boardwalk casino was, how could we build these two enormous "wings" and support them on thin air? One reason I describe Vinny as "brilliant" is that he devised an elegant answer: We would cantilever both wings over Mississippi Avenue. That meant that although both wings would appear to join the buildings on either side of the street, they would actually stop a couple of inches short of "kissing" the other properties. This was yet another example of how Trump thinks outside of the box or else finds people like me who can find people like Vinny who can think in such fashion.

While the construction documents were being produced and the subsequent bidding and negotiations with contractors and subcontractors took place, I again had occasion to observe The Donald's refreshing combination of old-time developer smarts, melded with his own brand of megachutzpah.

One prime example involved the contract for supplying the numerous elevators and escalators, a very expensive element of the undertaking. When an architect puts the vertical transportation on his drawings, he can either incorporate the specific criteria of a particular manufacturer or simply include a generic set of dimensions, then readjust the plans after the winning bidder is chosen. Donald instructed me to use the criteria for Company A's elevators. That gave the representative for Company B's elevators angina. At a meeting with the Company B rep, Donald explained that he had chosen Company A because they had given him a great deal. I mean, really low prices, Donald maintained, because, hey, they were going to have the bragging rights to say that Donald Trump himself had specified their elevators, and everyone knew that Donald always chose the best of everything. Yeah, they weren't going to make any money on the price they gave him, but they would get a hell of a lot of business because of the Trump name.

All this, of course, was pure fiction, but nevertheless Company B came back and undercut its competitor's purported price.

The elevators, aside from the machinations over which company they would be purchased from, were otherwise a routine installation. Not so for the escalators from the first to second floor. The logical place for the casino was on the ground floor, but New Jersey officials were adamant that the gaming area not be visible from the hotel's entrance. No less an authority than Joseph Lordi, head of the Casino Control Commission, had high-handedly proclaimed that "Atlantic City will be a resort with gaming, not a gaming resort." My reply to Lordi was, "Isn't that like saying that all those guys visited those houses in New Orleans to hear the great piano music downstairs?"

Given how narrow the Trump site was, placing the casino on the first floor would have left no room for amenities such as a lobby, administrative offices, and a loading dock that belonged on that level. So the gaming tables were destined to end up on the second floor, a heretical plan that left Donald speechless. Well, almost speechless. I assured him I would design this arrangement in such a way that it would not only work but be a tremendous plus, and would also succeed in his winning permits from the state in record time. That mollified him. Now all I had to do was figure out how to pull this off.

Mindful of what I had learned from Jimmy in Las Vegas, as well as the teachings of my father and John Hench of Disney, I put in two big and fast escalators leading up to the second floor and surrounded them with a wealth of mirrors and glittering lights. I knew people riding on the escalators would be looking up, not horizontally, and I wanted the trip to be a magic carpet ride for them, up to the gates of wonderland, in Disney terminology. What mattered was what people would be seeing from eye level, and eye level alone. The design was the physical manifestation of Jimmy's precept that the patrons must leave their everyday mentality behind and enter the casino world reborn as big-time gamblers whether they were playing the dollar slots or in the highest-stakes card and dice games. The public did love the magic carpet ride effect, and Donald did receive his permit approvals in short order.

Donald attended a lot of the conferences with subcontractors who were bidding components of the job. This is, in and of itself, unusual. The Big Kahuna usually delegates these meetings to his construction people. The subs were in awe to be meeting with the big guy himself.

Prior to one of these sessions, Donald took me aside and spread out the technical drawings.

"Alan, show me something."

By this time I was well versed in Donaldspeak.

I focused on a complex detail of how the windows were to be flashed. Flashing is the all-important joint between the manufactured windows and the building frame. If this junction is not designed and installed with extreme precision, the building will leak. The beach location next to the Atlantic Ocean, of course, was vulnerable to high winds, rain, and the occasional hurricane.

Donald sat patiently as I explained the complex drawing. As soon as I finished my tutorial, he and I walked into a meeting with prospective subcontractors. At one point early in the general discussion, Donald turned to the bidders and said, "Now, I want you guys, before you give me some kind of a bullshit lowball bid, to look carefully at the flashing details."

Donald proceeded to regurgitate the information I had just imparted to him. All the subcontractors were astounded that this fabled developer had such a complete mastery of the complexities of putting a building together. There was no lowball bid bullshit.

His method of making sure that the building was built both correctly and on budget was unique as well. A structure of this size and expense must be constructed by a contractor large enough and financially stable enough to secure a completion bond. A completion bond is an insurance policy issued by a reputable company, guaranteeing that the building will be completed.

As his general contractor, Donald selected Perini Construction, a fine and respectable Boston-based builder, which staffed the project with seven on-site managers. But it so happened that Donald did not trust most of the large corporate builders. So he went out, scoured the industry, and hired a dozen top building managers from smaller companies. He put them on his payroll and paid them considerably more than they had been earning. Their job was to watch Perini the way a chicken hawk watches a chicken. It was a stroke of genius on Donald's part. The building was completed both on time and on budget.

Trump Plaza opened in 1984 with 612 rooms, which I designed so that every one of them has an unobstructed view of the ocean. It is spread over thirty-nine stories (making it Atlantic City's tallest building at the time), contains sixty thousand feet of gaming area, the space that produces the bottom line, and was built for $210 million, less than a quarter of what both Tropicana and Bally spent on their buildings, although those two contained almost exactly the same size gaming area as Trump Plaza. The bottom-line profits reflected this discrepancy.

The grand opening on April 9, featuring performances by Bob Hope and Sammy Davis Jr., was one of my proudest moments. I admit to getting emotional as I looked out at the thousands of guests and the three thousand employees and thought back over details like the one hundred thousand square feet of mirrors installed throughout and the nearly eight hundred construction workers who had brought my dream to life.

Another reason I felt sentimental during the gala events held as part of the opening was because of Morris's presence and his reaction. He and I stood together on the Boardwalk, looking at my building, which adjoined Convention Hall, the site of his first job as a young architect for the prestigious firm of Warren & Wetmore in 1926, drawing plans for the toilets in the vast structure! As Morris himself described it, "For two weeks I did nothing but draw toilets." Gazing at my million-foot design, Morris declared, "This is better than the Fontainebleau." I was stunned! Not to mention confused and embarrassed. I protested that Trump Plaza didn't come close to his Fontainebleau (I meant it, too; Trump Plaza was a pretty cool building, while the Fontainebleau was a classic), but my father repeated that it was better than the Fontainebleau. I demurred a second time, and then both of us were too overcome to continue. It was a moment that amazes me to this day, the only time anything like that happened—as well as a wonderful memory of my father.

Was working with Trump always fun and games? Of course not.

Donald had bestowed upon his wife (as of then), Ivana, the mantle of "interior designer" for Trump Plaza. Given her background as a runway model for lingerie, this was not exactly a natural fit. But, hey, we're talking here about The Donald. The *actual* interior designer was a soft-spoken man named Jerry Floyd, who worked with Ivana throughout development of Trump Plaza. Some of the interior design meetings involving Donald and Ivana were held at my office, and they were unusual. At one session the subject was the carpet Ivana had picked for the casino floor. The total area of this room was ninety thousand square feet (it was the legally described "gaming area" that was sixty thousand square feet), so we're talking about one hell of a lot of carpet. Moreover, the casino was the area that would take the most abuse: Every night this space might hold more than ten thousand people, many of them spilling drinks, dropping cigarette ashes, and tracking in dirt and snow. Ivana had picked out an Axminster carpet, top of the line, and about as appropriate here as a mink coat on a mountain climber. When Donald saw the price of this material, he exploded at her. Veins bulging, purple-faced and wild-eyed, he accused her of trying to bankrupt him. She gave as good as she got, denouncing him as a barbarian who would sully their reputation by trying to use cheap and shoddy goods. The screaming went on for a while, with everyone else present trying their best to stay out of the line of fire. Future interior design meetings between Mr. and Mrs. Trump were held elsewhere, to my immense relief.

Those were the days before Donald started believing his own publicity, and in public he was still conscious of the image he was crafting. One day, he and I were on our way to meet with one of the regulatory agencies. The meeting called for a lot of explanatory drawings, and Donald and I were each carrying an armful. Just before we entered the meeting room, he stopped suddenly and handed me all the drawings he had helped carry. "Hey, Alan," he whispered, "you take all of these. It won't look right for 'the great Trump' to be schlepping plans."

I would go on to work with Donald on several more projects in A.C. and in places as nearby as Manhattan and as distant as Moscow, where we planned the restoration of the historic Hotel Moskva in 1997 (see Chapter 17). I've counted him as a friend for decades and I've always respected him because with Donald, what you see is what you get. If you work for him, you have to be willing to accept that he's out to get the better of you in any deal, negotiation, or dispute. Donald never tries to conceal it, either—during bargaining sessions he does not come on as your friend or as a sweet man who just happens to be a developer. I'm well aware that he has his detractors, but I question whether any of them know him as well as I've been privileged to over the years.

Allow me to make one thing crystal-clear: To this day, Donald Trump remains the most honorable developer I've ever done business with. Yes, he always tries to get the best of a bargain—what you might label "the art of the deal." The flip side is that he *always* lives up to his end of any deal he strikes. I wish I could say that about every builder I've worked with.

11

"It's the Magic Kingdom and Magicians Never Give Away Their Secrets"

The phone call was from Mouse Central.

It came in 1979, when the Walt Disney Company was about to start planning a new eight-hundred-room theme hotel at Disney World in Orlando, Florida. The hotel would be the first new one in the park since it opened eight years earlier, and Disney executives had decided to look outside their own organization for an architect. One of them, on the line from Disney headquarters in Glendale, California, wanted to know whether I would be interested in making a presentation to the board of directors.

Youbetcha!

I was given a date and a time to appear at the Disney offices on Flower Street in Glendale. Several days later, a Disney secretary called to ask me what type of audiovisual equipment I would require for my presentation. Those were the days before computers, PowerPoint, and virtual reality tours. She sounded a little surprised when I answered that I intended just to pass around copies of a brochure about me and my firm and talk to the board. The nice lady volunteered that there were five other teams, and all of them were utilizing slides and film. I assured her that all I planned to do was talk.

From years of teaching, I knew that when the lights are turned down, some of the audience always zones out. I also intended to use this interview as a forum to find out what *they*—the Disney people—expected, and for that, eye contact was essential. I was also the only "team" that would consist of just one person.

On the appointed day, I waited in the modest yet pleasantly furnished offices of WED Engineering, situated in a very prosaic low-rise building. This was the Disney design office; WED stood for Walter Elias Disney. The team preceding me was just leaving. I counted eight people, all loaded down with large presentation boards and many, many slide carousels. This was the group from Skidmore, Owings & Merrill, my alma mater. The Skidmore folks shot me a glance, sitting by my lonesome with just my attaché case. It was not a collegial look.

I entered the conference room where a dozen or so executive types were yawning, sat down, passed around my brochures, and started talking. Since there was just one of me and about twelve of them, I had a hard time keeping track of everyone, but my recollection is that the Disney group included CEO Card Walker; keeper of the Disney flame John Hench, whom we've already met; Richard Nunis, a strapping blond former Southern Cal Trojan football player who was in charge of the theme parks; and Marty Sklar, vice president in charge of creative development at Disney World as well as Epcot Center, which would open in 1982.

I explained that I had a relatively small staff, and the name on the letterhead was the name that would be handling the project from start to finish and attending all meetings. I pointed out that I would not have been invited there if they did not already know that I knew hotel function as well as most hotel executives. But, I emphasized, I was not about to tell the Disney Company how to design buildings that provided joy and delight to users. Disney was way beyond proving that it was the master of that specialty. In short, I would be there to apply my hotel design expertise to the project, and if I was selected as the architect, I intended to learn from Disney how to enchant people with a building and morph that with my hotel expertise. My presentation lasted a total of twenty minutes. The Disney board acted swiftly, too, picking me and my firm for the job.

The whole experience turned out to be a learning process for both sides. Until then, Disney had not used outside designers. Not only did the company have its own architectural and engineering staff, some of them known as "imagineers"—a combination of the words "imagination" and "engineering" conferred on those who devised important innovations at Disney facilities—it also had one of the most extensive design libraries I have ever seen outside of a university.

In those pre–Michael Eisner days, Disney was a small, somewhat lost, and mostly inbred organization. A large number of board members were Disney relatives, much given to what-would-Walt-have-done? discussions. Everything was very relaxed. I was subsequently to learn that in the Disney culture, first names only are used. When I was introduced to CEO Card Walker, I said politely, "Pleased to meet you, Mr. Walker." He explained that in the World of Disney there were only two "Misters": Mr. Lincoln, the animated statue in the Hall of Presidents, and Mr. Toad, from *Wind in the Willows*. Everyone wore an oval plastic name tag, maroon on cream, with his or her first name. It was a moment of great pride when, after several months, I was presented with my "Alan" name tag and the title of "honorary imagineer." I deemed that my proudest achievement since I made sergeant in the Fifty-ninth Engineer Company of the United States Army.

Disney's new resort was to be called the Mediterranean Village. I was handed a site plan and the program—meaning, how many rooms, suites, restaurants, conference and meeting rooms, and the like there were to be. I was also given many photos of the site itself, showing a parcel of totally unremarkable middle Florida land. No one ever mentioned a budget. I also had to sign the oddest legal document of my career, which stated that I could never let anyone know that I had designed this structure; I could not use it in my brochure or in any form of publicity. The Mouse had its own architectural license, and all the documents would list the architect as WED Engineering. In short, I was to be a nonentity. The company would even provide me with preprinted sheets of drawing paper, identifying WED Engineering as the architect, which I would use to produce the construction documents. This policy was reversed several years later, during the Eisner regime, when Disney decided to start publicizing its hiring of prominent outside architects. In any event, the nonentity provision was my first hint that Disney operated much like Japanese corporations did. Over the next few months I was to be immersed in the Disney culture.

The executive in charge of this project was a pleasant young man named Dick Vermillion. In his late thirties, Dick had been working for Disney for about twenty years, and his career experience was not unusual for this organization. When I expressed mild surprise that such a comparatively young man was in charge of a project this big, he explained that Disney liked to promote from within its own ranks. Disney was one of the few places where you could start at the very bottom and, if you had the smarts and the ambition, advance far up the corporate ladder. Dick had started working at the park, scooping ice cream, when he was seventeen and still in high school. He had been promoted to other food facilities, then became food and beverage manager at one of the hotels. Before he was assigned this project, he had been general manager of the Polynesian Resort at Disney World.

Dick explained in detail how Disney employees constituted a "family," glued together by an internal newsletter, company outings, sports leagues, and social activities. Marrying within the company was considered a good move, and Disney even published personal "in search of romance" ads in its newsletter as a means of encouraging socializing and possible marriages among employees. The park also had its own gas station that sold cut-rate fuel to employees.

As in Japan, the company was the benevolent parent and the employees were the loyal offspring. The Mouse would train you for a career, from which you would not be fired unless you did something un-Disney, such as being rude or committing homicide. If you were a good worker, the company would try to find you a mate, housing, and friends, and motivate and help you move up the ladder. All in return for unswerving loyalty.

As I toured the huge complex in Florida, I realized that, although I definitely wasn't in Kansas anymore, I surely was in a place that made Oz resemble a sideshow. Every square foot within a traditional hotel is referred to as "front of the house," places the public sees, or "back of the house," domains the employees alone have access to. In Disneyspeak, these areas are known as "onstage" and "backstage." This was showbiz on a scale to boggle the mind of P. T. Barnum. And the Disney way of life was constantly being drummed into your soul. Every "backstage" area contained ubiquitous signs with slogans that reinforced the mantra. Mirrors were placed about the premises, bearing an etched image of a grinning Minnie, asking, "Have you practiced your smile today?"

I had landed in a Stepford world. And it really was pleasant.

After many months, while I was attending some meetings in Florida, someone up the chain of command judged that I was worthy of being let in on the innermost secret of the Magic Kingdom. Like a mother who has decided to tell her pubescent daughter about sex, Dick Vermillion announced that he had authorization to show me "the tunnels." Trembling with anticipation, I was led around to the back of the park, to what looked like a hole in the side of a large earthen mound. Once we passed the security checkpoint, my jaw dropped. There was a world beneath the World: an underground city straight out of a science fiction film.

While you are merrily skipping through Florida's Magic Kingdom, with its landscaped walkways, trees, lawns, fountains, and lakes, you are actually walking on the roof of a gigantic megastructure. Below your sneaker-clad feet are buildings, roads, and hundreds of people. The first thing I saw were three Goofy characters walking side by side. In the street, a fleet of maintenance trucks constantly cruised along. Since the roof of this structure was actually the subfloor of the park, all of the piping, electrical conduits, sewer lines, and other utilities were hung in plain view of the repair vehicles. All these lines were being constantly monitored, inspected, maintained, fixed, or replaced from below, so nothing disturbed the peace and tranquillity of the kingdom up above. One enormous conduit was an internal vacuum garbage disposal system imported from Sweden. The trash from above was deposited in receptacles where this device sucked it down and deposited it in a dump a couple of miles from the complex, to be burned and converted into energy.

All the "cast members" (as employees are referred to) were headquartered in the area beneath the park, where they changed into their costumes and took their breaks. As well as maintenance facilities, there were changing rooms, wardrobe commissaries, and a host of other buildings. A vast network of hidden entrances to the park was concealed in various aboveground structures and landscape features. This is why you never see any of the employees go on break. Mickey or Goofy or Donald ducks into a building and then quickly reappears—except that it's a new

Mickey or Goofy or Donald. The setup also makes it possible for emergency vehicles to reach any part of the complex unseen by the vacationers above. A medical emergency can be attended to swiftly, without the ambulance having to navigate through the crowds or alarm the kiddies. I was dumbfounded.

"Dick, this is the most brilliant piece of urban design I have ever seen. Why hasn't the company shown this as an example of what is possible?"

He looked at me as he would at a slow child. "Alan, this is the Magic Kingdom, and magicians never give away their secrets."

I had yet another surprise coming. When I asked which government agency would be reviewing my drawings, Dick explained that Disney World was an autonomous government, complete with its own building department, fire department, police department, and all the rest. Disney World was the only true existing company town in the United States.

And it was the best-run municipality in the world.

When Walt Disney decided to build the Florida park, he learned from his mistakes in California. In Anaheim, he had built Disneyland, and Disneyland alone. In the process he made a lot of other people rich. The park was so popular that a host of hotels and other support businesses had sprung up around it. These local entrepreneurs were not only making money because of the Disney park, they were also screwing it up. It's kind of hard to get your mind into the Pirates of the Caribbean ride when you're looking up at a high-rise hotel.

So when Walt Disney decided to open a park in central Florida, he used surrogates and blind corporations to secretly acquire a huge parcel of land. By huge I mean forty-three square miles of undeveloped land— twice the size of Manhattan. Next he made a deal with the state of Florida. He would bring hundreds of millions of dollars into the state (it turned out to be billions of dollars) in the form of jobs and revenues, as long as he was granted the right to establish an autonomous civil entity. He got it. The official name of that tract (with less than 10 percent of the Disney parcel actually built upon) is the Reedy Creek Improvement District, or RCID for short, but it's popularly known as Lake Buena Vista. RCID has its own building code, fire code, and laws. Yes, there is an endless supply of jokes about the "Mickey Mouse" building codes.

After I started to fill out permit applications to the various agencies, I was stopped dead in my tracks when the local utility company sent me its forms. Now, many of us have had correspondence with our local electricity supplier. A utility's letterhead is usually sober and plain black typeface. RCUC, the Reedy Creek Utility Company, had a letterhead with Mickey Mouse in the upper left-hand corner, wearing his sorcerer's costume from *Fantasia* and flinging lightning bolts.

What can I say? I was mightily impressed by the mind of Walt Disney, who had conceived of all this. The man could do a lot more than draw magnificent cartoons; he was one of a handful of innovative geniuses who have marked our lives ever after. And some of his most brilliant accomplishments are known to comparatively few people.

Just as in the world of casinos, in Disney's world there is nothing by chance; everything by design.

This municipality was the only government entity I've ever encountered that seemed unconcerned about its budget. The park was so profitable that anything that kept it safe and humming amounted to chicken feed compared to park revenues, as opposed to a city that could spend only as much as taxes brought in. I presume someone was keeping track of expenditures, but that issue never was raised with me or the veteran imagineers.

As a result, services and equipment were the best that money could buy. If a new and better piece of firefighting equipment surfaced in some part of the world, Disney bought it. If there was a remarkably successful official in some city's government, Disney hired him or her.

One example: The director of the Reedy Creek Improvement District was Tom Moses, and his looks perfectly fit the name Moses. He had a shock of white hair and a no-nonsense manner. But he also was gifted with a reasonableness that I have rarely found in people who hold such important jobs. I proposed using a new type of sprinkler in the hotel's rooms. Called a "side throw" sprinkler head, it pointed horizontally out of the wall rather than straight down from the ceiling. The length of the room was eighteen feet. Tom looked at one of the sprinkler heads and questioned whether it could throw a jet of water the full eighteen feet. I replied that it had been tested by the Underwriters Laboratory and had received their seal for that distance. Tom explained that at Disney, they relied upon only their own experience—perhaps because Walt had spent his childhood in the "Show Me" state, Missouri. Tom set up the sprinkler in a warehouse, connected to a pipe with the same water pressure as would exist in the hotel, and he stood exactly eighteen feet away. He said if he got soaked when his people set off the sprinkler, we could use it. He did, and we did. The reason for the elaborate personal test, Tom added, was that Disney's fire code was the strictest in the country; one major fire would doom the Magic Kingdom.

At the weekly meetings in Glendale I was gradually folded into the Disney way of life. The meetings were with John Hench and a couple of talented young architects from WED Engineering. At our first session, I asked which type of Mediterranean architecture they were thinking of— Spanish Mediterranean, Greek Mediterranean, Italian Mediterranean? John Hench looked at me with an amused gleam in his eyes, laced his fingers together, turned his palms out, extended his arms, and replied in an amused tone, "Alan, we want Disney Mediterranean!"

I understood completely. That was the reason they had hired me.

As the process advanced, I became enamored of the milieu in which I had landed. It was wonderful and at the same time a little frightening.

"John, if I am doing a Mediterranean Village, it really should be sort of a fishing village."

"I think so too."

"But then we have to have a seaport."

"Absolutely."

"But a seaport has to have a sea."

"We'll build one."

"And a fleet of colorful fishing boats."

An assistant was soon on hand with several books of pictures of colorful Mediterranean-type fishing vessels.

"You pick them and we'll build them."

"How about some windmills?"

Books of windmills were produced.

This was fun!

As I started to design, I felt sort of like God. Although that's an occupational hazard with architects, this time I really did create the land and the waters and saw that they were good.

To unfetter my thought processes, I was later given a more complete tour of the "back lots" at Disney World, a huge yard well away from the paying customers. It was a combination of a kid's fantasy and science fiction. There was the shipyard, where all the Disney vessels, from large Staten Island ferries to pirate boats, were manufactured. There was the rock "farm" where huge boulders and small cliffs were produced by spraying a cementatious mixture on wire forms. And there were the two tree farms where the topiary in the form of Mickey, Goofy, and other characters were grown and trimmed to specification.

During this whole process, no one ever mentioned a budget. And no idea was ever dismissed as being impractical, unattainable, or undoable. In those days, Disney truly was a world to itself, an asylum run by the inmates.

The resort began to take shape as a series of streets with multicolored waterfront "houses" (actually, rows of hotel rooms of varying heights). There was a waterfront walkway with a mosaic serpentine design, a harbor entrance with a lighthouse, windmills, a breakwater, a marketplace, olive groves, and trellis-covered walkways leading to streets of "tavernas," market squares, and many hidden courtyards with a variety of fountains and outdoor cafés.

During the course of my work, I observed the imagineers designing a companion hotel to mine. It was just as large, and it looked great. Called the Grand Floridian, it was quite a bit more elaborate, with such inside architectural references as the Addison Meisner Room, in honor of an architect who established the classic 1920s Palm Beach architecture that symbolized the good life to the F. Scott Fitzgerald generation. Meisner was not exactly a household name, but it would be perpetuated by some very clever folks.

Seven months after I began, my design for the hotel was finished and Disney enthusiastically approved it.

It never got built.

After Michael Eisner took over as CEO in 1984, it was a whole new ball game. The people I had been working with at Disney told me Eisner had decided to delay the Mediterranean Village until the Grand Floridian was up and running and had had a year or so to demonstrate whether it would be a success. No one ever told me the village project wasn't going forward, just that it was being put on hold. Two or three years later, by the time the Grand Floridian had opened and started performing well, the Mediterranean Village had long since been forgotten.

My fee was paid in full, but not seeing the Mediterranean Village get off the ground was a major disappointment. This was one of my best and highest-profile projects, and I put my entire being into it. Architecture is a heartbreaking profession in many ways, not the least is that the architect usually has no way of knowing what goes on inside corporate boardrooms. Rest in peace, my prized Mediterranean Village!

12

The Four Mouseketeers

John Tishman is the quintessential New York developer. Like most members of the old guard, he is of German Jewish background, non-religious, rich with inherited money and reputation, bright, educated, smooth, and ultracunning. He's some ten years older than me, a small gnome of a man, about five and a half feet tall, bald, with glasses and a protruding stomach. John's eyes are what really grab your attention. He's one of those individuals who radiate power. When he walks into a room, he's instantly in command.

If the occasion calls for charming, John is that. Likewise, he can be compassionate, erudite, philanthropic, or diplomatic. But I think the most telling insight into his personality is that, in twenty years of working and traveling with John, which included several long conversations when he opened up about his life and career, I hardly ever saw him display any emotion.

John Tishman was late joining his family's business. He's an electrical engineer by training, but he started out as a teacher at the Walden School, a tony private school on the Upper West Side that my son also attended. But the Tishman family is large, their dynasty complex, and, as John told me during a flight from New York to Los Angeles, his mother was worried that his branch would be shortchanged if he did not join his uncles and cousins in the real estate and development industry.

Through evolution, the Tishman empire, which includes Rockefeller

Center and was the main contractor on the twin towers at the World Trade Center, as well as the original 7 World Trade Center and the one-hundred-story John Hancock Center in Chicago, split into two branches in 1978. Tishman Speyer, nominally the real estate branch, was run by Robert Tishman, John's cousin, and Jerry Speyer, Robert's son-in-law, while John Tishman became head of Tishman Construction. But John was far too smart and restive just to build buildings. He wanted the main chance. He got it when his construction company won the contract to build Epcot Center for Disney in the early 1980s. In the process John got to know the Disney board of directors as well as the financial side of the Magic Kingdom.

Resolved not to repeat the mistakes made in connection with Disney-land in California, Walt Disney insisted upon reserving all the financial rewards at Disney World and Epcot Center for himself and his company. Therefore, his first Florida amusement park was planned to include several fantasy hotels such as the Polynesian and the Contemporary, along with a separate area, the Village, where there would be a shopping center, bank, and sites he would lease to others to build plain vanilla hotels. But the lease terms were so onerous that none of the major hotel companies would bite. Therefore, the Village contained a pretty seedy assortment of no-name or low-priced hotels. There was one called the Dutch Inn, another known as the Plaza, and a Howard Johnson franchise. The hotel site lease terms may have seemed unappealing when Florida Disney was a new development, but as John Tishman was building Epcot, he realized it would bring considerably more business to the park. Disney, which kept complete demographic and financial profiles of visitors, predicted that even if Epcot Center failed to lure additional visitors, it would extend the stay of the existing audience by an average of two days.

As I said, Mrs. Tishman didn't raise a stupid kid. He ran the numbers. All the hotels in the Village, no gems to begin with, were old, tired, and hopelessly out of date. In those pre–Michael Eisner days, the management at the Mouse was pretty loosey-goosey, and John soon negotiated a favorable lease for a prime hotel site in the Village.

Then he asked Disney execs whom they liked for a hotel architect.

Before long I was invited to my first meeting with the man who was to become my primary client for the next two decades. John was charming, freely admitting that he had no experience developing hotels and would look to me to guide him through the intricacies of this new field.

I flew down to Orlando to "walk the dirt" (see the site) and pay a visit to the government officials I had previously worked with on the never-built Mediterranean Village project. The requirements for a hotel in the Village were slightly different from those of a theme hotel inside the park. Basically, the Disney theme hotels were an attraction in and of themselves, while the Village hotels had to be invisible from the park. Apart from the normal specified height restrictions, the Mouse's usual attention to detail mandated a test involving balloons.

What the hell, it's an amusement park!

This test involved letting several helium-filled balloons float upward from the buildings' footprints to the height of the proposed building to determine whether observers in the park could spot them. If the observers did, you didn't. Build the hotels, that is. Or at least you had to redo the buildings so they were invisible from Disney World. The balloons, fortunately, could not be seen from the park.

John was the perfect client. As the plans developed, he followed the design and asked all the questions a very bright student would ask. He absorbed information like a sponge, and he possessed that most valuable trait of knowing what he did not know. I also had the advantage of learning from him and his staff. In those days, the top executives at Tishman Realty and Construction had calluses on their hands. Most of them had come up through the building trades, and they knew how to build. Milt Gerstman, a construction man from before I was born in 1936, was head of the team. He was warm, friendly, and generous, a large, broad-shouldered, calloused-hand type whose construction background was written all over him. Milt liked to joke that he had worked for Tishman for so long that he had the company's red I-beam logo stamped on his behind. He and I got long fabulously because I knew construction, unlike other "classroom" architects he had worked with, whom he disparaged for not understanding the nitty-gritty of building. As I worked on my design, I kept in close contact with Milt, John, and a host of other construction types. They wanted a building they could construct really fast and as inexpensively as was prudent. But as the first new hotel in the Village, it had to be the showpiece.

Since many of its guests would be kiddies, one of the requirements for this eight-hundred-room hotel was that it have a friendly and welcoming atmosphere. But since it would be pricey, it had to be impressive looking at the same time. John had studied Disney's demographics and concluded that this facility must accommodate families with kids of disparate ages—say, a family with a three-year-old and an eight-year-old—as well as provide a vacation for Mom and Dad. In practical design terms, this meant solving the dilemma of what do they do when they have been to the park in the morning and the three-year-old is too tired for an afternoon jaunt? Another issue: If we included an upscale bar and dinner restaurant, how do we free up the parents so they can have a great evening and spend unconscionable sums of money?

The answer was a "children's hotel" within the hotel, one that was adjacent to the snack bar, so the staff, all licensed child care professionals, could feed the youngsters. The children's hotel had an indoor playroom full of Disney toys and animals, a quiet room with a big TV playing Disney films, an outdoor area with play fountains, and a bunk room with beds. Staffers were also available for in-room babysitting, to afford Mom and Dad a chance to dress up, go to the bar or the restaurant, or just get away for the evening and act like grown-ups. As you can see once again, designing a successful hotel involves so much more than simply drawing up structural plans.

The basic form of the building was a U with the arms spread out, which gave the hotel an open-arms welcoming appearance. Under Disney zoning and site restrictions, the structure was limited to ten stories, so it had to be a very long building. I placed two elevator banks, one in each "elbow" of the U. Guests were directed to either the left or right elevator bank, depending on where their rooms were, thus cutting in half the length of corridor they had to walk through. The walk through a lobby to a bank of elevators is usually interesting, since lobbies generally are vibrant, interesting places. Corridors, though, are deadly; the longer, the more deadly, especially with overexcited kids. My arrangement allowed guests to make a large portion of their walk to an elevator through the lobby instead of down a corridor. The spread U also had the advantage of breaking up what could have been an endless vista of hallway. Visitors could never look down the entire length of the corridor, due to the building's shape. This is a design philosophy my father initiated with his curved shape for the Fontainebleau. As a young architect traveling all over the country for his store designs, he always found it depressing to stare down a seemingly endless hotel corridor. So he bent his buildings, as did I, and it worked. That's one of those little subtleties that make a guest comfortable. Ironically, this simplistic bit of design rationale is something that guests cannot pinpoint. They just know that the place is "comfortable." Other subtle or subliminal features included setting the windows in the guest rooms below normal height. That placement enables guests, many of them children, to feel taller.

Since this structure was located in an ocean of verdant green landscaping, and since I had always hated standing in suspended animation while awaiting the arrival of an elevator, I put floor-to-ceiling windows in the elevator lobbies to give guests a "sense of place." To enhance the guests' excitement, I left out a section of floor at the elevator lobby on every other level, creating an unexpected two-story atrium throughout the hotel. By limiting these voids to two stories, I avoided the onerous and costly fire-mandated precautions required for higher spaces. In short, I used the whole bag of tricks to provide guests with a sense of comfort and interest, without having to resort to showstoppers like full-height atriums or indoor fountain lakes.

The main purpose of planning a hotel, to be sure, is to create one that will produce a profit. It goes without saying that in order to show a profit, a hotel must be appealing enough so people want to stay there. The trick is to make it appealing enough to attract paying guests, but not spend so much money on its construction that it can never be profitable. There is a mystical equation for the economics of hotels, probably handed down along with the Sermon on the Mount, which is obscure in its origin but unfailing in its conclusion. Simply put, a hotel must yield $1 of room rate for every $1,000 of project costs in order to break even. Thus, if a hotel produces $100 a night of average daily room rate, or ADR (the dollar income of the hotel divided by the number of days in the year) and the hotel costs $100,000 per room to build (the total cost of the project divided by the number of rooms), the hotel should be profitable. Following this simple empirical formula will result in a break-even cost at about 65 percent occupancy, which should be achievable. If it is not, you shouldn't build the hotel in the first place. If the occupancy exceeds the break-even point, you are in fat city. Every dollar that the hotel generates above the breakeven goes straight to the bottom line. A hotel built to hit its point at 65 percent occupancy that averages, say, 85 percent occupancy, will have a very happy owner.

During the wretched excess of the 1980s, hotel building seemed to become some sort of a weenie-wagging contest over who could build the most outrageously expensive facility. Nowhere was this better illustrated than in New York City. My future client, Bill Zeckendorf, built the Four Seasons Hotel in Manhattan (originally to be a Regent hotel) and used that paragon of profligacy, I. M. Pei, an architect who has never met a budget he couldn't bust. The Four Seasons ended up costing slightly over $1,000,000 a room, which meant that as long as it could fill its rooms with customers who didn't mind paying $1,000 for a night's sleep (as of about twenty years ago), the hotel should do fine. It didn't and it didn't. The Four Seasons resulted in one of the first bankruptcies of a Japanese company and then went through two more owners, until the third owner, who paid $375,000 per room for it, finally showed a slight profit.

In other words, as in so many forms of enterprise, the way for a neophyte in the hotel business to make a small fortune is to start out with a large fortune.

John Tishman was a neophyte, but, as I said, he's also a very smart man. Not only did he ask a lot of questions, he actually listened to the answers. The Hilton at Walt Disney World, as it came to be called, was actually completed *under* budget, receiving its first paying guest one year and one day after groundbreaking. It will never win any architectural awards, but the hotel operates at a steady profit, and more important, guests really like it and come back repeatedly.

By contrast, the Conquistador in Puerto Rico, my first hotel, gained wide praise from the important architectural journals, won some nice awards—and went broke. True, I "made my bones" with Conquistador, but I derive my jollies now from hearing guests at hotels that I designed talking about and enjoying my creations. I also get repeat business from developers whose facilities are filled with happy paying customers and whose offices are filled with smiling and happy accountants.

One day John Tishman called me into his construction trailer at the Hilton site and delivered some startling news: He had just negotiated a deal with Disney's board of directors to lease two additional hotel sites. John was going to radically change the Disney image by building a convention center that would include a fifteen-hundred-room Sheraton and an eight-hundred-room Loews hotel. They would be marketed as a package and would include a huge state-of-the-art convention building, the largest convention center in the southeastern United States. John wanted to know if my midsized office (I had thirty-eight architects working for me at the time) could handle a project of this size.

What a question!

After I finished my rant about how we would dedicate ourselves to his project, slave night and day, weekends and holidays, and never rest until the projects were done, John nodded. He said he would hold me to my promise, and for the duration of the project I would be contractually obligated not to take on any other work. I agreed.

Not that I had much choice. John, known as J.T. to those of us who worked with him, but reverentially as the Chairman within his organization, is an absolute control freak. Once while we were working for Disney, all of us got together in my Manhattan office. The meeting ran through lunch, and my secretary ordered a platter of sandwiches from a nearby deli. Afterward, John's secretary called my secretary and gave her the name of the caterer we were to order from in the future, whenever the Chairman was present. Most of our meetings took place not at my offices but in the boardroom at Tishman headquarters on Fifth Avenue. The place was decorated in 1950s boardroom chic: a conference table that seated about twenty, dark-paneled wood, and portraits of many Tishman ancestors. There was a kitchen off the main room, with an elaborate motorized sliding wall that opened to a smaller conference room; at the appropriate time a button would be pushed, and the wall glided away to reveal a sumptuous luncheon spread.

At most of these sessions, John was accompanied by his entourage. The names and faces of many players changed over the years. Early on he had with him Milt Gerstman, with whom I worked on the Disney hotels, and other hands-on construction types whom I liked. Later, as the firm grew rich and fat, the old guard was replaced by yuppie snots with suspenders and rimless eyeglasses.

At one meeting while I was designing the Hilton at Disney World, about ten of us—including John, Milt Gerstman, and Irwin Miller, president of Tishman—were going over the project when the building fire alarm sounded. The meeting continued. As the alarms continued to ring, J.T. said, "I think it is interesting that no one seems to care that the fire alarms are sounding."

"John," Irwin Miller answered, "you know when we built this building, it was designed in conformance with the old fire code. If there really is a fire, and we go down the fire stairs as we are supposed to do, all of us will die."

"I know, Irwin. But it *is* my name on this building and I am the designated fire warden. If we do not evacuate, and there is no fire, it will probably be in the *Daily News* tomorrow. We are going into the fire stairs."

And so we did. I stayed very close to J.T., figuring if it was a real emergency, they would probably try to save him first. It turned out to be a small but smoky fire on one of the lower floors, and the fire stairs did in fact fill with smoke. Had it been a more serious event, all of us would have been in deep trouble.

When John made the offer to work for him on the Disney hotels (my firm was employed directly by Tishman, not Disney), all I could think of was three years of high-profile work for clients I liked, on a project that was breathtakingly imaginative. Until John Tishman came up with the concept, no one had ever thought of the Wonderful World of Disney, with Mickey and Donald, Mommy and Daddy, and happy screeching kiddies, juxtaposed with the seamy world of big conventions that typically were identified with Daddy, booze, and women named Trixie and Fifi.

That's where John Tishman's brilliance truly emerged. He had closely examined the Disney World operation and noted that just two out of five visitors to the park were kids. That meant that a lot of adults were coming without their progeny. Epcot had indeed lured a new type of visitor, and in the years since the original park had opened, the little kiddies that were the first wave of visitors had grown up but still liked to visit the scene of their youthful joy. John also knew that Disney had two excellent golf courses and was a short drive from Sea World as well as a number of other tourist attractions, including the Kennedy Space Center, only about an hour away. This would also be the first major convention center where you could actually be comfortable bringing the wife and kids; Las Vegas, to name one competitor, still had its Sin City image. At the same time, Trixie and Fifi and their colleagues were alive and well and plying their trade on the bar stools of downtown Orlando. In short, all comers welcome and fun for all in Orlando and environs.

I started drawing. The project was enormous and intensely complex. Hotels of this size are always a challenge, but the gigantic convention center was a world unto itself; it had to be all things to all people at all times. There were to be 250,000 square feet of convention space and 84 meeting rooms, ranging from one that contained 56,000 square feet of space and could seat almost 7,000 people to a 400-square-footer that would accommodate just 36. The main hall had to be able to accommodate 5,000 people at a sit-down dinner, but also had to be easily subdividable, like a paramecium, into an almost limitless number of smaller spaces. All the spaces, no matter how configured, had to be situated so they connected to the kitchen. In addition, the subdivisions had to be autonomous enough so a prayer meeting could be held in one area while a rock band was blaring in the adjacent space. And all these rooms had to have discrete areas for their users to congregate beforehand (the prefunction space). Plus, everyone had to be able to get from one spot to another without crossing through someone else's event. Each area, no matter how subdivided, had to be capable of being lit to accommodate everything from an intimate dinner dance to a lecture where attendees would be taking notes. The hall also had to handle events ranging from industrial shows, which had all the trappings and appearance of a Broadway musical, to highly focused academic symposia, supported by audiovisual facilities that required a phalanx of experts and consultants. Then the "back of the house" had to have room for literally thousands of waiters and other transient staff. As well as the big box for the hall, there had to be a separate, equally huge, exhibition space, where vendors—obviously an essential feature of most conventions—could set up their booths.

Moreover, the convention hall had to have huge clear spans (there could not be columns that interfered with sight lines), but the exhibit hall had to have a forest of columns where electric and water outlets could be placed. The convention hall also required an extremely high ceiling, so that, when opened to its full capacity, it would not be oppressive and would provide adequate height for an intricate lighting system and a complex air-conditioning layout.

Another vital consideration was that sound can be conveyed through the air-conditioning ducts. Since the space was infinitely subdividable, the layout and engineering of this ceiling took months to lay out and months to coordinate. Speaking of sound, the hall needed several different speaker systems. One was dedicated to sounding alarms, tied into the safety system; the others were given over to the various speakers for voice and music. The structure also had to have "pick points," specially reinforced areas of the roof from which you could suspend a theatrical lighting bar or the newest model vehicle for an auto show. The ceiling required intense coordination so the smoke detectors, sprinklers, alarms, speakers, lighting apertures, tracks for the sliding walls, those pick points, and assorted other devices didn't overlap each other—and did not look like the chicken pox.

In short, the entire space had to look great but not *too* great. Most large conventions have a theme, usually the product they are selling, so the hall cannot have too dominating a personality. Large groups usually will want to decorate their own space.

The romantic image of the architect as the master builder somehow never shows the poor slob going crazy as he tries to weave air-conditioning ducts, electrical wiring, long-span trusses, simultaneous translation booths, and three different primary lighting grids (incandescent for atmosphere, fluorescent for lecture hall, and high-intensity halogens for cleaning) into a cohesive ceiling space the size of a couple of football fields.

The concept of form following function sounds fine in theory, but what do you do about the form when the space has to be able to accommodate about three dozen different functions all at once? You tear your hair out.

This particular convention hall, when filled to capacity, had the population of a small American city. Except that in this particular city, everyone was on vacation at the same time.

After six months, the drawings were far enough advanced so that the pricing could be done, and the estimators confirmed that we were on budget. The project was a go.

Disney and Tishman staged a lavish groundbreaking ceremony in January 1988, featuring Mickey Mouse driving a bulldozer over an earth berm and accompanied by a chorus of singing and dancing Disney characters with full orchestral accompaniment. Plus, of course, all the usual congratulatory speeches, none of which mentioned the architect. Also as usual.

With the groundbreaking behind us and the construction beginning, I took a long-overdue work and pleasure trip to the Orient, where I was researching a Japanese hotel, my first vacation longer than five days in more than ten years. In that pre–cell phone era, I made a habit of checking in with my office at least once every day. One day, while I was in Hong Kong, my principal architect, John Bowstead, remarked with considerable annoyance that Tishman had asked him to come to his office with every scrap of drawing we had done on the Disney project since its inception. He reported that when he arrived, the new CEO of Disney ("some guy named Eisner") had been there, and J.T. was not in a happy mood. My guy was ticked off because it had taken five people all day to gather and print copies of the hundreds of documents we had so far produced.

I felt nauseous.

I realized instantly that there could only be one reason why the new CEO was at Tishman's office and why John had wanted to show him the volume of our work.

The project was being canceled by Eisner, just like he had done four years before with my Mediterranean Village, and J.T. was negotiating a payout.

That is the difference between being the head of a firm, as I was, and being an employee. I could see the writing on the wall, while my oblivious band at the office was merely disturbed at the inconvenience.

I flew home immediately, accompanied by that sick feeling in the pit of my stomach. Anticipating three years of steady work, and pursuant to my agreement with Tishman, I had not sought out any additional work and had turned down several juicy projects. Now I was looking at a total disaster.

My meeting with John Tishman confirmed my worst fears. Michael Eisner, following in Walt Disney's footsteps, did not want others to profit from the traffic generated by the park. Eisner had been so impressed with Tishman's concept of the Disney properties as a convention center that he had decided to co-opt it.

Tishman's contract with Disney had stated specifically that Disney could not go into competition with him, but Eisner had decided to ignore that section of the agreement and build his own convention center *inside* the park. This would completely kill John's project to be located in the adjacent Village.

Michael Eisner had come to Disney after being head of Paramount Pictures. In Hollywood, if the studio boss trashes your contract, you do not sue the Big Kahuna—assuming you ever want to work (or have lunch) again in that particular town. Eisner would come to learn that Tinseltown is just a tad different from the world of big-time real estate development, where lawsuits are as much a part of business as the coffee break.

But while Eisner was learning all about real estate development, I, the innocent bystander, could easily be ruined. John assured me that should negotiations fail, his attorneys were already gearing up to put this Hollywood hotshot in his place. I should just hang in and he would resolve the situation.

Meanwhile, though, I was ordered to stop work.

I have always tried to avoid letting people go when there is a lull at the office. That's made it hard many times for me to earn any significant profit at my profession, since having a staff that's underemployed is the equivalent of pissing away money. But as a professional I've always tried to treat the architects who work for me as fellow professionals. This has usually paid off in the quality of architect I've been able to hire. Many other offices lay off staff as soon as a job stops or slows. Now here I was with an office full of people just sitting around, which left me facing a payroll of $100,000 a month—but no income. The catch-22 was that if I laid off my staff, I would not be in a position to resume work when and if the project proceeded again, but, meanwhile, with no other work in the office, I had nothing for them to do. Architecture is not a profession that allows you simply to go out and bring in a job that will immediately utilize the services of thirty-eight professionals. I swallowed hard, had my staff do make-work tasks, and called everyone on my Rolodex to try and find some work. I was able to farm out some of my staff to other architects who were shorthanded, and after a couple of weeks I found some small projects and a fortuitous renovation job. All that helped slow the bleeding, but my resources were draining fast.

The situation was unusual only in its scope. It is not uncommon for projects to have some form of "hold," and an architect has absolutely no protection against such delays. When a project hits an unanticipated stop, it is not likely that the people working on the job can be easily moved to other projects in the office. The result almost always is an enormous economic hit.

In my eagerness to design the convention complex, I had been seriously stupid. In retrospect, that constant tormentor of souls, I should have negotiated some form of compensation if the project was stopped or terminated without adequate notice. Isn't hindsight grand!

Eventually, after several months, Tishman and Eisner reached an agreement. For me, it was just past the nick of time. I was seriously in debt, and several of my employees, thinking that termination was imminent, had moved to other firms.

The breakthrough came when John resorted to that indispensable tool of the real estate developer: He sued Disney! For $2 billion! Not only did he sue them, but he also brought a RICO charge. RICO is the federal Racketeer Influenced and Corrupt Organizations Act, originally enacted by Congress in 1970 as a tool to use against organized crime, and amended many times since. This law provided both doubled penalties for violators and potential criminal sanctions. The possibility that the Mouse could become a convicted felon was enough to bring Eisner back to the table.

At the opening of the complex several year later, Eisner would joke that when Tishman brought his lawsuit, Eisner's attorneys had said words to the effect that unless Disney had a couple of billion spare dollars, he should reach an accommodation with J.T. At the time, however, the whole affair was no joke to me. The settlement provided that Tishman's convention center and hotels would be located inside the park itself but the names on all the buildings would be preceded by the Disney name and logo. Tishman would finance, build, and own his buildings, subject to the aesthetic control of Disney. The lease for these structures would be far more expensive than at the Village site, but Tishman realized that with the in-park location, he could command a significantly higher room rate. Our previous work would be scrapped and we would start over from scratch.

There was just one hitch: the provision that Disney would control the aesthetics. This was a large hitch, because Michael Eisner wanted to make *his* bones on this project. *And* he wanted Michael Graves as lead design architect for the complex. At the time, Graves, the dean of Princeton's School of Architecture, was thought to be on the cutting edge of architectural design, but presumably not based upon his previous work. He had designed a total of two large buildings in his life!

Tishman was aghast. This was to be the largest building project in the United States, involving extraordinarily complex structures that had to be built on tight budgets and be designed to produce income sufficient to pay the rent and throw off a profit. Graves's two prior buildings had both been client-ego-inspired office buildings, one a municipal structure and the other for a wealthy foundation, and they had exceeded their construction budgets in awe-inspiring terms.

Tishman and Eisner finally agreed that Graves and I would have a design competition, to be judged by Eisner himself, since Disney was Tishman's client and therefore in the driver's seat. Graves came up with a project that was certainly eye stopping but could not easily accommodate any hotel functions. This was a problem, given that two hotels were to be built there. So there was never a serious question about the outcome: The hotels would have to be *working* hotels, not simply showplaces.

Further negotiations resulted in two additions to the agreement:

First, it was obvious that these buildings would cost considerably more than the ones I had just designed for Tishman, so Disney would compensate Tishman for the additional expense by abating the rent to the amount of the "design premium."

Second, Graves and I would collaborate on the redesign of his concept, in order to produce buildings that actually functioned as hotels.

Graves and I would be locked into the Disney Design Studio in Hollywood, and we would not be let out, at least figuratively speaking, until we produced a complex that looked like a Graves and functioned like a Lapidus.

At one meeting, a completely frustrated John Tishman asked Eisner why he was going through this expensive and tangled process. The hotels would look bizarre, which John acknowledged might be a plus, but they would cost a whole lot more and function, even with my input, nowhere near as efficiently.

Peering intently at Tishman, Eisner replied, "John, I'm forty-four years old, I've already made more money than I ever dreamed of. Now I want to be on the cover of *Time* magazine. By using the most controversial architect in the country, I will establish Disney as a serious patron of the arts." So much for form and function! On a more practical note, Eisner was quoted as saying, "In movies, we use the finest minds, the best writers we can find. I don't see why we shouldn't use the best design minds." Thus, calling in and publicly crediting renowned outside architects for the first time instead of using his in-house team, Eisner said his goals were to "build something people can't see at home, buildings that make them smile," and to "create a sense of place that is unique."

It was while Tishman and Eisner were resolving their differences that I got to know Eisner. A tall man with the slender, muscular look of someone who works out frequently, he usually wore dark blue or blue pinstriped suits, which certainly bore the look of having come from the hands of a fine custom tailor. He's courteous to the point of courtliness and has an open and friendly demeanor and a way of putting you at ease. He loves and really gets architecture, and he would put his knowledge to use when he wanted to flatter me: "Alan, I *love* your father's work, and I've heard great things about how you are carrying on the tradition." He'd say these things all the while looking straight into my eyes with a gaze that made me feel I was the only person in the world who mattered to him at that moment, a device he employs with whoever he happens to be talking to. Eisner and Frank Wells, Disney's president and the number two executive at the company until his death in a helicopter crash in 1994, made an interesting pair. The scuttlebutt was that Disney had agreed to hire the relatively wild but creative (and obviously Jewish) Eisner as CEO on the condition that the reserved and towering (even compared to Eisner, a big man himself) WASP Wells, formerly a top officer and bean counter at Warner, be brought aboard to keep Eisner in check. With Eisner I've always felt I was schmoozing with an old friend, but any time I spoke to Wells it was like being on a never-ending job interview. At the same time, it was clear that Wells himself was stuck in his job and had risen as high as he would at Disney; given that he was ten years Eisner's senior, Wells was unlikely to succeed Eisner or otherwise advance from number two to number one.

Eisner is a class act in my book. A personal example: Twenty or so years ago, my son Adam was working his way up to a career as a television writer in Hollywood. He was a lowly production assistant on a Disney show. One day Eisner visited the set, leaving almost everyone struck dumb with awe. But Adam, never shy, walked up to him, introduced himself, and said that his dad, Alan Lapidus, was working on a Disney project in Florida, the Swan and the Dolphin. Michael told Adam how talented his dad was and how glad he was that Adam too was a member of the Disney family. A couple of years later I ran into Eisner and his wife in the lobby of New York's Mayfair Regent Hotel. Michael has an uncanny ability to remember names, and as we shook hands, he asked me, without hesitation, how Adam was doing.

With all the legalities resolved once and for all, I flew to Los Angeles and my home for the next couple of weeks, the Beverly Hills Hotel. Everyone was converging there. We had the CEO of Sheraton, a representative from Westin Hotels (which had replaced Loews as operator of the Swan), the chief development executive of MetLife (which was financing the project), plus Eisner, Tishman, Graves. And Lapidus.

Everyone held their breath when Graves and I met. They assumed that when the two architects who had vied for the design finally got together there would be friction.

Wrong! Graves and I got along famously. Michael's structures were colorful and weird, and flew in the face of the sedate glass boxes I had always hated.

After all, I was bred, raised, and trained by Morris Lapidus himself, the guy who originated the concept of the hotel as fun palace.

Michael, almost always dressed in "architect chic" (low-key sport jackets and casual slacks in neutral colors, wireless eyeglasses), has a patrician I'm-more-aesthetic-than-any-living-creature attitude, or at least that's how he can be perceived. But underneath it is a wicked sense of humor. Many times when he and I were alone, he would poke fun at our client and make repeated Mickey Mouse remarks, but he could change on a dime in the presence of the high and mighty, such as Eisner and Tishman.

Graves and I were shown to the design studio and provided with drawing boards, loads of pencils, pens, and Magic Markers, and then we began a two-person charrette. *Charrette* is an architectural term (as well as the name of a large company that sells architectural supplies) that originated in eighteenth-century France. Back then, architectural students lived and worked in their garrets and attended the university only for lectures. When a project was due, the school sent carts—charrettes—to their lodgings to collect their large drawings and models. Then, as now, their assignments never were finished on time, and the students would climb into the carts and try to finish as they rolled through the streets of Paris. The local folks would have a chuckle at the young architects in the carts, or *en charrette*. The word has endured in the profession and still means a hurried design project. It is also used as a verb, as in, "Were going to have to charrette this project."

So it was that Michael Graves and I sat down at adjoining drawing boards and commenced to have more fun than should be legal. Both of us were teachers, and we thoroughly enjoyed reverting back to being two students working together on a project. This was Graves's largest commission to date and an entry into the real world of commercial architecture.

Michael Graves was eager to learn, and I was equally eager to learn from him and see how his design aesthetic would turn out. Others as well were eager. Each day, when we knocked off, the assembled corporate honchos were sitting outside the studio, like expectant fathers, wondering if the project had been delivered. The old advertising jingle, "Is it soup yet?" came to mind.

The first issue we had to confront together was Graves's shape for the fifteen-hundred-room hotel. It had been designed as a long, straight, slope-sided bar of a building, with a mysterious and somewhat somber sphere half sunk into the middle of it—clearly a variation on a hypothetical building designed by the eighteenth-century visionary French neoclassical architect Étienne-Louis Boullee.

Earlier, when Michael and I had presented each of our designs to Eisner and the Disney staff, Eisner asked John Hench, the Disney executive in charge of aesthetics, for his opinion. Hench, well aware that this was a variation of Boullée's structure, which in fact was a funerary monument, replied, "Well, this should undo the sixty years of goodwill Walt generated!"

Eisner may have been a powerhouse executive, but he was not about to contradict the last remaining person actually to have worked side by side with Walt Disney. Moreover, I told Graves the basic shape was unworkable. Like any smart professional, he asked why.

"Michael, imagine a guest getting out of the elevator. He looks down the hotel corridor, which is six feet wide, eight feet high, and nine hundred feet long."

"Got it!" Graves answered.

And indeed he did.

As a result, the building was shortened by the addition of four wings perpendicular to the main linear structure, thus making the path of travel for a guest a more manageable trek. The sides were changed so that the building was now in the form of a pyramid. When it became apparent that even with multiple banks of elevators, there still was no practical way to make use of the last eighty feet of the pointy top, we decided just to build the thing, put in fake windows, and let it go at that.

On a tour after the building opened, Eisner discovered this enormous empty triangular cathedrallike space. Astounded, he asked what it was, and Graves, ever the glib professor, replied, "Why, Michael, this is for your apartment."

Graves had decided to call the two hotels the Swan and the Dolphin, believing the nautical symbolism evoked fun and delight in the aquatic world of Florida. Despite the fact that there are no swans or dolphins in Orlando, his rationale had a certain charm. It was also a rich source of visual theatrics, a subject dear to my heart.

The corridors of the Beverly Hills Hotel, our home away from home, were decorated with wallpaper that featured giant banana leaves. Graves used this exact design for the façade of the building. I mean, from the top to the bottom of the structure. Which was about as appropriate to mid-Florida as swans and dolphins, but it *did* look neat.

Michael Graves and I soon got into a routine. Each morning, promptly at 8 o'clock, we were picked up by a limo and delivered to the studio, where we worked side by side, figuring out how to bend hotel function to these two whimsical buildings. It really was like being back in our student days. We would draw, bullshit, trade jokes, and, not incidentally, conduct a lot of serious hands-on design work.

In the end we emerged with two buildings, one festooned with giant swans, the other with giant dolphins. But they were functioning hotels. Well, sort of functioning.

Graves and I headed back to the East Coast, congratulating ourselves for devising a convention center that John Tishman could operate—not to mention that Graves had produced his first two major commercial buildings, I had earned the money that allowed me to avoid financial ruin, and Michael Eisner, as per his dream, was destined to grace the cover of *Time* magazine.

There remained one significant problem to be dealt with: Mother Nature. She sends the occasional lightning and thunderstorm, all the more often to Florida, the new habitat for our twelve-story Swan Hotel and our twenty-six-story Dolphin. As a matter of fact, I learned firsthand while making many trips to Orlando in my small plane that this part of the country is Lightning Central, so I always try to arrive at night, when convective activity is at its ebb.

Together, Michael Graves and I came up with a truly bizarre answer. You say the problem is lightning? Hey, no problem! Let's remember that Michael Eisner was looking for "smiles" and "unique"—qualities the team of Graves and Lapidus was born to produce. As in five-foot-high statues of turquoise dolphins and turquoise swans, a waterfall dropping into oversized clamshells, and those huge banana leaves embedded in the exterior. The two huge swans sitting on pedestals on the roof of their namesake hotel were elegant beasties, their wings spread out over their backs. But not only did these sitting ducks—that is, swans—add twenty-eight tons apiece to what was atop a structure built essentially in a swamp, these figures, with their upraised wings, would also act like giant sails in any hurricane or heavy storm. Massive infusions of money could buy some serious foundation reinforcement, but the wings of the swans would still be the highest point of the building.

Normally, a building's high point is where we put lightning rods, since that is where lightning likes to go. Michael Graves would not hear of such crass and unlovely appendages to his elegant birds.

Okeydokey!

To add the cherry on the cupcake, a building's high point is usually decorated with a flashing red light to discourage low-flying aircraft from arriving in an ungraceful manner.

At this point, I didn't even bother asking Michael Graves about what I was planning. I figured there was no sense in letting these two gigantic birds just squat there; let them *do* something. So I converted them into forty-foot-high lightning rods, complete with flashing red eyes. (I am not making this up!) We could layer metal mesh into the molds the fiberglass is poured into—the same principle used in the most modern airplanes made of carbon fiber and other forms of fiberglass, which protects them from lightning strikes. The most up-to-date aircraft on the market today, including many private airplanes, are made entirely from composite materials containing carbon. Unlike all-metal aircraft that are naturally grounded and simply convey an electric charge out the rear of the plane, however, composite material can be fried if it's hit by lightning. The solution, which I adapted to these hotels, was to lay metal mesh into the fiberglass building shell as the shell was being poured and formed. After weaving metal strands into the fiberglass the swans were made of, we brought the lightning protection up internally to the swans' wingtips. And so it is, to this very day. If you have a camera and aren't too afraid of

lightning, you can get a nifty picture of bolts of lightning seemingly coming out of the wings, as the swans' beady red eyes flash to ward off way-
ward aircraft.

I came to greatly admire the Graves way of working. Not only his architectural chutzpah but also the way he interacted with his clients. From
having spent his life in academia up until then, he had a solid professorial way of talking that was devastatingly effective.

Graves had been commissioned to design the interiors of the buildings as well as the exteriors. A series of presentations to show what he intended for the various interior spaces was called for. Instead of delivering
typical design presentations, Graves staged his reports as lectures on the
history of architecture.

Traditionally in an interior presentation, the designer has a series of
drawings and sample boards that show what the finished space will look
like. (Three-D computer modeling has since changed this process, making possible virtual tours of the space.) In the 1980s, though, an architect
or designer typically represented the final look of a space by using highly
illustrated floor plans that depicted furniture placement, catalog photos
of the furniture we selected, and samples of the wall and floor coverings,
all keyed in to the plan to illustrate where they were to be used. In addition, samples of the lighting fixtures, moldings, and colors, along with a
series of perspective drawings to illustrate the appearance of the space
were offered.

Graves did none of that.

For example, the coffee shop of the Swan was to be called the Or-
angerie and was modeled after sunny greenhouse-type structures ap-
pended to buildings, most typically in France in the eighteenth and
nineteenth centuries. Graves presented a slide show illustrating classic
examples of the genre in Paris, the French châteaus, and the English
countryside. Most were photos of ancient engravings. His was an en-
chanting talk, filled with historical allegory, the evolution of the form, its
modern interpretations in different locales, and the symbolism of its design. When the lights went up, I could see that Eisner and Tishman were
enthralled. They were going to get a coffee shop that offered both rich

desserts and rich historical and architectural heritage. The plan was approved enthusiastically. So impressive had Michael Graves's presentation been that I was halfway back to my own office before I realized he had not shown anything to illustrate what he intended to do in the hotel. The design for a major restaurant in the complex had just gotten compete approval based on a theoretical concept. Yes, Michael was not only a terrific designer, he was a born showman.

A significant chunk of the financing was to come from a Japanese company, Aoki Construction, and Tishman had requested that one of the spaces have a Japanese theme. We assembled in the Tishman boardroom. Michael had decided to name the bar and cocktail lounge Kimonos. The walls of the conference room had been hung with a series of dramatically displayed antique kimonos, hung on horizontal wooden rods through their sleeves. As soon as J.T. and Eisner seated themselves, the lights were lowered and Graves's interior designer (and live-in lady friend), Susan Butcher, entered the room carrying a black velvet–covered tray on which rested a single fine porcelain teacup. Susan was not only a talented designer but also one great-looking female. For this performance she was dressed in a black minidress, which made it extremely difficult to concentrate on the teacup. I noticed that Eisner was also admiring her foundations (as most males with an eye for the female form would) rather than the ornament she bore.

As Graves continued his lecture on the aesthetics of Japan, Susan periodically replaced the object on the black velvet with an exquisite plate, a piece of antique fabric, and other lovely specimens of Japanese design. After twenty or thirty minutes—it was hard to keep track of time—the lights came up, Susan sat down, and Kimonos was approved. Once again, no one had seen the design for the space itself.

Another feature of Michael Graves's design was a series of false columns marching down the center of Kimonos. I guess their purpose was to provide an esoteric rhythm, or some such thing beyond my pedestrian comprehension; most of them performed no function structurally. We put the phony columns in. But as soon as the building opened, it became painfully obvious that these ponderous columns blocked so much of the room that patrons couldn't see the waitstaff to let them know they wanted some service. It was like playing hide-and-seek! Tishman had them all torn out almost immediately. It undoubtedly would have helped if we had seen the design before the columns were constructed.

After all the ups and a few downs, my collaboration with Graves proved a success, winning such plaudits as a citation from *Progressive Architecture* magazine, whose jury commented that our work was "fantasy architecture, and it belongs in Disney World," and that "It's good for Disney World. It upgrades what architecture can be there."

The whole adventure reminded me of a classic statement by General Dwight Eisenhower. When asked whether he had ever served under General Douglas MacArthur, he replied, "Yes, I studied drama under him for several years."

I learned a lot from Michael Graves.

When John Tishman and Disney signed their contract, John assured me that it provided that Graves and I would always receive equal billing, Graves as design architect, and I as architect. All press releases were required to honor this arrangement. It never happened. As the project progressed, Tishman was noticeably impressed that his project was being hailed as a daring breakthrough in hotel architecture. He and Eisner were being lauded as the new princes of aesthetics who would invest prodigious sums of money to give one of America's leading architectural lights an opportunity to take cutting-edge design out of the classroom and apply it to commercial architecture. These kudos were not about me.

Even so, I was truly enjoying myself. I had always been slavishly devoted to creating buildings that would be financially successful yet elicit delight from their users. I had come to regard the strictures of fiscal responsibility as another hurdle to be overcome on the way to creating a worthwhile building.

Now I was faced with a whole set of new rules. Graves and I had no fiscal restraints. All we had to do was make the whole project work. We finished our drawings and the construction process started.

In 1990, two years after we began, the complex was ready to open. The mother of all galas was planned. Disney was piggybacking on the event with a premier of its new movie, *Dick Tracy*, starring and directed and produced by Warren Beatty. The afternoon before the formal opening, I was checking some last-minute items in the lobby of the Dolphin. Eisner was standing next to me, overseeing the comfort of the VIPs who had been brought in. At that moment, a distraught room clerk rushed up to Eisner and blurted out that Beatty had called down to complain that there were mice in his suite. (It is not uncommon for field mice to take up residence in a building under construction or recently completed.) Eisner, the horrified host, ordered the clerk to get the exterminator up there on the double. I turned toward Michael and asked what the ramifications would be if the *National Enquirer* were to learn that the chief of Disney himself was murdering defenseless mice. He didn't seem to think it was all that funny. I heard no more of those mice.

The grand opening was a lavish affair, complete with a formal dinner, a private visit to the park, and much speechifying. On the evening of the great day, the park was closed to the public and a couple of thousand tuxedoed and begowned guests walked past hordes of Hawaiian-shirt- and sandal-clad tourists shuffling grumpily if not bashfully or sleepily out of the park. What a weird sight it was! But having the park to ourselves was incredible—every ride and attraction was open, and, best of all, there were no lines.

That afternoon I had been able to indulge my own fantasy ride *over* the park.

The major funder of this project was MetLife, and Charles Sayers Jr., vice president for real estate at MetLife and my contact there, asked me if I'd like to fly one of their Snoopy blimps over the park.

Wow!

I sailed awestruck over my own buildings, for the first time viewing the actual constructed buildings the way we architects usually see design drawings: looking straight down from a stationary vantage point (the God's-eye view). There was only one restriction on my aerial adventure, and it offers additional evidence of the Disney mind-set: The company had an ironclad rule that only Disney characters could be displayed in the park or in the air overhead. Since Snoopy was emblazoned on the blimp's left side, I was instructed to circle the outer perimeter of the park clockwise, executing right turns only, so that the blimp's left side bearing the unwelcome beagle would be invisible to anyone within park boundaries.

It was truly a great day—until it turned truly shitty.

I had never been too bothered by being left out of all the publicity. My ego isn't that big. I have often remarked that all of the ego in my family was appropriated by my father. But the opening of these buildings was the culmination of close to five years of effort on my part, and I was really proud of the role I had played in their actualization. For all the problems, I think that what we created in and around Disney World and Epcot Center was terrific and certainly constituted a new twist in building design that would be both profitable and imaginative.

John Tishman had the honor of delivering the opening address to the thousands assembled in the main hall of the new convention center. Unfortunately, John may have started celebrating a little too soon and a little too enthusiastically. Slurring his speech, John congratulated Michael Graves for his genius. He congratulated Michael Eisner for his boldness. He thanked all his financial partners. And then he sat down.

To say I was humiliated is an understatement for the ages. As Tishman concluded his oration, everyone at my table of twelve, among them my wife, Nancy, and senior architects at my firm, was looking down, looking off toward space, looking anywhere except at me.

The next speaker was Michael Graves. To his eternal credit, his opening words were: "The first thing I would like to say is that there would be no Swan and no Dolphin without the effort and talent of Alan Lapidus, the architect of these buildings." That is how I define a class act.

Even though Michael Eisner had initially wanted to replace me with Graves, he, too, was acutely sensitive to what had just happened. He began by declaring, "I would like to congratulate Michael Graves for his magnificent vision for this complex, and I would like to congratulate Alan Lapidus, who actually made the Swan and Dolphin work as hotels." Eisner, who has often been spoken of unflatteringly, rose to the occasion.

Ironically, my patron, John Tishman, had slighted me, no doubt inadvertently given his condition, while Eisner, originally my antagonist, expressed his appreciation for several years of my hard work that helped transform his vision into reality.

To the two Michaels, Eisner and Graves, I will everlastingly be grateful.

13

"The Most Gorgeous Building in All Manhattan"

On the island of Manhattan lie several older established neighborhoods that feel in many ways like a small village and are known collectively as the Upper West Side. For almost fifty years after I fled my native Brooklyn and enrolled at Columbia University during the mid-1950s until early in the twenty-first century, that is where I made my home.

The Upper West Side is loosely defined by Lincoln Center at its southern point, north to Columbia University, and from Central Park to Riverside Park. Prior to the 1980s, little new construction had taken place for many years. This area had not been considered very chic or fashionable, though it did possess a certain élan, as the home of a collection of world-famous writers, professors, and theater people. During part of the time I lived there and as a way of giving back to my beloved native city, I volunteered my services as an auxiliary police officer with the Twenty-Fourth Precinct (the Two-Four in cop talk). I spent many evenings on foot patrol walking through every street and avenue, which gave me a deeper understanding and appreciation of this domain's ethnic mix, small shops, and eclectic character. The rough part of the sector was north of 96th Street, up to 110th Street, the beginning of the Columbia University neighborhood. As in any evolving urban landscape, the major question was whether the unpleasant part in the middle would harm the value of the older, middle-class locale, or would the expansion pressure from the other areas drive out the bad.

As of the early 1980s, a large tract of corner property at Ninety-sixth Street and Broadway had been vacant and available for at least ten years. A department store and a variety of other uses had been proposed for the site, but these projects had all been abandoned in the face of the economic realities of the immediate area. Better than a slum, but with its share of single-room occupancy "boardinghouses" and a number of halfway houses, the vicinity could not be called middle class but indeed was several notches below.

Into this void stepped William Zeckendorf Jr., one of those rare developers who actually changed the face of New York City. He didn't do it by building bigger and flashier structures but rather by understanding the dynamics of how the city evolves. Zeckendorf's father, William Sr., was one of the most important and powerful developers in the country during the years after World War II. He developed Century City in Los Angeles and owned the land on the East River where UN headquarters are located. Bill Jr. used to point proudly to a handwritten bill of sale—for $1!—hanging on the wall of his Midtown office. As I understand it, John D. Rockefeller Jr. bought the land from Bill's father for $8.5 million and then "sold" it to the UN for $1. The senior Mr. Zeckendorf ultimately went bankrupt in one of the most spectacular falls in U.S. real estate history. However, as we will see, a developer going bankrupt is not the same as you or me going broke. Zeckendorf Sr. retired in ignominy, but he had mucho bucks squirreled away, some of which Bill Jr. used to start his own business on a relatively small scale before I met him. And thanks to his brains and balls, he eventually saw it evolve into a vast empire.

Bill Zeckendorf Jr. is a large, fleshy man plagued with the chronic health ailments of the grossly overweight. He's had back problems (that he complained bitterly to me precluded him from riding horses, one of his favorite pastimes) as well as pain in his feet; I once referred him to my own podiatrist.

For a man with the sort of "golden gut" that distinguishes successful investors in everything from real estate to movies to stocks and bonds, Zeckendorf seems curiously naïve in some ways. During my architectural presentations I've often felt he didn't fully comprehend any of the

technical or aesthetic points I was talking about or demonstrating graph-
ically, and over the years he seldom raised questions. When he does have
something to say, he's so soft-spoken that he's hard to understand. He has
explained to me that he has a hard time grasping architectural documents, including even painted renderings showing a building in three dimensions, and that he needs a model in order to fully follow what's being
planned.

Zeckendorf pondered over the Ninety-sixth Street site and saw to the
north space-starved Columbia University, with its community looking
south; to the south the headquarters of ABC, with culture vultures in
that neighborhood looking north; the culturally emergent neighborhood
of Lincoln Center; a prodigious number of tony private schools; and a
series of arts and religious centers sprouting up like mushrooms after the
rain. Zeckendorf realized that decaying old Ninety-sixth Street was
squarely in the middle, with all the opportunities that presented. After
acquiring the northwest corner, he built a classy, handsome mid-income
condominium apartment house designed by Frank Williams. (I believe
in giving credit to architects. It always makes us feel good.)

The Zeckendorf condo, called the Columbia, sold out quickly, opening the floodgates for developing the entire area. Soon to come were several other expensive high-rise apartments, as the seedy hotels were
renovated and targeted at a more affluent clientele. Hard on the heels of
these improvements came the inevitable blizzard of Gaps, Banana Re-
publics, and the like. On the streets where you once could buy the best
sandwich Cubano in the city, as well as many other ethnic delicacies,
you now found "haute cuisine."

Zeckendorf followed his first condo triumph by building an even
more upscale residence on the once truly run-down corner of Seventy-
ninth Street and Columbus Avenue. It too was a knockout success,
thanks again in part to architect Frank Williams. The Upper West Side
was now officially gentrified.

The two Zeckendorf structures led to improving a major section of
New York. The developer followed them with Zeckendorf Towers (in
honor of his father), which did much the same for Union Square. As I
mentioned, Bill just has a knack, a gift that cannot be quantified or cod-
ified, for spotting a neighborhood that's ripe for change, coupled with

the resolve to put his money and reputation on the line and build the catalyst that will produce that change. None of the feasibility experts, focus groups, and other esoteric and mysterious studies can come close to the instincts of a truly talented entrepreneur.

During the mid-1980s, the city of New York faced a challenge. The fancy East Side of Manhattan was way overbuilt. Since it was *the* address to have, it was much in demand. The prevailing wisdom was that only an East Side location was suitable to signify an enterprise of quality; an East Side residential address served notice to the world that you had arrived. Manhattan is all about status, and a person's business and personal addresses told it all. The West Side, by comparison, was rather déclassé at the time.

While developers and the public were focused on East Side vs. West Side, Manhattan's historic Times Square was trying to hold on to the last shred of its once glamorous reputation, and failing miserably. It had deteriorated into a cluster of porn theaters, sex shops, and other sleazy enterprises. The stretch of Eighth Avenue around the Port Authority Bus Terminal had become known as "the Minnesota Strip"—referring to the many underage midwestern blue-eyed, blond runaways who cruised the area, earning a living for their pimps. In police argot, Forty-second Street was known simply as "the Deuce." At risk were the Broadway theaters and the venerable headquarters building of *The New York Times*: elegance amid the garbage.

Several proposals from both the private and the public sectors sought to address this issue, but they dealt only with the Forty-second Street corridor. That was the wrong approach, because it amounted to merely excising a lesion, not killing the disease. A much more comprehensive strategy was needed.

The New York City planning department finally devised a strategy it hoped would solve both problems: overcrowding on the East Side and the deterioration of the West Side. This was a wonderful example of how, every so often and by some miracle, city planning can actually work. The key to the plan was harnessing the three principal motivations involved in real estate development: greed, greed, and greed.

City officials realized that in order to transform the Times Square zone from sleaze to slick, development could not be limited to just a couple of buildings; virtually the entire area would have to be rebuilt at the same time. A critical mass of new buildings to reverse the decades of downward trend was called for.

The type and maximum size of buildings in New York City are determined by the zoning district in which they are located. The entire city is divided into zoning districts, and each district has a letter, such as R for residential or C for commercial, and a number. If a piece of land is zoned R-8 (the highest density is 10), that means the area is designated residential, and a structure can be built that has a volume of eight times the square footage of the land. To illustrate, if you own a piece of land in an R-8 district that measures ten thousand square feet, then in theory you can put up a building containing eighty thousand square feet of enclosed area. But that's just the beginning of the exercise. Most zones have required setbacks, which dictate how close to the property lines you can build. Maximum building height and setbacks are also limited in part by the width of the streets the structure faces. Taken together, the zoning, the maximum density, and the required setbacks define the "building envelope."

One more consideration is the "sky exposure plane," which specifies that you must set the building back farther as it rises higher—which is why most Manhattan high-rises have a "wedding cake" appearance. When you walk through the dark canyons of Wall Street, you can see what happens when setbacks are not required. In fact, it was these sheer towers downtown that led to the inclusion of setbacks in later zoning laws.

In addition, there are light and air requirements for any form of dwelling unit in the city of New York. Residential units must have at least thirty feet of open space outside their windows, and the number and location of windows is also spelled out by the code. Certain spaces, such as mechanical areas, including pipes, do not count for zoning floor area purposes. That's not all: You can increase the amount of allowable square feet by buying the unused floor area ratio (FAR) from any adjacent buildings that have not used all their allowable FAR—provided that the setback requirements for your building allow it. You can also increase your FAR if you include certain "bonus" amenities, such as building a park or improving a subway station. To cite one example, Donald Trump was able to raise the height of his supercondo on the East Side near UN headquarters by purchasing the unused FARs from a string of adjacencies. Thus, the price of real estate in the city is determined by the gross square footage that can be built on the land.

If all this sounds convoluted, that's exactly what the process is—to the benefit of several zoning consultants in the city who earn a very good living interpreting the code. No large building is planned without hiring one of these advisers to help unravel the mysteries of the zoning laws.

In an effort to encourage developers to turn their attention to Times Square, city planning passed a regulation stating that anyone who agreed to construct a building in the newly designated Times Square Redevelopment Zone within a specified five-year period would be allowed to raise the existing limit of ten times the square footage of a lot to a multiple of thirteen.

Since Times Square was then a combat zone/cesspool, real estate was not expensive, and the city's one-time offer to let builders build 30 percent more space sent developers into a feeding frenzy.

Bill Zeckendorf, who by now had an impressive record of effecting changes in several neighborhoods, assembled the block fronting on the west side of Broadway between Forty-eighth and Forty-ninth streets. This block had the densest collection of XXX-rated theaters and related enterprises in the city, including that paragon of porn, the Pussycat Theater.

Realizing that most of the hotels in this area had rooms that were rented by the hour, Zeckendorf decided that there was demand for a relatively expensive hospitality facility. The deal he put together was for a 770-room upscale brand of Holiday Inn that the Memphis-based chain dubbed Crowne Plaza.

Meanwhile, John Tishman, aware of the huge amount of building Zeckendorf had in mind, decided to become Bill's new best friend. To strengthen their bond, Tishman took up part-time residence in Santa Fe, where Bill spent much of his time. Tishman also proposed that he would build the hotel for Zeckendorf and that I would be the architect, all of which was agreeable to Zeckendorf.

For me this was a very promising project, although quite challenging. The site's entire available building area was more than a hotel could prudently use, so Zeckendorf decided to include an office building component, an immense outside membership health club, and a large convention center, complete with grand ballroom, at a total cost of $300 million. Although all of these pieces were to be in a single building, the office portion was to have its own elevator banks and a totally separate entrance and lobby on Forty-eighth Street. Using all the allowable FAR and including offices subsequently turned out to be a huge mistake, as Zeckendorf would later concede. By the time the building was completed in 1989, the office market had dried up, and he was stuck for several years with two hundred thousand square feet of unoccupied space. The cost of including the office component, compared to amortizing the burden of carrying it without income, could never be recouped.

Irwin Cantor, the structural engineer, and I had to figure out how to incorporate all these parts into one whole, in which the upper segment of this forty-seven-story skyscraper contained the 770 guest rooms.

Let me present a brief primer on how high-rises are configured. Hotel planning standards call for columns to be thirteen feet on center, which yields rooms twelve and a half feet wide, fairly standard for hotel rooms. Since it would be way beyond strange to have a column run through the middle of the bathroom, columns are placed in the six-inch-thick walls that separate the rooms, known as demising walls. If this entire building had been planned as a hotel, there would have been nothing unusual about its design, but in this case there were those office floors and other elements below the hotel component. Office buildings require columns on a twenty-five-foot grid, in order to accommodate a standard office layout that calls for private offices that generally are ten to fifteen feet wide, plus adjacent secretarial space normally ten feet wide, hence a design module of twenty-five feet. But hotels are built on a thirteen-foot grid, with thirteen-foot column centers that yield two rooms, twelve and a half feet wide with a six-inch demising wall between each. So for a hotel with thirteen-foot center columns on top of offices with twenty-five-foot spacing, we had to "pick up" all forty stories with the thirteen-foot space, set it on a huge transfer beam, and then have the lower beams supported by twenty-five-foot spacing—a very costly endeavor. Don't worry about all that math. Trust me, it was a big headache.

Making it more difficult to design this building, the hotel ballrooms were beneath the offices, and ballrooms cannot have *any* columns that would interfere with sight lines. Therefore, the twenty-five-foot columns that supported the transfer beams that in turn supported the thirteen-foot columns had to be completely picked up over the ballrooms by a *gigantic* beam that in turn had to be supported by other columns running down through the lobby. These huge beams, known alternatively as transfer or pickup beams, are not a problem structurally, but they must be very deep and be concealed in the ceilings of the public space below, making them extremely expensive. On a normal site for a hotel, the room tower is located to the side of or in back of the public spaces so that the lobby, restaurants, and meeting rooms are not cut up by its forest of columns. It is on a constricted site that this problem is most formidable.

But the cost of purchasing additional real estate, especially in a place as pricey as midtown Manhattan, usually outweighs the cost of the pickup beams. I had faced a similar situation while working for my father when he was designing the Americana New York (now the Sheraton) on Seventh Avenue between Fifty-second and Fifty-third streets. That sixty-story hotel, the tallest reinforced concrete structure in the world when it opened in 1962, encompassed nearly two thousand rooms on a very small site. The Tisch brothers, Larry and Bob, the developers, decided that the cost of a transfer beam would be less expensive than trying to acquire additional real estate. The transfer beam at the Americana was so enormous that we were able to put the entire administrative floor within it—actually a girder made up of horizontal and vertical members, like bridge girders, that you could walk through.

In addition to all these complications at the Crowne Plaza Times Square, the developers wanted to include a swimming pool, the largest at any hotel in the city. Or, more to the point, not on top of the complications, but directly on top of the grand ballroom, which was the only space in the project that could accommodate a pool that large. I still have nightmares about what would happen if thousands of gallons of water from a leaking swimming pool cascaded into the ballroom below.

All in all, Irwin Cantor and I had our work cut out for us: We had to deal with a mixed-use structure, in a special zoning district, on a small site with separate primary entrances. Just to make sure that I didn't get bored, we had to incorporate into the lot an overlaying set of special requirements for this district that required a through-block drive to enable vehicles to travel from Forty-eighth to Forty-ninth Street. Economic reality required that most of the Broadway frontage be used for high-value retail space. Maddeningly, the grand entrance for this imposing hotel had to be as small as possible. Given the relatively tiny entrance, the retail space, the drive-through requirement, and the necessity for a separate office building entrance, there was no space for me to include a grand lobby. The solution, not elegant but workable, was to have a small entrance space from Broadway and the through-block drive, which would lead to a bank of tall escalators to carry guests to the second-floor lobby. I included a huge sloping glass roof over the escalators, so that when visitors ascended from the street level to the lobby they would have the sensation of climbing to the sky. This glass roof is one of my pet features in the building. Moreover, I realized that up to that time there was not a single hotel lobby in the city that afforded an outside view. I felt that guests who elected to stay at a hotel in this new Times Square would want to be able to *see* all the action in Times Square. And so, in an unprecedented step, I designed a hotel lobby from which people could actually look out. I also situated a restaurant–cocktail lounge on the south corner of the building; given the second-floor location, it provided a terrific view out over Times Square.

My hope was that as Times Square rebounded, presumably resulting in the eradication of the existing landscape of hookers, pimps, and drug dealers, it would morph back to the exciting, blinking, flashing fun venue I remembered from my youth. I fondly recalled how inspiring this locale was when, as a teenager during the 1950s, I would occasionally subway out of Brooklyn for a special occasion in "the City," as we outer-borough folks called Manhattan. When I had a really *big* date, I would emerge from the BMT into the riot of lights that defined Times Square and head to the Paramount Theater for a stage show and a first-run movie. Then, as a proven bon vivant, I would squire my date back to Flatbush, where I would have my passionate advances rebuffed yet again.

With my New York City background and genuine love for the city, I was thrilled to be part of the group that would restore this historic area back to the glory days when the Camel cigarette sign blew smoke rings over Broadway and the Bond clothing store had a waterfall as its rooftop display. My high school classmate Woody Allen and his scenic designer, Santo Loquasto, brilliantly portrayed this moment in time in the 1987 film *Radio Days*. Woody's vision of Times Square in *Radio Days* meshed perfectly with mine, and while I was designing my building there, I rented his film for research.

So I set to work with not only profit as my motive but also the dream of beautifying the iconic Crossroads of the World. My mind was filled with images of flashing neon. But almost immediately I was stopped dead in my tracks. According to the city zoning code, *large signs were prohibited in Times Square.* Huh?

In high dudgeon (actually in a subway car), I rode downtown to the Municipal Building and visited the Office of the City Planner to discuss the city code as it related to the lighting of high-rises, laws that had been adopted during a politically correct era when flashing lights were considered vulgar, which was out of touch with present-day reality.

The nice thing about political correctness is that it changes every decade or so.

By the time I was designing the Crowne Plaza, it was coming to be understood that all those lights and razzle-dazzle were what Times Square was really about. In a city whose leading industry was tourism, and whose leading tourist attraction was *still* Forty-second and Broadway, the Brahmin definition of "good taste" wasn't going to cut it. New York was determined to bring back all the whoopee of the "Bow Tie" — that area around Duffy Square where Broadway crosses Seventh Avenue in a large, flat X.

One obstacle remained: It was up to city bureaucrats to define and legislate "whoopee." Like obscenity, whoopee does not easily lend itself to the language of legislation. Nevertheless, the city and the Municipal Art Society determined to make a try. Like any good group of civil servants, they overanalyzed everything, overlooked the obvious, legislated the impossible, and even resorted to fake scientific terminology to mandate the ridiculous.

They did all of this because I had complained that the code wouldn't let me use a lot of big signs. The net result was more or less, "You say you *want* big signs? Okay, you are now *required by law* to have big signs. But only according to our definition of signs, and only up to a height of one hundred and twenty feet."

Heaven protect us from government-mandated jollity!

By the time the city got through drafting the regulations for the new Times Square District, I was confronted by a set of rules that required signs of a wattage and brightness to be measured in something called a LUTS (Light Unit Times Square). This silliness was promulgated by the keepers of the moral and aesthetic flames, people who considered all bright signs to be in "bad taste." Otherwise reasonable and able lighting designers had been retained by the city in an attempt to accomplish the impossible: codify emotion. LUTS turned out to be a totally meaningless unit of light measure. You had to have a sufficiency of LUTSes (or maybe the plural is LUTSi?) in order to be allowed to build your building. The LUTS measurement did not allow for the use of lasers, projection images, total building illumination, or any of the other advances that had occurred in illumination over the previous half century.

The signs also had to contain advertisements, instead of being purely ornamental, and they counted toward your approvals *only* if they were in the lower 120 feet of the structure. Why just the lower 120 feet? Because our earnest young city planners had pored over old photos of the area in the thirties and forties, and deduced that that is where all the lights *used* to be.

My plan was to light the entire building, since it was to be the flagship of the Crowne Plaza chain. And, yes, I had designed a "crowne"-like cornice that I wanted to be illuminated. And, yes, this is the very same new Holiday Inn facility that the company's representative was discussing with Donald Trump in 1982, when Donald snookered the company on the Atlantic City deal (see Chapter 10). There was absolutely no connection between that experience with Trump and the Holiday Inn people, however, and this commission from Bill Zeckendorf—just another of my life's many coincidences.

I tried my best to convince the city planners that they were taking things a little too literally with all this micromanaging of the lighting and LUTSes. After all, I argued, in the 1930s lighting technology was not quite what it was by the 1980s. The technology of the 1930s did not permit the innovative effects that had since become possible. I spoke of creating a refracting laser canopy over Broadway, with computer animation projections on the face of the buildings that would be vacant at night. I asked the planners to consider continuing the evolving tradition of fun lighting in our new modern era, rather than slavishly trying to re-create the past. I pointed out publicly that "the signage requirements are OK for hotels but not for office buildings, and the setback requirements are OK for office buildings but not for hotels." In February 1987, I wrote an op-ed piece for *The New York Times* titled "Let There Be Light in Times Square," which I hope was more understandable to the readers than the curious illustration accompanying it. Even I was totally confused by the newspaper drawing until I realized it was a rendering of my hotel— *upside down*! In my article I argued that "people, like moths, are fascinated and attracted to light. . . . Requiring that [only] the lower 120 feet of a building be illuminated, because that's where lights were placed in the 1920's, and insisting that signs be the key mode of ornamentation, is as obsolete as trying to light a Broadway show with gas lights." What was needed, I insisted, citing the lit tops of skyscrapers like the Empire State Building and the Chrysler Building and the genius of Abe Feder, who lit up the entire RCA Building in Midtown, was to give pedestrians reason to look up higher than the normal cone of vision that extends just fifteen degrees above horizontal. "The spontaneity and exuberance of the old Times Square," I added, "were not created, and cannot be replicated, by legislation. . . . There's more to visual excitement than advertising signs. The city should really turn Broadway on—with lasers, holograms and the newest in lighting techniques." As for elitists who regarded the bright lights of the big city as tawdry, "Broadway and Times Square evolved into the most famous visual symbol of New York City because the area had to appeal to the public, not the critics." What the city should have as its goal was to "move light-years ahead." In a separate news story, *The Times* quoted me as commenting that "the regulations are geared for the old technologies, and we have a unique opportunity in Times Square to create visual excitement for the sake of visual excitement."

I might just as well have held my breath.

Eventually, however, events overtook dogma. I had envisioned a new Times Square of hotels, theaters, restaurants, and entertainment. In fact, mine was one of the few hotels in the initial batch of buildings. Most of the other developers looked at the Crossroads of the World and unfortunately saw nothing more than a new venue for sterile glass and aluminum office buildings. There even was babble about creating a new Champs-Élysées, complete with trees, museums, and sidewalk cafés.

On Times Square!

To these builders, the Great White Way — its history and traditions, its status as an icon in the nation's cultural memory — would have had all its energy sucked out just for the sake of erecting yet a few more boring midtown high-rises.

Not only were the majority of other structures planned for Times Square office buildings, but they were to be designed by architects known for creating buildings of impeccable "good taste." I was familiar with the designers, including my onetime employer, Skidmore, Owings & Merrill, as well as the planned style of the buildings that were to be the neighbors of my hotel. I did not have to see their specific designs to know that their palettes would run the gamut from light gray to black.

I decided to make my building pink.

My choice of color was for all the obvious reasons, plus it was my homage to Joni Mitchell, whose song "Big Yellow Taxi" has always been a favorite of mine. She talked of a pink hotel with a swinging hot spot, and I felt it was a personal call to me. As I anticipated, the other developers resolved to fight City Hall and build tasteful, unlit gray and black office buildings. They succeeded. Whether it was a fluke of the economic cycle or God's judgment on self-important developers, most of the office buildings that went up during that period were completed just in time for the 1990 real estate bust, and the owners went stone-cold broke. By the early 1990s, Broadway was home to an array of empty, grim-looking office buildings. Plus at least one moneymaking, neon-lit, flashing, sparkling pink hotel — "a great pink tongue of lasciviously rounded brick and glass sticking up at the sky," as *Newsweek* described it. With a swinging hot spot. The restaurant and lounge with the great view of Times Square were quickly booked for every New Year's Eve for the foreseeable future; in fact, Michael Silberstein, the hotel's first managing director, observed to *The Times* that within twelve hours after the Crowne Plaza opened on December 1, 1989, they had 129 reservations for New Year's Eve without even advertising. Having inherited and then had drummed into my brain over and over the first design rule of Morris Lapidus, I had adhered to my custom of designing with my client's clients in mind.

At least two other Times Square hotels were built about the same time. The Ramada Renaissance sits directly on the "Bow Tie" bounded by Broadway, Forty-seventh and Forty-eighth streets, and Seventh Avenue. Relatively small, with just 315 rooms, the Renaissance's primary reason for existing is as a support for the gigantic signs that adorn its south face and beam messages down on the square. The rest of the building is black glass. In addition to its revenues as a hotel, this project generates a fortune in sign revenue. Another hotel, just across Broadway from the Crowne Plaza, was also a Holiday Inn brand, Embassy Suites, with 460 rooms on top of what had been the Palace Theater at the southeast corner of Seventh Avenue and Forty-seventh Street. The builder was Larry Silverstein, for whom I had done some work previously; he is best known today as developer of the World Trade Center site. In one of those wonderful moments of developer idiocy, Larry and his chief construction executive retained the architectural firm they used on their office buildings—an outfit that designs excellent office buildings but had little or no experience with hotels. This is roughly akin to going to a dermatologist after you've had a heart attack. Predictably, the patient died. The Embassy Suites was a mess from the beginning: People couldn't even find the front entrance, and it went bankrupt within a year, while the Crowne Plaza was coining money.

As for the pretentious developers who owned the pretentious office buildings, most of them went broke and their buildings were sold at a fraction of the original cost. The new owners subsequently covered these structures with "zipper" signs and more flashing neon, LEDs, and video screens than can be seen anywhere this side of Tokyo's Ginza.

In the face of economic reality, the LUTS got lost. The final product was exactly what *I* would have designed if I could have planned all of

Times Square by myself. Perhaps I would have done a good job on the rest of the square, if what the press said about the Crowne Plaza represented the majority opinion: "It may be the most gorgeous building in all Manhattan," *Newsweek* gushed. "It will be even more gorgeous at night, washed in the lurid megawattage of its billboards, raining gorgeousness down on the radiance-starved multitudes. You can imagine the gasps of the guests stepping off the escalator to the second-floor lobby, onto a landing in the glass-filled Roman arch stretching a hundred feet high on Broadway." Or, as the *New York Post* put it, "If you think Times Square has lost its glitter, you haven't seen the dazzling neon display that lights up the new $300 million Holiday Inn Crowne Plaza on Broadway between 48th and 49th streets. . . . The light show was designed by architect Alan Lapidus."

In the end, my hotel turned out to be one of the more sedate structures—but one that sheds some brilliant light on Broadway and, as the first building to use the city's new guidelines for Times Square, would play a leading part in the rebirth of the Great White Way.

The finished product was said to resemble one of the old Wurlitzer jukeboxes and "certainly is different," *The Times* observed shortly after the Crowne Plaza opened on December 1, 1989. "The Wurlitzer Company," I explained to *The Times*, "designed a jukebox that imitated the design of the buildings that went up around Times Square in the 1930's and 1940's, and now I'm imitating Wurlitzer. . . . I think people long for the good old days when buildings made us smile, so I deliberately chose to use pink and burgundy on the outside of the Crowne Plaza as a happy way of inviting people to come inside."

For me, the defining moment on the entire project was the 1987 groundbreaking, a festive occasion with moral overtones. Since this block had been home to a particularly sordid assortment of porn theaters, the neighborhood groups, led by the pastor of a local church, had long crusaded for the demise of these establishments. The big ceremony, heralding all that was to come and ignoring what had gone before at this location, was held in front of the Pussycat Theater, where the display for that film classic *Hot Doctors in Lust* still graced the marquee.

While representatives of the Big Apple Wrecking Corporation stood poised with their implements of destruction in front of the movie house, the head of the Municipal Art Society, standing with the clergy, praised city officials and Bill Zeckendorf for their civic virtue that was ushering in a new era for Times Square. Then, as the speeches wound down, the representative of the Art Society looked pensively up at the sexually provocative marquee and commented to Bill that perhaps he should preserve the sign and reuse it somewhere in the new building because, after all, it was an "icon of the neighborhood."

Bill strolled over to the men from the wrecking company and whispered, "Tear it down! *Now!*"

14

The Ungrateful Living

More jobs, more lessons in human behavior. At least a segment of humanity known as *developer Americanus.*

This time, in 1990, the call came from John Tishman (again). He wanted to see me. When I arrived at the Tishman boardroom, John entered with his usual entourage and spread some design drawings on the table. They were for a hotel in Puerto Rico. I found myself looking at yet another case of a preliminary design drawn by architects who did not have a clue as to hotel function and design. John explained that one of his enterprises, Tishman Caribbean Holdings, was about to develop a six-hundred-room oceanfront convention hotel and casino to be called the Rio Mar on the eastern end of the island. The money for this project was coming from a Puerto Rican government fund to promote tourism. He said he was using a prominent local architectural firm, Sierra Cardona Ferrer, the principal of which was the first cousin of the governor of Puerto Rico. The resort had great political significance because by the time it finally opened in 1997, it was the first new hotel built on the island in almost thirty years. I interjected that I was very familiar with the situation, since I had designed the last hotel built there, El Conquistador, in the late '60s. J.T. went on to add that because of local regulations, he would not be able to use me as the lead architect. Instead, he said, the Puerto Rican architects needed "a little guidance" in their functional designs. He allowed as how, if I agreed to work for a relatively small fee, he wanted me to do a schematic design, so he and his Puerto Rican contingent would have something feasible on which to base their drawings.

The whole plan outlined by Tishman seemed really strange, given that to the best of my knowledge he had never built a hotel or anything else outside the continental United States and had absolutely no experience working with Latin American architects and construction firms. I was surprised that, knowing of my involvement in several major projects on the island, he did not appear interested in getting any input from me. After weighing his offer, I did agree to produce a "quick schematic" and to charge a low fee.

My chief architect, John Bowstead, who went with me to the Tishman meeting, was outraged. He demanded to know why I was bothering with this insulting offer. We were practically giving away all of our hard-won expertise so a bunch of locals could make a fat profit using our smarts, he pointed out.

I assured Bowstead that I had an intimate knowledge of how things are actually done down in the islands, and that Tishman would be back. We did the schematics.

Nothing had changed since I had worked there. The local architects were primarily interested in the aesthetic designs of their buildings, and hotel function was usually not their strong point. There was another zinger that I knew was waiting to cause Tishman tsuris: American-style construction documents were unheard-of in Latin America. But I didn't mention it at the time, because I had learned from experience that you did not volunteer advice to John Tishman.

My next meeting was with the principals of the Puerto Rican firm. They were friendly and garrulous. By time-honored Latin custom, we spent a while complimenting each other. J.T. walked in while we were in the midst of an enthusiastic discussion in Spanish and asked snidely if we could switch into a language "the client" understood. So English it was. The Puerto Ricans had produced a set of preliminary drawings, based on my schematic. Of course they had totally ignored my plans; instead they had spent a considerable amount of time and effort refining the details of their wonderful red-tile roofs and their striking but functionless bell towers. John asked me to take their drawings and "fine-tune" them so they were just a tad more functional. In other words, include details like having the kitchens connected to the restaurants, having a way for the guests to get from their rooms to the beach without going through the cocktail lounge, and perhaps having a space to put such unaesthetic trivia as the mechanical equipment. It would also be an improvement if guests could actually walk from the lobby to the restaurants without having to go outside—in a part of the world where rains are frequent, not to mention that this part of the world is located less than ten miles from El Yunque, the rain forest. The Rio Mar site actually was right next to El Conquistador.

This time I negotiated a reasonable fee, since I was faced with a reprise of the Swan and the Dolphin. I would have to stuff a working hotel design into a fanciful set of shapes and forms. After grudgingly agreeing to let me go forward with this exercise, he pointedly remarked that "of course all the working drawings would be done down there," meaning by the Puerto Rican architects.

My office had been limping along, still trying to shake the effects of a major recession that began in late 1989 and was catastrophic to the architectural and development scene in New York. I had been doing some consulting work, as well as small projects such as a planned casino for the Yurok Indian tribe of Northern California. I was still trying to keep as many of my old employees as I could, so I was not operating at a profit and I viewed this project as a lifesaver.

I was mystified that John had not sought to discuss with me the way things worked in the "Pearl of the Caribbean." It puzzles me to this day. John Tishman is many things, and one of them is undeniably smart.

Sometimes.

I also knew with certainty that he would be back and that I would end up doing the drawings for this resort.

Then one morning my secretary leaned into my office with a puzzled expression. J.T. was on the phone and asking for me. This was strange because John always observed a strict protocol: His secretary would not put him on the phone until I was already on the line. He was, after all, superior to me or any other of the scores of architects he could hire and fire on a whim. Busy people do not like to be put on hold.

I picked up the phone, and a bizarre conversation ensued. John was at his vacation home in Santa Fe. He was also extremely friendly, in distinct contrast to his typical reserve. That alone made me apprehensive.

"Alan, I seem to remember that you have family in Miami."

"Yes, John, I'm the only one who stayed in New York. What can we do for you?"

It turned out that a friend of his, whom I had met at Tishman's house in Westchester, had been arrested for possession of cocaine and was in the Dade County jail. Did I know someone who could get him out?

"John, give me the phone number where you can be reached for the next couple of hours. You will get a call from Richard Lapidus. He is my brother, and he is one of Miami's most prominent attorneys. If anyone can sort this out, he can."

I called Dick and explained the situation. I also explained that I was about to start negotiating with John about a very large and critical project.

All this occurred at 10:30 in the morning.

At 4:30 that afternoon, Dick called and said that John's friend was out of jail and the charges had been dropped. He would not bill Tishman for his services, so that Tishman could chalk this up as a favor from me.

Dick is the kind of big brother you really want to have.

The whole thing was handled very discreetly. There were some minor expenses that Dick had fronted, and, as Dick later told me, John paid him with a personal check sent to Dick's home address.

About two weeks after the incident in Miami, the long-awaited call came. John had finally found out that they don't do working drawings in the land of sun and fun. I should come to his office to negotiate a fee for my office doing all the work. Of course I was still to receive no credit.

What followed was the most insulting meeting of my life.

John offered to pay the salaries of my staff, with no multiple. Just their salaries. Nothing for profit, nothing for overhead. Desperate as I was for a big job, I still could not afford such a one-sided arrangement.

I was shocked, almost beyond speech.

I told him what he already knew: I had to pay rent, insurance, Social Security, administrative expenses, and other costs. Doing a job of this size on this basis would put me under.

With a tight smile, John acknowledged that he was aware that my office had very little work. So I should be grateful to him, since this would allow me to keep my doors open.

This was the man whose first hotel I had designed. I had taught him the basics of hotel design and function and how to develop a profitable hotel. His firm had since gone into business as hotel developers and was becoming one of the giants of the field. John and I had flown on long trips together, broken bread together, and shared our life stories with each other. And he had made a profit on every project I had designed for him.

But all that counts only if you have blood in your veins.

I thought of the very large favor my brother had just done for John and his friend. I was seriously tempted to grab him around the throat and choke him.

But survival has a way of tempering rage. All I did was explain to him that I could not and would not agree to such an arrangement.

He calmly explained that since these were hard times, he had his pick of other architectural firms.

After a long and humiliating session, he agreed to pay my staff's salary plus a lump sum to cover most of my basic expenses.

John was right, of course. I made just enough to keep my doors open, and I had to lose just a relatively small sum on this "commission" for the privilege.

At its start, 1989 shaped up as a spectacular year. The Crowne Plaza at Times Square was well on its way to completion. The Dolphin and Swan hotels for Disney in Florida had opened and proved successful. My office was operating at capacity, with a couple of new hotel projects. One was another job for Bill Zeckendorf. Bill had just completed a large office building called Worldwide Plaza, on Eighth Avenue at Fiftieth Street, a block from the Crowne Plaza. And he was about to start another hotel across the street from Worldwide Plaza, which he commissioned me to design.

I have always been proud that my practice has consisted largely of business from repeat clients such as Zeckendorf, Tishman, Disney, and Trump. My buildings almost always generate a profit, so clients usually come back to me whenever they have a hankering to build another hotel.

Bill Zeckendorf is as gracious a client as I've ever had. He's unfailingly courteous, always reasonable, and quick to complement my work. I was flattered that he offered me another hotel to design—another satisfied client.

I thought it a mere formality when Bill said the financial world was tightening up, which meant he was having problems getting the up-front financing for this project. Up-front financing includes all the work on a project until the first draw of the construction loan. A large part of the initial costs are the architect's fees, since the construction financing is obtained by using the completed construction documents. Bill asked me to "front" my fees. In those days, when I was operating in a euphoric cloud of major completed and successful projects, great publicity, and a gracious client, it never occurred to me to ask why he didn't dig into his own pocket to pay my fees. Especially since he certainly had a lot more money than I did. But such a question would have been considered downright rude in New York real estate circles. The developers' first sacred rule is that all of their efforts are to be financed with the classic OPM, meaning, of course, "other people's money." Bill put his proposal to me in an almost offhanded way, and he offered to give to me and my attorney copies of the all the financial agreements regarding this project.

Bill was proposing to erect a thirty-three-story Marriott Hotel, financed by funds from Adachi Steel of Japan, with help from Marriott and a construction loan from Crédit Lyonnaise. Bill also provided proof that he owned the land, so in case of any problem I could always put a mechanic's lien on the real estate to secure my interests. The papers were all in order, and Bill gave me a reference to National Westminster Bank for a line of credit so I could obtain the funds to do the project.

Of course I had put all thoughts of the huge recession of the mid-1970s out of my mind. That catastrophe had occurred more than a dozen years earlier, and, I reasoned, it was only an aberration.

In short, I had fallen victim to that most common of self-delusions: Today is forever.

Meanwhile, I had also been designing a twelve-hundred-room Sheraton hotel in Chicago, along the Chicago River, for John Tishman. That was a difficult project because the parcel was very contorted, as it fronted the river, and the zoning was quite complicated. John had told me that the project was a definite go, and that as soon as the zoning board approved our plans, he would give the green light and I could begin work. While I waited for the Tishman hotel to begin, Zeckendorf's Marriott would occupy my time and efforts. The timing couldn't have been more perfect.

As I said, it was definitely *my* year: two more high-profile center city hotel projects. I was in hog heaven.

Which turned out to be more like a fool's paradise. Guess who the fool was?

But at the time, all I focused on was the design problem of my new project.

As is all too common among architects, my main concern was aesthetics, not finances.

Eighth Avenue is only one city block from Broadway, but stylistically it is a world apart, the decrepit heart of Hell's Kitchen. Bill, as usual, had taken a huge chance building his office complex, Worldwide Plaza, in that location. He was having a hell of a time luring big upscale tenants to the "wild west." As one of the enticements to any major firm that would rent a large block of space, he had contractually obligated himself to build a new hotel directly across the street. The neighborhood had no discernible attraction, and as far as I could remember, it never had. Instead, there was an eclectic mix of small ethnic restaurants, novelty stores selling sex toys and tourist-style junk, pawnshops, and run-down low-rises with judo halls and dance studios on the second floors. Since Zeckendorf's office tower was of quasi-classical design with an elegant retro street-level arcade, I decided to make my building Art Deco.

When the drawings were finished, Zeckendorf and I visited Marriott headquarters outside Washington, DC. Marriott's offices were huge, modern, bustling, and impressive in every way. After our presentation, Bill Marriott came over to congratulate me, hands were heartily shaken, and Zeckendorf and I returned to New York with corporate blessings.

Just as I was starting the construction documents, I got a strange phone call from a totally unexpected quarter. Marvin Mass is the founder and owner of Cosentini Associates, one of the biggest and best mechanical engineering firms I have ever worked with. When I had created the preliminary drawings for John Tishman's Chicago Sheraton Hotel, Cosentini did the preliminary engineering. Now Marvin was calling with a peculiar question.

"Alan, you're still the architect for John's Chicago project, aren't you?"

"Yeah, sure, Marvin. Why do you ask?"

"Because I just had a call from the Solomon architectural firm in Chicago, asking me to give them a price for the mechanical engineering work on the project."

Having one of those blinding flashes of insight with which I am cursed, I immediately understood the unfolding catastrophe.

The two somber office buildings that would flank my Broadway Crowne Plaza were being developed by David Solomon, whose father had an architectural firm in Chicago. John Tishman wanted to be the builder of those Manhattan buildings. It was obvious that John had made a pact with David, ignored his deal with me, and given the work to David Solomon's father. One hand washes the other, as they say.

Once again I made an appointment to visit John at his headquarters on the thirty-eighth floor of the Tishman Building. The address is 666 Fifth Avenue — the sign of the devil, which I learned when a Haitian cabdriver refused to take me there. It's a number that at times seemed perfectly fitting. Now, as I trudged over to this one-on-one meeting with John, I was disappointed, hurt, and angry. I wasn't angry at the loss of a project; I had spent my life in New York and understood the ethos that ruled the city's real estate world: the bottom line. Period. The reason for my anger was that Tishman had not had the common decency to call me to tell me that "my" project was no longer mine. In the tight world that is Manhattan, every new development and its players are immediately known and extensively discussed. While I was innocently awaiting commencement of the Chicago Sheraton, the job had already started. It was crushing to find this out from one of my consultants rather than directly from my client, Tishman.

When I arrived at John's office, he actually looked sheepish. Not a common look for John Tishman.

He explained that the project "had gone in a different direction." He did not elaborate. Nor did he need to.

Since I might have to work for him again, I was more gracious than my seething guts were dictating. I assured John that I understood the underlying reasons for the change but I told him I would have preferred knowing about it before my consultants informed me. I made nice and offered to supply any helpful information to his new architect. We shook hands and I left.

Hey, I can be just as big a hypocrite as anyone else.

Over the last dozen years of working together, I had spent a lot of time with John. On long flights together, he had talked extensively about his past, how he had come into the business, his schooling, and his life as a very young officer in the navy toward the close of World War II. I had come to appreciate his intelligence and keen intellect. We were also both pilots. I had a single-engine propeller plane, called a Mooney, and John owned a twin-engine aircraft, a Beechcraft. On one occasion, we flew down to Atlantic City in John's plane with his corporate pilot. The pilot was mainly for insurance purposes. J.T. was the CEO of a large corporation, and insurance companies like the warm, fuzzy feeling of knowing that a professional is in the cockpit to back up their flying executives. On this occasion we both were at the controls while the pilot, with many misgivings, sat in the back.

At that time I also owned an antique airplane, a de Havilland Chipmunk, that had once been a Royal Air Force trainer, which I flew in air shows. One show was held at Westchester Airport, very close to John's country estate. He came to the show, wearing a leather flight jacket, and admired my plane and invited me back to his house for lunch. Something else John and I share is an affinity for Chinese food, and his Chinese butler served us delicious wonton soup and stir-fry. After lunch, John eagerly showed me around the house. He was especially proud of the new darkroom where he could develop his own color prints, along with a CAD machine that he was beginning to get the hang of. (I never did.) Afterward, he drove me back to the airport and watched me take off into the wild blue.

Seeing this personal side of John, I had come to think of our relationship as more than just business. Now I was in the process of learning that in New York real estate circles there is no such thing as "friendship," just ever-shifting strategic alliances.

Even after the Sheraton fiasco, I was still full of residual good feelings for John. He had given me the opportunity to design his hotels and had recommended me to Zeckendorf. One misadventure, humiliating as it had been, was not sufficient to deplete the reservoir of goodwill I had for this man.

The construction docs for the Marriott in Hell's Kitchen were nearing completion, and I was growing concerned because the usual steady stream of new projects was starting to dry up. At about this time I happened to be in Donald Trump's office. He leaned back and started to wax philosophical. This is not unusual for The Donald. He swiveled his chair around and gestured at the endless expanse of the city outside his window.

"Alan, it's the end of the world out there."

By this time, even I had begun to realize that some bad economic times were approaching.

"Donald, I know that you are heavily leveraged. Aren't you worried?"

Steepling his fingers, he turned to face me with one of his infrequent smiles and replied with a version of a statement that would come to be identified with him: "Hey, Alan, if you owe the banks a couple of million dollars, you're in deep shit. If you owe the banks a couple of billion dollars, *they're* in deep shit."

With a typical non sequitur, he abruptly switched subjects. "Alan, do you think I should buy Bloomingdale's?"

It wasn't as if Donald valued my opinion so much. He had a habit of asking everyone their views on a vast array of subjects, no matter how unqualified the source.

After assuring him that I shopped *at* Bloomingdale's but didn't know anything about shopping *for* Bloomingdale's, I left his office and started to genuinely worry. I had taken out a line of credit for $1 million to finance the Marriott project. Since I was owed more than twice that amount, I wasn't panicked, but I was certainly concerned. Once Zeckendorf paid me, I would be okay financially, but with no new work coming in, the question was, for how long?

The answer was soon to come.

Plans for the Marriott were completed, submitted, and approved. Crédit Lyonnaise approved the construction loan and champagne corks were popped.

It all came crashing down the next day.

With stunning swiftness, the real estate world imploded. The great crash of 1989 had just occurred, bringing down almost every component of the industry. The trouble had begun with the collapse of the Japanese economy. The stock price of Adachi Steel, our project's principal funder, bottomed out. Adachi was no longer able to finance the hotel. Even the Marriott Corporation was in trouble and unable to stand by its commitment. Bill Zeckendorf was not going to pay me for almost a year of work. The project was canceled. That design for the Marriott remains one of my favorites. I liked it so much that I could truly "see" it, walk around it and through it, as if it were real. But it wasn't. The operation was successful, but the patient died.

Bill and I met at his office, and he commiserated with my plight. He explained that he understood and sympathized with the economic devastation this was causing me. Even though he was causing me to lose my $2 million fee, he hoped I would find consolation in the knowledge that he was losing $5 million. I honestly believe that in his heart of hearts, Bill, who has always been a gentleman and a very nice guy, sincerely believed that what he was doing wasn't all that harmful to me, nor did he intend it to be. In a state of shock, at least on my part, we shook hands (weren't we civilized?) and I walked the cold, dark winter streets back to my office.

The loss of $5 million—nothing more than a paper loss on his books—would not alter Bill Zeckendorf's standard of living one little bit. He was staggeringly rich. I owed National Westminster Bank $1 million—in real, not paper or play, dollars—and I had used all my personal assets to keep this project going.

I was more than broke. I was totally wiped out.

On both the Zeckendorf and Tishman jobs, I hadn't even realized I was gambling. And I lost.

At Christmastime 1975, when another recession wracked the nation, my father had abruptly closed the New York office, fired everyone with two weeks' severance, and left for his Florida empire. He also left with several million dollars.

At Christmastime 1989, I had no choice but to let go most of my office. At the time I didn't even have my next month's rent. No one got any severance.

The confluence of events was particularly devastating to both my staff and me. Because of the total collapse of the real estate industry, there would be precious little work anywhere. Architecture, as is true of any field that is fun, is overcrowded. Except in boom times (defined as those brief periods prior to a crash), there are too many architects trying to work on too few jobs. When real estate develops a cold, architects come down with pneumonia. Now the entire real estate industry had developed pneumonia.

Letting this group go was the worst single day of my life.

No architect who works on major projects can be a sole practitioner. No matter how great a designer you are, you must depend on your staff to produce the voluminous documents necessary to construct a building.

The Morris Lapidus office had been run by a thick set of rules, which spelled out not only the policy on sick days and vacations but also the frequency and duration of coffee breaks. There was a fearsome chief draftsman who glowered at the staff from his vantage point at the head of the drafting room, keeping careful tabs on tardiness, overly long lunch hours, and undue bathroom breaks. Sounds almost like an elementary school classroom, doesn't it?

I resolved that my own firm would not treat professionals as if they were errant schoolchildren. My sensibilities were formed during the 1960s, when peace and love were in the air. I would treat my employees as colleagues, not wage slaves. To that end I've never had a sick day or personal day policy. If you're sick, stay home. If you have something to do that can be done only on a weekday, just consider it your personal time and take care of what you need to. Nor have there ever been prescribed office hours. Everyone is expected to work thirty-seven and a half hours a week, but those hours are flexible. No one in my office has ever kept tabs. I reasoned that if I treated professionals as professionals, they would act accordingly.

For the most part, I've been proved right.

I've also had a policy of dividing the profits of the firm so that at least half of each year's profits are distributed as bonuses.

Early on I realized that the few women in the profession have usually had a much harder time than men. Traditionally they're paid markedly less and are rarely given the opportunity to be project chiefs. Starting with one remarkably competent woman from the Morris Lapidus office, I set out to hire female architects. I've found that having had to overcome many more obstacles than their male counterparts, women are usually extremely dedicated and generally just better at what they do. I've always paid them exactly the same as the men, and I soon had an office where all my project architects were women.

My practice has always been more an informal studio than a corporate type of firm, with a collegial and relaxed atmosphere. I've gotten to know most of my staff well, and their families too. Now, a week before Christmas 1989, with no warning, I had to let most of my employees go and send them out into a world that had no immediate use for architects. Fortunately, through contacts I and some of my employees had, and with glowing letters of recommendation from me, every member of my staff was able to find employment in our field, even if they didn't earn as much in the new jobs as they had when they worked for me.

As had happened before, I was partially saved by a series of small jobs. One was a renovation project for a French developer named Leon Cohen, who purchased a forty-seven-story midtown apartment building at 135 West Fifty-second Street, abutting the Sheraton (formerly the Americana). The building was planned as a condo but got caught in the same meltdown that wiped me out and never opened as condos. Cohen wanted to convert it to a hotel, which meant reconfiguring the rooms — turning large apartments into numerous hotel rooms, converting apartment kitchens into smaller kitchenettes, creating a restaurant and bar, upgrading the lobby, and bringing fire systems and the like up to code requirement for a hotel. Cohen's idea was to rent what he called "flats," as opposed to simply standard hotel rooms—hence the name Flatotel. He called me the day after the massacre at my office. The job was enough to keep a few of us busy for a few months. When you are desperate, a few months seems like forever. I slashed expenses. Anything that wasn't essential for keeping the doors open had to go. My landlord, realizing that many of his tenants were about to be in big trouble, cut my rent in half. The remaining staff had their pay cut by 15 percent. I borrowed money from friends and took no pay at all.

Meanwhile, NatWest Bank started breathing down my neck, demanding that I repay my loan. They made impolite queries as to when they could expect me to pay back one million big ones. I was fifty-three years old, and my options were few. Since more than half the profession was unemployed, I could not just go out and find work at another firm. In the superfirms, partners were now working as draftsmen. This is how it must have been during the Depression.

Moreover, I felt that if I closed the firm, I would never be able to get it going again. I either had to change fields, or survive somehow and keep my doors open.

I called my big brother.

Richard is a litigation attorney, one of the most relentless in south Florida. In legal circles, he is known as "the Tiger." His only specialty is winning.

I should explain that I am a somewhat solidly built, brown haired, cow eyed, softspoken man of medium height. My soft and gentle disposition is not an act.

Then there's Richard. He is lean, short, and tough (he entered triathlons well into his sixties), and in his professional life he has the disposition of an irritated timber rattler.

I told Richard my story.

Having mellowed a little, he did not call me an asshole. He just implied it.

Be that as it may, he came to my rescue. He instructed me to retain local counsel in New York and start filing for bankruptcy. I was horrified. Richard had reviewed my list of now uncollectible receivables from a who's who of New York developers. Richard interrupted my objections with a question: "Do you really want to spend the rest of your life paying off Bill Zeckendorf's and John Tishman's debts?"

Following my brother's advice, I hired a kind and understanding New

York bankruptcy attorney, James Pagano. He was part legal practitioner and part counselor. When I voiced my misgivings about becoming "bankrupt," he gently explained that practically all my clients had already put their shell corporations into bankruptcy. This had, unfortunately, become just another way of doing business. The land that Zeckendorf had owned was worth $11 million when we began the project. I assumed that would secure me. Pagano looked up some figures and advised me that in this crash the land was now worth zero. No one was buying New York real estate.

I had mortgaged my condo to the hilt to pay personal and office expenses, and I realized it was just a matter of time before I lost it. I had sold my airplane, my car, and everything else that had any cash value. Pagano walked me through the whole excruciating process. He told me the bank could still cause me some serious grief by foreclosing on my condo before I had a chance to sell it. I told him that my brother had foreseen that and had set up a meeting with NatWest. Pagano wished me luck.

As soon as Dick arrived in New York, the two of us went down to the impressive headquarters of the National Westminster Bank on Water Street. In the early '90s, the "work out" guys were the stars of the banking industry. With all of the failures, defaults, and bankruptcies, these vultures were the ones who made sure that all the corpses were picked clean before burial.

My brother and I entered the cavernous conference room, with its panoramic view of the East River, the Brooklyn Bridge, and my home borough of Brooklyn. Five flinty-eyed suits sat down with all the magisterial ceremony of a posse of hanging judges.

Before they could open their mouths, my brother shot them a vicious look and snarled, "You guys are in deep shit!"

As you might imagine, that stopped them cold.

Giving them no time to recover, Dick continued, "Why did you loan my brother a million bucks? He doesn't have the equity to securitize that kind of a transaction, he has no inventory, no equipment of any value, no personal assets that would warrant this loan. For God's sake, he's an *architect!*"

Adding in a soft and sinister voice, "Why did you make this loan?

Could it be because he had receivables from Trump, Zeckendorf, and Tishman? That would be very interesting," Dick went on ominously, "because the way I see it, and the way the court will see it, you were simply using my brother to make a secondary loan to these big guys. They all seem to have existing loans with you. I believe that this sort of transaction is illegal under the Federal Banking Regulations."

By this time, the bankers' mouths were hanging open. It was clear that they wished they had called in sick.

My brother, ever the gentle conciliator continued, "Alan is filing for bankruptcy. If you guys so much as send an attorney to the proceeding, I will file papers and a lawsuit against you in federal court *that very day*. Do we understand each other?"

They understood. On our way out, one of the suits admiringly asked Dick how long he had been practicing bankruptcy law. Dick replied that he had never before done bankruptcy work. What was his field, they wanted to know. With a big smile, my brother looked at them and revealed, "I represent banks."

The court proceeding was anticlimactic, even somewhat reassuring. After weeks of preparation, James Pagano and I sat before a federal bankruptcy referee in Manhattan. The papers were fairly straightforward. Nobody from NatWest showed up. The only money I owed was to the bank.

The referee, upon looking through the file, said the most reassuring words I could have wished for: "It's a crying shame what they are doing to you architects!"

It turned out that this was the fourth bankruptcy of an architect he had handled that month. He shook his head and actually commiserated with me, declaring that all the developers were abandoning ship like rats in a storm and leaving their architects to go under.

Instead of feeling like an abject failure, I got a measure of comfort from the referee's words.

I also no longer owed NatWest $1 million.

Of course at any time I could have refused to work for developers who had screwed me. With most of the giant developers, however, shafting the architect if necessary is just standard operating procedure, the same as in Hollywood, where it is not only routine but almost required for the studio to screw the writer. If you piss off a developer in the tight world of New York real estate, he will bad-mouth you to his friends and you will never eat lunch in this town again. Developers regard throwing the architect overboard as "nothing personal, just business." The sad part is they really believe it. For Tishman, Zeckendorf, and others, maintaining good relationships with them, almost no matter what, has usually paid off for me in additional jobs. In fact, staying on the good side of developers is an excellent way to get referrals: Disney recommended me to Tishman, who in turn recommended me to Zeckendorf. And of course Trump knows all of them, and all of them know him. Bottom line: Everybody knows everybody.

To illustrate how small a world it is: In 1988, Zeckendorf hired me on behalf of himself and several partners to redesign the legendary but outmoded Plaza Hotel into 308 upgraded hotel rooms, plus condos and major new commercial space. The hotel was built at two different times—the north part near the beginning of the twentieth century and the south section during the 1920s. The original entrance was on Central Park South, while the Fifth Avenue entry was called the Champagne Terrace because bluebloods riding through the Park on horseback or in their carriages could canter up, tie their steeds or carriages to hitching posts, and have a "stirrup cup." I placed a lot of retail space where the seldom-used ballrooms were; one tenant was to have been Harrods. Ironically, part of the Plaza is currently being converted into private residences selling for $2.5 to $40 million and "hotel condos," similar to time-shares, going for $1.6 to $9 million.

One day while I was researching and redesigning the Plaza, Donald called me.

"Alan," he said, "I hear you're doing the due diligence for Zeckendorf."

"Yeah, I am, Donald. Who's doing your due diligence?"

"You are. I know your work and I know you will give them an accurate assessment on which they'll base their price. I'm relying on you, then I'm going to bid five million more."

Donald actually did outbid my group, then sat on the Plaza for a while and eventually lost the project.

So there just isn't any point in indulging in righteous indignation that might cost me future work. How many people hate their bosses but continue to work for them? Most people, I dare say.

What I did take away from the bad experiences was the understanding that on future jobs I would have to protect myself by estimating and billing high, as a means of making up for losses I might incur unfairly. Call it my UUE (unforeseen and uncalled for eventuality) insurance.

15

A Walk on the Wild Side

As the United States struggled to shake off the effects of the 1990s real estate meltdown, the rest of the world was busily gearing up to take advantage of global tourism. In the mid-1990s, the fastest-growing segment was ecotourism. There was a large group of people that wanted to experience nature in the raw. Well, maybe not all that raw.

The call came from a Brazilian architect named Edo Rocha. He was in New York (like many South Americans he kept an apartment in Manhattan) and wondered if he could meet with me about a new hotel in Brazil. I was still trying to keep afloat as an architect in a recession, and foreign work was a bright spot in an otherwise bleak architectural landscape. Besides, this was Brazil, home of the world's largest rain forests and the world's smallest bikinis. How could you not love such a place? Edo was beautifully tailored, much traveled, and multilingual. This, as I was to find out, was not atypical in cosmopolitan Brazilian society.

Edo explained that the government of Brazil, in an effort to protect the rain forest, had offered huge tax incentives to companies that would spend money to help preserve this enormous resource. One of the largest landholders in this region was Pirelli, the Italian tire company. Historically they had grown hundreds of thousands of hectares of rubber trees in Amazonia, the heart of the forest.

But blight had virtually wiped out the rubber industry in Brazil, and Southeast Asia was now the growing area. This left Pirelli with enormous holdings that were now unproductive. Edo had been speaking with a representative of the tire company and they had discussed the idea of building an ecohotel on part of the Pirelli-owned forest. This would ease their hefty tax burden, as well as present the opportunity to cash in on the hot new wave in tourism. Could I design a hotel that was "environmentally neutral"? This got my attention on several different levels. First and foremost, it was a paying job. Second, it was a fantastic challenge. Third, there were those bikinis.

First I would have to find out what, precisely, was meant by "environmentally neutral." Edo arranged a trip to Washington, D.C., to visit the headquarters of the Nature Conservancy, an entity that was to be an integral part of this project. It was an interesting meeting. The people in the conservancy were not a bunch of wild-eyed tree huggers, at least not the group I met with. We discussed the idea and they were quite clear that they would lend their name and expertise to this venture only if it could be designed as a true four-star resort, with air-conditioning, TV, faxes, and all the bells and whistles. They allowed as to how they had a sufficiency of facilities for people to live in huts in the forest, but that was like preaching to the converted. You didn't go to those places unless you were already an ardent preservationist. What they wanted was a facility that would cater to the mainstream traveler, where ordinary people could see and learn about the wonders of this part of our planet while still enjoying great meals, showers, air-conditioning, CNN, and flush toilets.

While providing all the wonders of the modern world, it could burn no fossil fuel; leave no waste, human or otherwise; and in no way impact the natural environment. The site was deep in Amazonia, on the Rio Guamá, and of course it was nowhere near any sources of electricity or potable water. It was, however, plentifully stocked with piranhas, crocodiles, jaguars (the kind with claws, not wheels), a huge variety of snakes, and multiple other creatures that would regard the future guests as the bill of fare.

We discussed the idea of providing a research station for the conservancy as an integral part of this complex. This would be a symbiotic relationship: The hotel would provide food and lodging for the researchers in a separate facility, and the conservancy would provide the hotel with a staff of expert guides for the guests. Off the main lobby would be an orientation lecture room, where the guests would get a course on the Amazon and its environment, as well as being told what they could do and, more important, what they could not do. We would establish trails for walking or navigating by electric vehicle (yes, shades of *Jurassic Park*) as well as daily lectures on the ecology, wildlife, plant life, and indigenous people of this place. By the time we boarded the flight back to New York, I was stoked.

Edo promised to send me a site map and a retainer. Two weeks later, I received both and a date was set for my trip to São Paulo, Edo's headquarters. The night before I was to leave, I was studying the site plan when I noticed that cable TV was showing a film called *At Play in the Fields of the Lord*. The film was advertised as having been shot on location in Amazonia. As I watched the film, featuring Daryl Hannah cavorting buck naked about the rain forest, I kept looking at the site plan. It showed the site at the confluence of two rivers, one of which was much larger than the smaller tributary. So did the film. I realized that this was undoubtedly a fairly common situation in this part of the world. As I was soon to discover, it was a common situation, but the hotel site was, in fact, where they had shot this film. I was later to see the remains of the fake "native village" set smack in the middle of our site.

I flew to São Paulo and spent several days examining site plans, soil analysis, and background information on the rain forest. I also talked with a few contractors to find out how they would build this type of a structure, and we concluded that the major framing would be prefabricated near São Paulo and moved by barge some three thousand miles up the coast to Amazonia.

I also met with some very smart mechanical engineers about designing a system that produces copious quantities of electricity to power this complex without burning any fossil fuels. Then there was the problem of getting rid of the sewage without leaving any pollution, and of getting sufficient quantities of safe water so that everyone could take multiple showers in the hot, sticky environment of the rain forest. It was estimated that each room would use a minimum of two hundred gallons a day and the project was to be designed for two hundred rooms plus the housing and research station for the conservancy. Do the math, it was a tall order.

The Pirelli jet flew us to Belém, the jumping-off point. It had been a major staging area during World War II. Most of the matériel that was shipped to Africa and the CBI (China, Burma, India) theater of operations flew down to Belém, and then across to West Africa, and then onward. The airport was huge, having once serviced the thousands of United States Army aircraft that supplied the fighting fronts. A stone marker noted that this spot was 0.0.0 latitude; we were standing on the equator.

During the height of this area's rubber-growing opulence, the plantation owners had decided to make this a city to rival Paris. French architects and planners were brought in and a metropolis of grand boulevards equal to the Champs-Élysées was mapped out. With the help of European artisans and craftsmen, they set to work and got the place half built, before the rubber blight wiped out the industry. It resembled a science fiction film depicting a ruined ancient civilization crumbling back into the jungle. The grand boulevard was spectacular, but it ended abruptly and turned into a slum. The rest of the city consisted of imposing structures overcome by neglect and decay, with hovels in close proximity. The waterfront, like waterfronts everywhere in the third world, stank of decaying fish and other unidentified and unpleasant substances.

We stayed at the Hilton, a building of indeterminate age, but most of the facilities were working.

It was here that I first began to realize that the rain forest was, in fact, another world. The breakfast buffet consisted of fruits that I had never even heard of. Instead of orange juice, there was something called acerola juice. I remembered that I had once bought some vitamin C tablets to ward off a winter cold, and a clerk at the health food store was touting the C made from acerola. I never gave it much thought, but I stayed sneeze free. As I was to learn, acerola has one hundred times more vitamin C, ounce for ounce, than oranges. And it is green, tastes far sweeter than other citrus, and grows in profusion in this part of the world.

We met with several more builders and had meetings at the zoo in Belém, an experience that I highly recommend. I stared in awe at some of the creatures that inhabited a domain like no other. At the zoo, we met with conservancy people as well as veterinarians and other specialists in the life of the forest. Next morning, a car and driver were waiting. I had not asked the particulars of our agenda, since Edo and the local folks had arranged everything and I just went wherever they pointed me. I was wearing my usual traveling outfit of a lightweight blue blazer, khakis, blue button-down shirt, and penny loafers. The car drove us to the river, where we boarded a small open boat with an ancient outboard motor. Surprised, I asked our destination. With some amusement they informed me we were heading into the rain forest for a site inspection. I was going into the heart of darkness dressed in Bass Weejuns.

After a surprisingly short ride we arrived at the wooden dock that I had seen in the film. The rain forest begins abruptly at the outskirts of the city, and the transition is sudden and intensely dramatic. One minute shacks and run-down buildings, the next minute we are back in the prehistoric era. As we stepped from the boat, the Pirelli guy looked up at the enveloping forest canopy, the gigantic trees whose exposed roots were taller than us, and the chattering flocks of strange birds. He spread his arms and exclaimed: *"Un vero paradiso!"*

Great! I was in a Fellini film!

Pirelli had supplied us with guides who met us at the dock and took us to the compound that serviced the caretaker crew of the tract. We went into an open wooden building that was sort of a lounge and dining hall. We had lunch as they briefed us on this portion of the plantation. As we finished our meal, the heavens opened and the rain came down in sheets. Quite literally *sheets*. It was precisely 2 P.M. After about a half an hour, the downpour slackened somewhat, and within an hour it had turned into a light drizzle.

Welcome to the rain forest.

A little after three we set out along a forest trail, accompanied by several of the Pirelli guides, complete with machetes. These guides all came from this area and were eager to show us the wonders of this strange world. They would go into the forest and bring back various fruits and other substances, and we sampled what we could. At one point they emerged with a medium-sized pod of what I took to be a small melon. When sliced open it had a pale, slightly orange flesh and a large cluster of seeds. It was cacao, a Hershey bar in the raw. If you discarded the fruit, dried the seeds, ground them up, then roasted them in an oven, added sugar and stuff, you got chocolate. It still amazes me that someone figured all this out. Not exactly a logical progression.

We arrived in a broad clearing that contained a large building. It had no walls, a rusting corrugated tin roof, and a series of abandoned ovens and cauldrons. This was where the raw rubber sap was reduced by boiling and then baked into "biscuits," a few of which were still lying around. They were about one yard around and a foot and a half thick. These in turn were brought back down to the dock for transshipment to plants where they would be refined into the finished product.

The temperature in this area was in the high nineties, and the humidity was the same. I asked who could possibly work in this place, tending boiling vats and hot ovens. "Slaves" was the answer.

It was further explained that after those bleeding-heart liberals outlawed slavery, the plantation owners had made a deal with the government to provide them with prisoners. Spending your life working here would have made Devils Island seem like Club Med.

Before we continued back to Belém, we took another walk through the forest. I was cautioned always to keep on the cleared paths. As we walked, I saw a narrow path leading off to the left and, like an idiot, decided to explore it. As I walked along, I noticed that the ground was moving. Not only was the path moving, it was carrying a bunch of tree leaves along with it. Slightly too late, I realized that I wasn't walking on a dirt path; I was walking on a moving stream of fire ants.

As they swarmed up my legs, I let out a scream that was loud enough to have brought help from New York. The guides came running, tore off my pants, doused me with water (*not* from the river), and one of them came running over with some sort of fruit that he was slicing open. They rubbed my legs with the juice of this plant, and within minutes, the stinging and itching vanished. During the next couple of days that I spent here, I had my legs washed with this juice, and had no further problems. (On the flight back, everything started to itch. None of New York's best dermatologists could come up with anything to give me much relief. After about two weeks, it subsided. I have no idea what that rain forest plant was, but I had observed that the major pharmaceutical companies had extensive research facilities in that area.)

That evening, at the edge of the forest, we had dinner in a "restaurant" — an open-sided wooden building that extended out over the river. At one end was a large open charcoal grill, actually a fifty-gallon drum sliced in half laterally, with a grate across the coals. Dugout canoes were coming up to the building and the cooks negotiated with the natives and then hoisted up some of the ugliest fish that I had ever seen. It looked sort of like a sturgeon, but uglier. This was the specialty of the house. When it was served, it looked like a pork chop. What was truly weird was that it tasted like a pork chop. Apparently I was eating a creature that appeared to be some sort of transitional form of life between surf and turf. Of course, when I returned home, no one believed a word I said about this creature until *The New York Times* did an article about a huge benefit dinner in East Hampton. The proceeds were to go to aid the rain forest and they had flown in some of the fish that were native to the Amazon. The headline of the article was: "A Fish That Looks and Tastes Like a Spare Rib."

Since there was no precedent for this type of a structure, I was forced to resort to logic. The final design was a series of two-story structures connected by open covered walkways, the whole complex being elevated six feet above the ground. This would keep the wooden buildings off the forest floor. It was designed this way so that the wood would not be in constant contact with the perpetually damp ground, and it would also enable all the plumbing, utilities, and electrical lines to be run aboveground and be readily available for inspection and maintenance. This was a page right out of Walt Disney's playbook. The rooms were configured so that each had at least one right-angle corner to provide cross ventilation, but they were also air-conditioned. The air-conditioning would be necessary in the hot, humid mornings, but the cross venting would make that unnecessary in the pleasant air of the evenings. I also had the walkway ascend to the jungle canopy and continue through it, to make the varied ecology of this world accessible to the guests. Since this area of the forest had a fairly low tree canopy, about thirty to forty feet, I could do this without having to resort to heroic means.

The space below the buildings and walkways had electrical-charging stations for the golf carts that the guests would use to explore the forest. A dock provided a mooring for a seaplane to take people farther upriver to such places as Manaus, a town with a Victorian opera house (made famous in Werner Herzog's 1982 film *Fitzcarraldo*) and an abandoned ghost village called Ford Town. This was a now ruined replica of an American midwestern town, which had been built by Henry Ford to house the workers on his rubber plantation.

Our complex would also have boats of differing sizes and capacities for local touring, fishing expeditions, and dinner cruises. A large swimming pool was located at the riverbank. Since this was to be built on the "black" side of the river, the waters were too acidic to support mosquitoes, so it would be relatively bug free. To keep our large slithery friends from climbing up the steps to the rooms, I put metal "nosings," or edges, on the stairs and wired them to transmit a very low voltage that would be harmless to people but highly annoying to serpents. It was all low wood structures that would blend into the environment. That was the easy stuff.

I returned to São Paulo to tackle the crux of the problem. On my first trip, I had met with several local engineers and we had begun researching the subject of powering this environmentally neutral complex. I realized that the power source would have to have redundancy. The Caribbean projects had taught me that anything mechanical can and will fail. Redundancy was not a luxury, it was a necessity, especially here, where any repairs or replacement parts could be days away. If we could somehow generate sufficient electricity, we would be home free. We finally worked out three different systems for this.

The local engineers came up with a dandy device called a "biodigester." It could provide copious quantities of power, fueled by an inexhaustible resource—human waste. When feces decomposes, it emits H_2S, hydrogen sulfide, commonly known as sewer gas (it has the smell of rotten eggs). H_2S is highly flammable and can be burned like any other volatile gas with a heavy hydrogen component. This system worked by pumping all the toilet effluent to a large sealed tank, where decomposition would be accelerated, the gas piped into burners that would boil the collected rain- and river water to distill it into drinking water, and the steam thus generated would power turbines that would generate electricity. The by-product of this process would be water vapor, hardly a problem in the rain forest. The sludge from this process would be the same as from any sewage disposal plant. It would not smell and it was a nitrogen-rich fertilizer.

I presumed that if the hotel was fully booked with tourists who had their air conditioners on full, and every other appliance going full blast, they could simply serve lots of fresh fruit and a prune stew, and everything would work just fine. Sort of gives new meaning to the phrase "power to the people."

I came up with the second system. I remembered that the New England colonies had used tidal dams for power. This was a simple system of building huge troughs that would be filled by an incoming tide, and, when the tide ebbed, the water would flow out over a spillway and turn waterwheels, or turbines. The Amazon had a nine-foot tide, so the power would be ample. The third system used windmills. Another unique feature of this section of the Amazon was that a constant five- to ten-knot wind blew down the water. This was another source of nonpolluting power.

When all of this had been designed and integrated into a low-slung series of elegant wooden buildings, I got on a Varig jet and returned to São Paulo. Pirelli, the conservancy, and the government all approved the complex. I was interviewed on local television in a unique fashion. Portuguese is the language of Brazil, but every other country in this part of the world speaks Spanish. Therefore, most Brazilians understand Spanish. By this time my ear had become enough accustomed to the language, which is close to Spanish, so that, given the context, I could understand what was being said. Therefore, the interviewer spoke to me in Portuguese and I answered in Spanish. Much champagne was consumed and the toasts were elegant and multilingual.

After I returned home, Edo kept in touch about all the mounting difficulties in Pirelli coming to terms with the sale of the property and the problems of getting acceptable funding for the project. After a while, the calls stopped and I went on with my life. It still hasn't been built.

But I bought a copy of *At Play in the Fields of the Lord.*

16

"A Little Favor"

A developer client invited my wife and me to join him for a weekend at his Easthampton estate. This was weird—I was rarely invited to socialize with my clients, and he was quite guarded when I asked who else would be there. When we arrived, he gave us a tour of the grounds, stables, swimming pool, and all the other necessary appurtenances of a successful developer.

When we returned to the main house, I was introduced to the other couple. I had seen her, quite often, on television. She was in then-president Bill Clinton's circle of close advisers. (No, it wasn't Monica.) The conversation that weekend ranged over a wide variety of subjects, and I was slightly in awe of being with a lady who was so close to the big guy himself.

The conversation was never about politics. At one point my client brought up the interesting fact that I had, during my student years, lived for a while in Cuba. I had mentioned this to him one day when we were having lunch at a Cuban restaurant in Manhattan. At the time, I thought nothing of this, other than it being polite conversation. Later that week, during a meeting on one of his forthcoming projects, he asked me to dinner at his apartment. With cartons of take-out Chinese food on his stately walnut dining table, he casually asked if I had a mind to do "a little favor" for my country. Like in a bad spy movie, I asked the nature of this "favor." Like in that same bad spy movie, he allowed that it would involve some foreign travel, there would be some danger, and if anything went wrong, this conversation had never taken place. I had definitely seen this flick, and I fully expected to see my old friend James Bond enter stage right. At least I was hoping to. No such luck.

He explained that the Helms-Burton Law prohibited trade with and travel to Cuba, but one of its exceptions was for architects traveling to Cuba for the purpose of restoring historic buildings. His "friends" in Washington had been looking for an architect with a national reputation, *not* of Spanish descent, and with a working knowledge of Spanish. How would I like to go to Havana to restore the only remaining synagogue in Cuba? Of course I would be taking four of my "associates" to help me with this task.

I met my "associates" at Kennedy Airport and we boarded a flight to Nassau, the Bahamas. We spent the night in the Atlantis hotel and ended up in the casino. Utilizing my casino experience, I pointed out which of the slots were most likely to pay off, and they all won big. One remarked that with such insight, I should go into their line of work.

The next morning we took a short flight to Havana on an old, ratty Tupolev airliner. As we came in for a landing, I was fascinated by all the old aircraft lined up by the side of the runway. There were several Antonov biplanes (these were current production airliners with a design straight from the 1930s) and a collection of other outdated Soviet aircraft. The terminal was a chaos of shouting, pushing humanity greeting loved ones. We were the only people who looked like we were on some sort of business. A handsome young man in a sport shirt and white slacks came pushing through the crowd, corralled us, and, bypassing all the customs and immigration officials, ushered us into a waiting minivan. We barreled out of the airport and drove straight to the same hotel where I had stayed with my parents in the midfifties. At dinner that night our mission (we're still in the bad spy movie) was explained to me. Two of my companions worked for "an agency of the U.S. government" and the other two were involved in the generic pharmaceutical industry. One of the latter, a man whose name I had instantly recognized, was a former top official in the Kennedy administration. The current administration was covertly working to normalize relations with Cuba, and a bargaining chip was the Cuban pharmaceutical industry. One of my Cuban hosts explained that since Cuba lacked marketable natural resources, they had invested most of the money the Soviets had given them on medical education and medical research. He explained that their country's only resources were their brains, and they had better figure out how to translate that into a marketable bargaining chip.

Purportedly, they had developed a host of vaccines and other medical breakthroughs that they were willing to share with their grumpy neighbor to the north. They had developed these drugs but did not have the ability to manufacture them. Yes, they could easily sell them to the Swiss or other European pharmaceutical companies, but they were not seeking a trade relationship with Switzerland. The major problem was Miami's Cuban exile population. This group voted as a solid bloc, so this matter had to be handled with extraordinary delicacy. The danger was not from the Cuban KGB (our affable young driver, I found out later, was a high-ranking officer in that organization) but from the exiles themselves, who were dead set against anything vaguely resembling a rapprochement. In that respect, it was that group who would stop at nothing to sabotage this effort. My companions illustrated this point with some graphic examples. I will not go into those details, as my family lives in south Florida.

Next morning I was driven to the synagogue and introduced to the elders of the congregation. One hundred and thirty-six Jewish families had elected to stay in Havana. As my companions were driven to various places around the city, I set up a makeshift drawing table in the sanctuary and started sketching. Each evening we returned to the hotel and swapped stories. The pharmaceutical guys were bowled over. The Cubans, they reported, had seventeen vaccines that our guys were still trying to develop, including ones for some very deadly diseases.

On our last day, I went with the group on a little trip. Even my companions had no idea where we were going. We were just told to bring a lot of bottled water, as the drive would be long and we would not be stopping often. We were taken on a fairly long drive in a van with blacked-out windows and ended up at a nondescript house in a nondescript suburb of an unknown town. Inside were a group of men in their seventies. The conversation was long and out of my league. One of the men, who was identified only as "Barbarossa," was, judging by my companions' reaction, a very important dude. The others were not minor players either. They were part of the group of sixteen who had journeyed from Mexico with Fidel Castro to start the Cuban revolution.

Since I have no way of knowing how much of that day's conversation was accurate and how much was posturing, I will not attempt to repeat any of it. This is a book about architecture, not international intrigue. Suffice it to say, it was mind-boggling. Part of the conversation was about the Cuban missile crisis. I was listening to two people who had been at the very center of power on each side, giving an hour-by-hour recap of what they were thinking and what they were doing. They had never had this type of debriefing and each was fascinated by what the other had done and thought as the crisis reached its flash point. No fictionalized or "reconstructed" history that I had ever heard or read could compare with what these two were saying. The hair on my arms was literally standing up.

We then drove to a sugar plantation. After some further indoctrination on the economics of this Socialist state we were taken to the "clubhouse," the former house of the plantation owner and now a club for the use of the workers. We were being given a farewell banquet. Joining us were a group of workers, managers, and our hosts, the gentlemen from the government. There was much toasting to the future of our two countries, our inevitable rapprochement, and the success of our "mission." As an example of diplomatic one-upmanship, they alluded to the past military and governmental background of two of my companions and how they hoped that I had found Cuba changed for the better. They knew exactly when I had been there and the family with whom I had stayed. Our guys did exactly the same type of I-know-who-you-are game. If I hadn't been quite so drunk, I probably would have been nervous.

Upon our return, we cleared U.S. Customs in Nassau. We had all been taken, as honored guests of the Cuban government, to several of the cigar factories, where we bought copious quantities of that forbidden product. When we cleared customs, we all had written Cuba in the space on the form that asked about other countries visited. With gleeful smiles, a horde of customs guys descended on our luggage and started triumphantly pulling out the boxes of cigars. Finally one of them noticed that one of our group was holding an unfolded sheet of stationery in front of his chest. An agent finally read it, said "damn!" and put all the boxes back in our luggage.

I do not smoke, but, back home, to all my cigar-smoking friends I was a god. One of my "companions" casually remarked that, since he spent a good deal of his time in Moscow, I should call on him if I ever found myself there.

Not bloody likely thought I.

Wrong again.

P.S. A year and half later, Congress repealed that portion of the Helms-Burton Act that prohibited the shipment of pharmaceuticals between Cuba and the United States.

17

The Return of *Gospodin* Lapidus

My return to my roots came courtesy of Donald Trump. He called to announce that he was going to buy the most prominent hotel in Moscow, the Moskva. He wanted me to go over there, survey the building, and redesign it as a modern facility for a hotel, condominiums, a health club, and a casino.

The Moskva was a large polygonal structure on Red Square, which was actually set into the Kremlin wall. It had been built on the personal orders of Joseph Stalin and was intended to house visiting dignitaries and others whom he wished to impress with the power of the state. The location of the hotel was as strategic as could be imagined. It was opposite the Duma (the Russian Parliament), the Kremlin, the Bolshoi Ballet, and Lenin's tomb, and its windows looked down the length of Red Square.

My host, a representative of the Moscow Architectural Commissariat, spoke English and was eager to learn as much as he could about the ultimate capitalist, *gospodin* Trump. He took me on a walk-through, starting on the roof and working our way down. Standing on the top of this building, looking over the seat of power of one of the mightiest nations on earth, I couldn't help musing about my grandfather. Less than a century ago he had fled Ukraine, which he continued to love, to start a new life in a strange land. His grandson had returned and was now standing atop the cornerstone of the Kremlin itself, a place he could have imagined only in a fantasy. It was a heavy moment for me.

We walked through the still functioning building. It had grand public spaces, now in the last stages of decrepitude, and mean little rooms with small low beds (often four to a room). It was now mainly used by representatives to the Duma and for bargain-basement tourism. I could see the remnants of the Soviet-era opulence in the fading murals and frayed tapestries. The weirdest feature was the fact that the two main façades, behind which were identical rows of rooms, were completely different from each other. My host explained that the Soviet architect had submitted two different elevation studies to Stalin. He had expected him to select the one that he preferred. Instead he got back both studies with Stalin's approvals. Rather than tell Uncle Joe that he was supposed to have picked his favorite, he simply built both façades, one on each side. Since they were on opposite sides of the structure, Stalin never noticed.

As we made our way through the subbasement parking garage, I noticed that a large portion of this valuable area was taken up with a huge concrete box along the entire length of one wall. It was only about eight feet tall in a space that was twelve feet high. I assumed that it was a utility tunnel, a not uncommon feature in some countries. This would normally be a concrete-encased space in which electrical, water, and sewer mains ran within the protective cocoon. I casually suggested that since we were going to do a total rehab of the building, that it might be better to remove this ponderous tunnel and run the utilities underground in a normal conduit. The Russian architect stopped, looked straight at me, and announced, "You do not move tunnel!"

Okeydokey, I will not move tunnel.

An American who dealt with the Russians later informed me that this was the passageway that connected the Kremlin with the much dreaded Lubyanka Prison. All those stories about people going into the Kremlin and never being seen or heard from again were apparently true. They just made a slight detour through the hotel on the way to their more permanent quarters.

I continued to study the hotel, meet with the Russian architects and engineers, and interview potential contractors. It was fascinating, both architecturally and socially. The contractors were from Turkey, Italy, and other countries. Their operations resembled an occupying army. Everything, from concrete, steel, and even the water used in the construction, was trucked in. All their support, including food, was imported. Huge truck convoys were always coming and going great distances to supply these operations.

I had gotten in touch with my companion from the Cuban adventure, and he invited me to have breakfast with him at the Marriott Hotel. When I showed up, I noticed he had brought a friend. I was introduced to a colonel general in the KGB, a tall, well-spoken man in his mid-fifties. He had a gray crew cut and wore a gray suit, a white shirt, a gray tie, and plain black shoes. He handed me his card, white with gold raised lettering, showing the Russian double-headed eagle, which identified him as an executive with something called the International Organization for Foreign Commerce. My American friend noticed the card and expressed surprise. He asked what had happened to the old KGB card. The reply was a Russian classic: "There is an old expression, 'When the cat has nothing to do, it licks its balls.'"

We got down to the business at hand. It was suggested that an American, especially an American representing such a tempting subject as Mr. Trump, might have need for some *protexia* (well-connected protection). There were three entities that pretty much controlled this country. The Russian Mafia, the KGB, and the civil government. He wrote down half a dozen phone numbers and told me that if I had a problem, he could always be reached at one of them. He was doing this as a favor to our mutual "agency" friend.

He then started to talk about the recent machine gun death of a prominent American hotel executive in Moscow. After lamenting the fact that the old Soviet Union was now being manipulated by "thugs," he said that one still had to admire their "craftsmanship." The Kalashnikov, the rifle that had dispatched the executive, was a fine weapon but not terribly accurate. He was mightily impressed that they had managed to put seventeen slugs in his body in a crowded subway station without hitting any bystanders. Even his bodyguard was unscathed.

"Now that is an excellent mechanic!"

———

I spent six weeks in New York working out the design for the transformation of the old Moskva into a modern hospitality facility, with all the bells and whistles. At this point in the development, I was not yet dealing with the aesthetics. The problem was to get this behemoth repurposed so that the hotel functioned to contemporary international standards with separate entrances for hotel guests, convention attendees, health club patrons (there was a huge demand for American-style health clubs to buff up the American-style Russian women), and the condo owners. The building, having four accessible sides, made this possible. Reshuffling the insides was the purpose of this phase of the development and it all worked out well.

I returned to Moscow to meet with my clients. They had two surprises for me. I was to make a personal presentation of the project to the mayor of Moscow, an old-style Soviet ogre who hated everything Trump stood for; and knowing my love of airplanes, they were arranging for me to take a flight in a supersonic MiG-23. They presented me with their best wishes for the presentation and a Russian Air Force flight suit complete with wings and my name embroidered in English and Cyrillic. I went to my hotel and had visions of being shot down literally and figuratively.

The day of the presentation, I was reading *The New York Times* when I saw a picture on page one that demonstrated yet once more that timing is everything. The premier of Russia was being challenged by an up-and-coming ruthless politician named General Alexander Lebed. The mayor of Moscow was a very close ally of the premier and a sworn enemy of Lebed, who would die in a helicopter crash some years later. The general was then on a visit to the United States, and *The Times* picture showed Donald Trump standing in front of Trump Tower with his arm around Lebed and declaring his enormous respect for him. With all the confidence of a Roman gladiator with a dull sword, I was thrust into the political arena.

After an hour's wait, twitching in the anteroom, my client, my translator, and I were summoned into the office of the mayor. I had never before made an architectural presentation with two policemen pointing their machine guns at me. I hoped that they were not tough critics. As my client listed my accomplishments, including the resorts I had done for Disney, the mayor bellowed that there would be no "Meeky Mouses" in the Kremlin. He also snarled something about Trump that was not translated. Judging from his tone, it probably didn't need any translation. After he vented for about twenty minutes, I finally had a chance to explain the scheme.

I assured him that there would be no "Meeky Mouses" and this would re-create the Moskva as the cultural center of the city, and it would allow foreigners to see that the new Russia could field a world-class hotel and conference center. Since I am not too good at interpreting loud snorts, I wasn't certain of hizzoner's reaction. But I hadn't been shot, so I took this as a sign of encouragement.

That evening, for the first time and at my specific request, we had dinner in a place that actually served Russian food. The building was an elegant old mansion called the Artists and Writers Club. The setting was straight out of those wonderful nights in the palace of the tsar, the waiters in formal cutaways and all the dishes served under silver domes that were raised in unison. I had last had these dishes at my grandfather's house, where the dress code was somewhat more relaxed.

The consensus was that the presentation had gone well (I hadn't been riddled with bullets—this was a good sign), the mayor was eager to see the tired old Moskva reborn as the center of the new Moscow, and the rest depended on the "negotiations" between Trump and the powers that be.

The next morning I was told that my MiG-23 flight had been postponed because of a mechanical problem, but I was assured that it would be there for me when I returned. It was not to be. The story I got was that when Trump learned the nature of some of the "partners" he had to have on his team, he decided to forgo his entry into the world of the "new Russians."

I still have the flight suit.

18.
Rich and Famous

While an architect's life is generally more prosaic than the Hollywood depictions, I have seemed to attract into my orbit more than my share of outsized characters. Not always happily. Two cases in point: the world's richest man and the world's luckiest man.

In 1970, my father and I did some work for Aristotle Onassis. We were brought onto the job through one of my favorite characters, Arthur Levien, a principal in Arlen Realty and Development, which had been behind many buildings, including 17 Battery Place in Manhattan and Seacoast Towers in Miami Beach.

Levien was by then a mogul, but at heart and in his booming voice, accent, and diction, Arthur remained the construction worker he had started as. I'll never forget a scene from my experience designing a Dallas office building for Arthur. At one point, I found myself partially paralyzed and in full body traction, awaiting major back surgery at Lenox Hill Hospital. Nevertheless, Arthur needed to talk to me, so he called and made an appointment. I had had my staff post all the drawings on the wall, and using the newly invented laser light pointer, I was ready to make a complete presentation right there in the hospital. Arthur, a large, muscular man with a full head of black hair and a penetrating voice, strode into my room along with his entourage. Taking in the scene, my drawings taped tastefully to the walls and me lying there immobilized in full body traction, he bellowed in his construction worker's voice, "Don't think you're gonna get any fuckin' sympathy from me! If the design sucks, you're gonna do it over."

Fortunately, he liked the design.

And so it was that my father and I were invited to a mysterious meeting with Arthur in early 1970. When Lapidus Senior and Junior arrived at Levien's office, it was clear that something big was up. Levien asked a number of questions about our workload. Could we devote our undivided attention to an important project? A *really* important building. He was about to begin a project with two partners, both of whom had agreed to hire us as the architects, and Arthur wanted to make sure that we could produce a building that would justify his faith in us.

We said all the right things.

Arthur's two partners turned out to be Meshulam Riklis—the largest shareholder in the Rapid-American Corporation, a conglomerate that owned such enterprises as Best & Co. department stores and McCrory, a chain of five-and-dime stores—and Aristotle Onassis, who owned most everything else in the world.

The building in question was to be a skyscraper on Fifth Avenue and Fifty-first Street, across from St. Patrick's Cathedral. That was the easy part. The real challenge was that we had a mere thirty-seven and a half feet of frontage on Fifth Avenue to build a fifty-story building!

The Best & Co. flagship store currently occupied the site. Next to Best was the Olympic Airways ticket office, sitting on that thirty-seven and a half feet of Fifth Avenue. The ticket office was to be demolished and rebuilt in the lobby of this new office tower, but Best was to remain. The consortium had purchased the air rights, the unused allowable building area, from adjacent buildings. Arthur slyly hinted that he and his people were currently negotiating with the archdiocese for all the unused zoning floor area from the cathedral.

It was an architect's fondest dream: a major high-rise in the best location in New York City that would be the most visible structure of its era, thanks in no small part to the involvement of Onassis. An even juicier aspect for me was the challenge of trying to design a skyscraper for a lot that narrow, a challenge that when overcome I felt certain was going to shake up the architectural world.

When we got back to our office, I realized that my father was actually somewhat intimidated by this commission. Ever since the avalanche of critical abuse that had been heaped on him for the Fontainebleau and subsequent hotels in Miami Beach, he had been less and less sure of himself. Sixteen years had passed since the Fontainebleau job, but he had not been able to reconcile the popular adulation and success of his masterpiece with the unprecedented lack of civility that the architectural critics had used to excoriate his work in Miami Beach.

The barbs had left an indelible scar on my father's psyche. Morris lusted to do a skyscraper on Fifth Avenue but was apprehensive over what *The Times* might say about the project. Morris would be in charge of this important work, he told Arthur Levien, but I would handle the day-to-day operations.

The building at hand was to be called the Olympic Tower, since Onassis owned Olympic Airways and was providing the financing for the project. My solution to the peculiar geography of the site was to design a thirty-seven-and-a-half-foot-wide granite-clad windowless tower containing high-speed elevators that rose two hundred feet over the roof of Best & Co., to a sky lobby, above which the building would widen, by means of cantilevers, to seventy-five feet. At this level, a bank of local elevators would carry passengers up to the thirty floors above. I put a heated outdoor park on the sky lobby level that would provide one of the great views of midtown Manhattan. The upper tower was sheathed in silver reflective glass.

Although I generally do not like mirror glass on buildings, I felt that this large rectangle floating above Midtown would be the perfect place for the biggest mirror in the world. Looking up or down the avenue, the effect would minimize the structure's mass, and people on the street would see only a reflection of the sky. Except at night, when the effect would be bands of light floating in the void.

My father thought the solution sufficiently idiosyncratic to bear the Lapidus name, even if the black granite monolith was a bit somber for his taste.

Showtime!

We built a model of the entire block, with the building towering above. After checking the schedules of all concerned, a date was set for the presentation. I am not normally nervous at these events, but my mouth was almost totally dry as I stood in front of the drawings of what was to be the most important building of my life, awaiting the arrival of the richest man in the world. And here he came—a small, quiet, beautifully tailored gentleman with a drooping eye: Onassis!

Introductions were made, and as I shook his hand I couldn't help thinking that this was a far cry from my Flatbush origins. I couldn't even begin to guess what was running through my father's mind.

We didn't have to wait long to learn Onassis's opinion: He loved the building.

I exhaled.

As Arthur Levien and Meshulam Riklis sat down with my father to work out the details, Onassis motioned me to sit on a couch beside him. He complimented me on the design and launched into a discourse on the design of the new Olympic Airlines ticket office. Almost bashfully, he explained that people in the United States thought that Greek architecture was limited to stark white buildings with columns that were Corinthian, Doric, or Ionic. Noting that he was from Minos, where an entirely different style of architecture had evolved, Onassis said he would prefer that the ticket office reflect his home region. To familiarize me with the style he had in mind, he offered to have examples sent to me.

While I was in architecture school, I read Mary Renault's novel *The King Must Die*, which portrayed life in the royal court of Minos. Intrigued by both the architectural descriptions and the steamy sex scenes, I had started studying the old steel-point engravings depicting life in the Minoan court. Here, as well, I was fascinated by both the architecture of the buildings and the amazing views of the ladies of the court. The court dress for the women of the royal household consisted of exquisite full-length, elaborately beaded gowns that ended just *under* the breasts.

Beaming at Onassis, I replied that I was familiar with the architecture of Minos, adding that I thought his was an excellent suggestion, especially if the ladies selling tickets were authentically costumed. There was the briefest of pauses, and then he gave me a big smile, clasped his hand on my shoulder, and declared that he and I would get along just fine.

Onassis and I met face-to-face just a couple of times after that, and we always got along famously. When I called him in Greece to tell him that the rendering of the ticket office was ready, he had Olympic Airways hold the departure of the evening flight from Athens so he could view the rendering the very next morning. It sure helps if you own the airline!

In October 1970, just as the construction documents were almost completed, my world exploded. Under the headline, "Good-by to Fifth Avenue?" *The Times* editorialized that our building amounted to "a glassy death." The editorial went on to add that the Olympic Tower would be "a product of the Miami Beach hotel architect Morris Lapidus, known more for tinsel than for polish. As they said when the Summit [Hotel] opened in New York, Fifth Avenue is awfully far from the ocean." (The "awfully far from the ocean" crack, about Morris's first New York hotel— now known as the Metropolitan, on Lexington Avenue at Fifty-first Street—resulted in the hotel's owners promptly ripping out its colorful lobby and replacing it with a sedate set piece in beiges and browns just after it opened as the Summit in 1963.)

Ada Louise Huxtable had struck again! And I was dumbfounded. She had never even asked to see the design!

The phone call that soon came was not wholly unexpected. Onassis explained that he had the highest personal regard for me and my work, and that as a Greek, he did not ordinarily let his wife interfere in his business dealings. But in this country, she was regarded as an authority on aesthetic taste and culture. *And* she had seen the editorial. *And* Jacqueline Bouvier Kennedy Onassis (who, like Ada Louise Huxtable, had never laid eyes on a single drawing for this project) had stated in no uncertain terms that her husband could not have his name associated with such vulgarity. Being as this was her domain, he would have to comply with her wishes.

We should submit our final invoice, Onassis said, before ending the call. The bill was paid promptly.

Best & Co. eventually went out of business; the firm's corner building was demolished; and a conventional glass office building, designed by my onetime employer Skidmore, Owings & Merrill, was built on the site.

The whole experience left me with a grinding feeling in my stomach for weeks. And I doubt that my father ever got over the humiliation. Although he was in general a nonlitigious individual who avoided confrontation, Morris was so incensed at *The Times* for trashing our building without even asking to see what it would look like that he threatened to sue the newspaper. During the legal maneuverings I had a private meeting with Huxtable, who had become kindly disposed toward me while she kept abreast of my plans for the Bedford-Stuyvesant swimming pool (Chapter 7). After studying a detailed photo of the Olympic Towers from the exact scale model of the project we had created, Huxtable looked up at me and said, "Well, Alan, it would have either been the best or the worst building ever built on Fifth Avenue. I'll be watching your future work."

My father ultimately decided not to proceed with his suit. All that existed from our efforts to design the Olympic Tower skyscraper was a short chapter I wrote about our pride and joy in a 1976 book: *Unbuilt America*.

As for the world's luckiest man . . .

Among the Atlantic City casino projects I worked on was one in the late 1970s that began with a phone call from a lawyer on behalf of a client he subsequently revealed to be Bob Guccione of *Penthouse* magazine. Before long I found myself at Guccione's Upper East Side townhouse to discuss ideas for the proposed Penthouse Hotel and Casino. Guccione arrived clad entirely in black, save for enough gold chains around his neck to pose serious peril in the event of an electrical storm. He was accompanied by two huge Rhodesian ridgebacks, hounds that regard dobermans as pussies and are bred to hunt lions, and just one huge human, an individual who was built along the lines of a concrete block. The huge human being, whose name was "Babe" Dinallo, owned a major New Jersey construction company called Terminal Construction. I sometimes wondered whether the name of his company was a fluke.

Guccione was doodling on a pad, and I noticed that he was drawing, with great panache, a high-rise shaped like a phallus. This was fitting, because he said he wanted a building that would "give me a hard-on." Adding to the distractions was a procession of ravishing young ladies not exactly dressed for high tea at Buckingham Palace. I was at even a further disadvantage because most of our meetings were held at midnight or later, to conform to Guccione's night owl lifestyle.

From the beginning there were several obstacles: Guccione wanted a sixty-thousand-square-foot casino (the largest then allowable), and since casino size is dependent on the size of the overall building and the amenities it contains, the facility simply was not large enough to qualify. Complicating matters, two elderly and eccentric ladies owned parcels on his block and refused to sell, meaning the building would have to spread over and around their places. In addition, Guccione had no firm commitments for the estimated $250 million cost of the casino.

Nevertheless, Guccione and Babe assured me they had "connections" who would take care of everything. As evidence of his New Jersey "connections," Guccione spoke with pride of how they had arranged to have him named grand marshal of Atlantic City's upcoming Columbus Day parade! Plus, Guccione himself had promised to include monthly puff pieces about Atlantic City in *Penthouse*!

I was horrorstruck by the incredible naïveté on the part of Guccione and Dinallo but was instructed to continue my designs, and I did, ultimately finishing the working drawings. Despite the pull Guccione and Babe supposedly had, the state turned down their plans cold. It seemed that the lot—surprise!—was too small. Also, the state frowned on casino-hotels that for whatever reason would not occupy an entire square block. After the rejection, Guccione and Babe exchanged knowing winks, and Guccione ordered construction to begin anyway. The casino was well under construction and Guccione had already sunk some $30 million of his own money into the deal when reality hit: He would need more money—much more.

Guccione did have a virtually foolproof plan for financing the place, at least in his own mind: His X-rated Roman costume epic, *Caligula*, that starred, among others, Sir John Gielgud, Peter O'Toole, and Malcolm McDowell. *Caligula* was, according to Guccione, going to throw off money by the tens, even hundreds of millions of dollars, which he intended to use to build his dream house. As we know, the world's movie fans voted almost unanimously with their feet, avoiding the movie en masse. *Caligula* actually did open, though. Unlike the Penthouse Hotel and Casino in beautiful Atlantic City by the Sea.

To his credit, Guccione did pay my fee in full for the first stage of the job. Of course the most profitable segment of my work was dependent upon his obtaining financing and going forward with construction. Never happened.

I've been done in by clients who failed to honor their commitments *and* had battalions of high-priced and often unscrupulous legal sharks at their beck and call (those legal sharks were always paid, even if I the architect was not); by the wife of the richest man in the world; by a celebrated architectural reviewer whose scathing critique of one project was read by the wife of the richest man in the world; by the king of a porn empire who planned to finance my fee and his Atlantic City casino project with proceeds from an X-rated film epic it turned out no one wanted to see. Among those and others, there has been a varied and in many ways sensational collection of characters whose machinations had the potential to spell my or my father's ruin at every turn. The leading exception to this rule is my friend The Donald. Yes, Trump lives and loves to drive a hard bargain, to master the deal, but once he enters into an agreement his word is gold, and he honors his side of the pact with the architect. Plus one other group: I have found that the word of Mob guys is always as good as gold.

It may have been Ada Louise Huxtable, of all people, who best depicted the architect's situation in her 1972 *Times* piece that heaped praise upon me for the Bedford-Stuyvesant public swimming pool. "The architect," she wrote, "is, by implication and legal agreement, victim and fall guy. . . . Everything is rigged to make him responsible for everyone else's sins, and he is treated as the one potential crook. No one shares his concern for good design and everything is stacked against it. In the end, it is the system that wins. . . . The system, you see, is foolproof. And the system always wins."

When have comments like that been made about doctors, lawyers, engineers, business executives, accountants, or members of any other profession?

Huxtable's assessment is accurate. I hope the public will have a realistic view of architects and that would-be architecture students will embark on this adventure with their eyes wide open. I still love my profession, but working as an architect does have its pitfalls.

Having learned Huxtable's dictum the hard way—from personal experience—I came to realize in the mid-1990s after more than thirty years of architecting that the surest method of getting rich from designing buildings is not so much to design them as to *own* them.

19.

A Way Out

According to an old and oft-told joke in Hollywood, a pretty young starlet is cast in a horrible movie. She asks plaintively, "Who do I have to fuck to get *off* this film?"

By the early 1990s, thirty years after I entered the field of architecture, I decided that I needed to learn what it would take to get out of the profession, at least to some extent.

In the wake of the real estate meltdown of 1990, several clients had defaulted on accounts receivable amounting to over $2 million, the bulk of it owed by Bill Zeckendorf. Although I survived bankruptcy and started to rebuild my shattered practice, I was beginning to fear that I was in the process of going through another painful recovery only to wind up devastated by the next economic upheaval. The hard reality was that I possessed no other marketable skills, leaving me without a viable alternative.

In those dark days, one architectural acquaintance, who had enjoyed a successful upscale practice, left the profession via the window in his Rockefeller Center office.

Another of my friends, Richard Roth, was a third-generation architect whose grandfather founded the eminent firm of Emery Roth & Sons. A New York mainstay, the firm designed some of the most elegant Central Park West apartment buildings, including the most desirable addresses in the city. After World War II, Emery Roth practically owned the office building design market. They were the main architects of the

World Trade Center twin towers. (Minoru Yamasaki was the design architect.)

Shortly after my debacle with Bill Zeckendorf, I had dinner with Richard Roth. As I was telling him my problems, he revealed that we shared more than just our architectural heritage. Déjà vu all over again: Zeckendorf was also an office building client of Emery Roth, and Richard said Bill had asked him to "front" the financing for his work on a new office tower. Richard said the outcome was identical to mine—Zeckendorf had simply walked away from $2 million he owed Richard.

Shaking his head, Richard added, "The Roth firm and the Zeckendorf family have been doing business on a handshake for three generations. Bill shook my hand, promised that I would not be financially hurt by 'specking' his job, and then he just totally screwed me." Richard made these comments without any hint of malice toward Bill. Like me, Richard understood that tough times had overtaken all of us in the industry. He said the lesson was clear: "It's time to get out of this field."

Richard took his own advice. He shut down the office that had done so much to shape the face of New York City, sold his apartment, and moved to the Bahamas.

My economic undoing had been so complete that I did not have that option. I had no choice but to continue trying to formulate some sort of exit strategy.

While I was trying to figure out what to do, I suddenly realized that a solution to my problems had been shown me years before. When my father had packed up all the marbles in 1976 and decamped to Miami for good, or at least forever, I started my own firm in borrowed office space. Once my Atlantic City work started flowing in, I knew where I wanted to establish my "real" office.

Living on the West Side of Manhattan, I had often noticed a building at Columbus Avenue and Sixty-first Street that was a classic example of Art Deco architecture. This was the twenty-seven-story Sofia Bros. Moving and Storage Warehouse. Periodically a sign would appear stating that there was office space to rent. One day I went over and met the owner. Mr. Sofia was in his late eighties and had been in the moving and storage business all his life. He took enormous pride in both his firm and this building. There was even a bronze plaque in the lobby to honor his deceased brother who had cofounded "the House of Sofia."

Mr. Sofia did indeed have a space to rent, and the size and price were perfect for my start-up office. He delighted in telling me the history of this beautiful building. It's a great New York saga: The structure had originally been built during the late 1920s as the first high-rise, fully automated garage in the world. Cars entered and were moved automatically via steel rails to a large elevator that delivered them to a preset floor where they were again moved to an assigned space. All this was done without human interaction. This technological innovation was to accommodate the upscale population of this then fashionable locale, who did not like to have garage attendants, in their greasy overalls, besmirching the pristine velour upholstery of their Packards and LaSalles.

The garage opened just in time for the stock market crash of 1929 and the Sofia family bought the bankrupt building a few years later. At that time, the world was gearing up for World War II. Scrap steel was a valuable commodity. The Sofias sold the thousands of feet of steel rails that had been used to move the cars around and did quite well. Then, after we actually went to war, young men were going away, families were relocating, and there was a critical need for moving services and storage warehouses. The same situation existed after the war, and the Sofias were in the right place at the right time. Now, with the coming of Lincoln Center directly across the street, they realized they could make more money by renting space to people than to cartons. Or to cars.

A lack of windows limited the types of businesses that could thrive in a building like that, so there was a truly oddball tenant roster. It included the venerable old Folkways Records and several of the service industries for Lincoln Center. My floor also housed a costume company. A not infrequent sight in the hallway was a bevy of cute little anorexic-looking females trying out their tutus.

Mr. Sofia treated his tenants like family. He took an active interest in our work and financial health. During one period when money was tight, I went to his office to try to explain my missed rent payment. He got up from behind his desk, put an arm around my shoulder, and told me that he understood hard times, I was a "good boy" and a nice tenant, and he knew I would pay him when I could.

Yes, those were different times in New York City.

One day he called and asked if I could come down to his office, saying that he would like my advice. When I arrived, he explained ruefully that although this building was his life, his deceased brother's two sons owned half of the business, and they wanted to sell the building to take advantage of the rising real estate values in this improving neighborhood. Knowing that I was involved with real estate people, Mr. Sofia asked if I could help with the sale. Having lived in this area for most of my adult life, I realized that this building was positioned to become a prime apartment facility. Lincoln Center was an obvious draw, but the less apparent selling point was the Lincoln Square Synagogue two blocks away. Its congregation consisted of wealthy Orthodox Jews. Orthodox Jews are prohibited from driving on the Sabbath, so they must walk to their house of worship. Ergo, they had to live within walking distance—*and* there was a lack of upscale housing in the area.

I told Mr. Sofia I had some definite ideas that would help him get top dollar for his building. He gave me a set of plans and I started to lay out the building as an apartment house. The obvious problem was the dearth of windows, but I felt that the cost of creating more would be minor in relation to the value of the property as an upscale condo. Another extra I discovered was that the building had gone up before the current zoning code was in place, so it was about 30 percent larger than any then allowable structure.

Excited by the possibilities, I felt sure I would have no trouble finding the right developer. At the time, I was so naïve that I didn't realize the profits that could accrue from developing the building myself; all I thought of was helping Mr. Sofia and generating an architectural fee.

When I went to the building department to check for any existing violations, I received a shock. The building had been redlined, meaning the structure was under active consideration for landmark designation. To look at the glass as half full, the redlining vindicated my conviction that the Sofia was an extraordinarily fine example of Art Deco architecture. The downside was twofold: It would not be easy to persuade the Landmarks Commission to approve punching out the 375 windows necessary to convert the building into apartments, and a possible landmark designation was a disincentive for prospective developers because of the restrictions landmark status entailed.

At the Landmarks Commission, staffers said I might gain approval to add windows, provided the final product still looked like a 1930s apartment house, of which there were plentiful examples three blocks away on Central Park West. The commission's staff, as is true in all municipalities, does all the analysis and makes recommendations to the actual commission, which hardly ever overrules the staff's advice. The employees with whom I dealt tended to be ardent young preservationists and great fans of my father and me. Two had been in a class lecture I once gave. They hated curtain walls and loved my populist approach. One even wore bow ties—a good sign. It also helped that I had graduated from and taught at the Columbia School of Architecture. I had also taught at Yale, Penn, and other universities, so I had good academic chops. Approval would be forthcoming.

Now all I needed was a moneyman. After turndowns from John Tishman and several others, I found the ideal person. Aaron Greene was not only a shopping mall developer but also an Orthodox Jew who lived on the Upper West Side, attended the Lincoln Square Synagogue, and was a regular patron at Lincoln Center. Aaron knew that with the Sofia just blocks from the synagogue, there was a lucrative, ready-made market for this condo. He had some reservations about the landmark designation until I assured him that would be no problem, because I would mimic the fenestration of the Art Deco apartment houses on Central Park West and create a building that indeed would look like it had been residential since the '30s. I even suggested the advertising tag, "Live in a Landmark," which Aaron loved. To our potential customers, this type of cultural cachet would be an important selling point.

Aaron bought my argument and agreed to buy the building, so I introduced him to Mr. Sofia. It was a classic clash of two cultures. Mr. Sofia was an Old World Italian who had bought the building for cash and had never even considered such a strange financial contrivance as a mortgage. As Aaron outlined various scenarios for the purchase, Mr. Sofia interrupted him: "It is very simple, I come to the table with the title to the building, and you come to the table with the twelve million dollars. You give me the money, I give you the title. Eh?"

Which is exactly how the deal went down.

I submitted a presentation to landmarks, first showing photographs of the building as it was, then how it would look with all the windows placed in the best Deco style. The landmarks department agreed that the windows were an improvement, and the project was green-lighted.

As a result of my negotiations with Aaron Greene, I ended up with a standard architectural fee plus, as a reward for my efforts, one of the apartments, which I rented out for several years. An instant success, the building sold out rapidly. When I sold my apartment several years later, I made more money than I ever had from an architectural fee.

As testament to my financial denseness, I didn't realize that I had stumbled upon a way to utilize architecture to earn a comfortable and relatively stable income. The experience taught me one definition of the word "wisdom": intelligence coupled with experience.

Twenty years later, by 1995, I had accrued the experience. That's when a new client, a Chinese gentleman who had made a fortune packaging soy and duck sauce in little plastic pouches and liked to dabble in Chinatown real estate, arrived at my office with a potential hotel project. He had purchased a small polygonal two-thousand-square-foot property in the Wall Street area that was being used as a parking lot. He thought it might be a good spot for a small hotel if one could be made to fit. A zoning variance would be required.

At that time there were scarcely any hotels in the Financial District, and not a single new one had been built in almost half a century, which persuaded me that a business-oriented hotel would be a natural. I developed a scheme with vertical as opposed to horizontal setbacks that would allow light and air to penetrate down to the street, which is the purpose of city-mandated setbacks. The conventional way of complying with setback requirements is to set the building back in progressive steps as the building goes higher—the classic "wedding cake" form seen in most big cities. I developed a scheme that was specific to this site. A hotel cannot easily step back, as the plumbing must run straight down and won't function properly if you "offset" it. Since this site was polygonal and very narrow, there was no way I could use conventional setbacks. Instead, I produced a plan that had the street wall running from street level to its maximum height, and rather than being set back horizontally, the wall stepped back in a series of vertical sawteeth that formed vertical slots for light and air to reach street level. I also put together a study showing that the same amount of light and air—in fact, slightly more—reached the street with this approach than would be true with a horizontal setback.

I went ahead and made a presentation to the city Board of Standards and Appeals.

The zoning change was approved. At that point, my client, faced with the realities of developing this property into a hotel, was intimidated by this field in which he had no experience. He asked if I could help him find a buyer for the rezoned site.

Shades of Mr. Sofia.

I proposed that I would form my own group and buy it from him. I was beginning to act like a true developer. Even though I had barely a couple of months' expenses in the bank, I offered to buy the property for $2 million. (My client had bought it for $800,000.)

My ace in the hole was an acquaintance named Jay Furman, a shopping center developer who was once married to the daughter of billionaire Ronald Perelman. Jay had recently asked me the classic developer's question: "Know of any good deals?"

I gave Jay a call and explained how I could fit 138 small rooms into this structure.

I had no qualms about small rooms. A dozen or so years earlier, two guys fresh out of federal prison on an income tax rap had come to my office to kick around ideas for a small, run-down one-time brothel they had just purchased. They wanted to renovate the premises into a hotel. The rooms were tiny, but the location, on Thirty-eighth Street with entrances on both Park Avenue South and Madison Avenue, was dynamite. I advised them that they didn't really need my services, adding that the only people who routinely charged pricey hotel rates for small rooms were the Europeans. I suggested they hire a European high-style designer and make the place small but chic. Eurotrash and the "smart set" absolutely love small but chic.

Ian Schrager and Steve Rubell of Studio 54 fame and infamy thanked me very much and followed my advice. The small but chic Morgans Hotel, which opened in 1984, quickly evolved into a New York classic and the start of a boutique hotel empire. In fact, it also served as the beginning of the much copied boutique hotel craze that remains with us to this day. I totally love the way I am able to gratuitously toss out these little ideas—without having the brain wattage to insist on getting paid for them. It's one of those rare and enviable gifts I possess.

The upside of this experience was that I knew I could do small.

I made a deal with Jay Furman. Jay put up the financing and I received my full architectural fee plus a limited partnership. At last I had created the opportunity to be the sole architect and interior designer, as well as one of the owners of a hotel.

Jay Furman is a tall, thin man with an Abe Lincoln beard who's way too smart to be just a shopping center developer and nothing more. A lawyer by training, he has taught law and also is both a very serious explorer and brilliant photographer. He would take off periodically, travel to some remote location, and return with incredible photographs. When I first met Jay, he was bored out of his mind by strip malls and was looking for something else to devote his formidable intelligence to. For that reason he jumped at the chance to enter the hotel industry, which has come to account for a significant portion of his business.

Since this was to be my baby, and since Jay had no background in hotels, I decided to rethink the concept of the hotel to be site-specific. I started by heeding my father's advice: Always build for your client's client.

I pondered over who would be the clients of this facility and started to design the building with them in mind. They would be people who came to New York to do business on Wall Street. Most of them would be alone. Each room should have ample facilities for them to do their work there. They did not need big closets, couches, or cute little coffee tables.

What they *would* need was a really big desk, a built-in computer with high-speed Internet connectivity, a comfortable easy chair with an ottoman and good lighting, along with no lines for check-in.

I came up with a project that to the best of my knowledge is like no other existing facility. In addition to the front desk, the lobby has automated check-in, much like an ATM. An automated concierge tells guests how to reach conventional attractions throughout the city and how to travel to them via public transportation, and then produces a printout of the directions. The various high-tech systems accounted for $2 million of the hotel's total construction costs of $18 million.

Also, because I have always hated staying in a hotel and needing more towels or an extra pillow and being told that housekeeping was closed, in this hotel there is a "guest amenity" closet on each floor, open twenty-four hours a day and stocked with extra towels, pillows, blankets, and toiletries. No charge and no security. People who do business on Wall Street are not prone to stealing towels.

Each room has an L-shaped desk with eight feet of working surface and a flat-screen computer, as well as a tray of paper clips, White-Out, a stapler, erasers, and a minilibrary consisting of a dictionary, a thesaurus, and a book containing standard business forms. In addition to such standards as a large-screen TV and minibar, there are marble bathrooms with English "rain showers."

There is also a small health club, but since by the time we were planning the hotel, nearly half the business travelers were women, any of the workout machines can be delivered to the room, so a guest can exercise in privacy.

One revolutionary precept we've lived by is our recognition that the clientele would be coming from out of town. Believe it or not, many New York hotels are designed as if it's New Yorkers who will be staying in them. Our out-of-towners are likely to have heard about all the varied cuisines available in the city but be too busy to go exploring for ethnic restaurants. We provide a leather-bound book in the room called *Beyond Room Service* that holds take-out menus from various ethnic restaurants in the area, so guests can sample New York deli, Chinese, Korean, Turkish, Japanese, or pub food in their room and charge the meal to their room through an arrangement we have with several eateries. Another option for our guests is eating in the well-regarded Italian restaurant off the lobby.

I view my insistence that the hotel be operated by Holiday Inn as the cherry on the cake. A Holiday Inn with shoeshine service and marble bathrooms, to be sure. Our place deviates from the Holiday Inn norm in so many ways that I like to call it my "waiver hotel." My reasoning was both practical and, sadly, prescient. Having had ample experience with recessions, I knew that when times are tough, the front office frowns on employees staying at upscale chains. But no corporate comptroller was going to insist that employees downgrade from a Holiday Inn, even if it did charge several hundred dollars a night.

Few hotels are owned by the companies whose logo emblazons their marquees. Most of the time, hotel companies manage hotels and get paid a fee. In years past, the big hotel companies (Hilton, Sheraton, Statler, etc.) developed, built, and operated their own hotels. By the 1960s these corporations realized that they were more in the real estate business than the hotel business because so much of their capital was tied up in these huge properties. They then "deacquisitioned" the hotels, selling them to individuals but agreeing that for a fee they would provide all their expertise, hire the staff, supply all the branded provisions (towels and other items with the company logo), and operate the property. This type of arrangement enabled the hotel companies to get all their capital back and keep the gravy. The initial management contracts were nothing short of rapacious. There were hidden fees up the wazoo; the chain's fee got first position for payment, even *before* the mortgage; the operating contract had a mammoth life span, usually twenty years; the hotel chains were not responsible for any losses; and the contracts were unbreakable. The contracts were structured so that they even survived the inevitable bankruptcies. These licenses to steal have been tempered by the passage of much time and the filing of many lawsuits. In fact, these one-sided packages came into being principally because the initial groups who bought into these schemes consisted primarily of people who had made their money in other fields such as doctoring and lawyering, knew less than nothing about the hotel business, and were in it for reasons having more to do with ego than with finance: "Let's all go to dinner at *my* hotel!" is a line almost guaranteed to get you laid.

Nowadays these agreements are a bit more reasonable, especially if the negotiating partner knows something about the business. Remember that initially, since most of the hotels were owned by hotel companies, there were not many people outside these corporations who really understood the business side of this field.

In the twenty-first century, there are two primary types of hotel agreements: management contracts and franchises. With a management contract, the hotel company operates the hotel, furnishes all the branded goods, and, most important, provides the reservation system. About

one-quarter of all the people who stay at our Holiday Inn find us because they call Holidex, the Holiday Inn reservation service, and ask
for a reservation at a specific location. ("I will be doing business in the
Financial District" gets them into our hotel, asking for Midtown leads
them to a different facility, and so forth.) The terms of the agreement are
more in favor of the investors if they know what they're doing. Critical in
our case (and in fact all cases) is our right to hire the general manager of
our choice. That makes him or her beholden to us, not to Holiday Inn,
for his or her livelihood. In turn the GM hires the staff, which gives the
owners more direct control over the operations. Terms like these are unusual. Most hotel management contracts have a "noninterference
clause" that precludes the owner from having direct input into the operation of his own property. If you don't like the way the facility is being
run, you have to complain to the management company, and what action they take is *their* decision. If the GM is yours, you can have direct
and immediate input. The fees for management contracts are totally ne-
gotiable, but the starting point is usually 3 percent of gross and 20 percent of profits, plus additional fees such as a charge for every guest who
comes through the chain's reservation service. Finding financing for a
hotel is easier if it is under a management company.

With a franchise, all the hotel company provides is the reservation system and the towels and other branded goods. The corporation retains
the right to kick you out of the system if your facility sucks. Management
fees are much lower in this type of setup, but it's harder to get financing.
A franchise is the preferred route if you have a plain vanilla 150-room facility just off the interstate and all you're offering guests is shelter from
the storm.

In either case, the facility must be designed to the standards of the hotel company. For our Wall Street hotel, I had to go to Holiday Inn and
get a variance because my rooms are eleven feet wide and their minimum was twelve feet. I spent two days explaining to their chief designer
why eleven feet would work (twelve-foot-high ceilings and less furniture
than was standard would make the room appear bigger). He was a young
architect who had written his thesis on my father, so it was an easy sell.
No guest has ever complained that the rooms are too small.

Once the facility opened in July 1999, it became the most profitable unit in the Holiday Inn chain. Because of all the automated features, we were able to operate the facility with far fewer employees than a more conventional one would need. Thanks largely to the general manager we hired, Frank Nicholas, it has also been the only Holiday Inn to be awarded a perfect score by the corporation's evaluators. In the past few years, however, with the good times truly rolling, we discovered that many of the big Wall Street companies were not booking rooms with us because they didn't want to put their people up in a Holiday Inn: too cheap an image for them. Even though many of these companies sent their personnel managers to inspect our place and the unanimous opinion was that it was a fine facility that they would be happy to refer their people to, corporate policy took precedence.

For that reason our ownership group, in which I am a nonvoting member, decided recently to terminate the Holiday Inn contract (another edge we insisted on, which would have been impossible in days gone by) and bring in a brand that is more acceptable to our upscale Wall Street clientele. While we were in the process of changing brands, we elected to go all the way, sell the hotel and recoup our money, and let the new owners pick their own hotel chain. Our hotel, given its location, would make money even if someone took out all the toilets and replaced them with an outhouse. The hospitality market in New York is so hot these days that almost anyplace with a bed and a sink is assured of making money.

My first experience as an owner of a hotel proved to me that, unencumbered by a developer, I could dream up a facility that would outperform the chain-mandated cookie cutters.

My deal with Jay Furman called for me to start receiving my percentage of the profits after he had earned back his invested capital. Two years after our Holiday Inn opened its doors, all this was on the verge of becoming reality. *And* we were finalizing plans to build and own additional hotel properties.

As the summer of 2001 wound down, everything seemed to be in place for my big breakout. September was shaping up as sensational. And so it was, but not in the way I was anticipating.

20.
End of the World

As the Wall Street hotel was in its finishing stages of construction in 1999, I realized it would be a winner. I had joined forces with Michael Callahan, a smart, honest, financially astute real estate developer. Mike has the ability and the smarts to generate feasibility studies, financial projections, amortization schedules, and internal rates of return—in short, all the things that leave me cross-eyed. The best aspect of our partnership is that each of us is aware of his individual fields of expertise and we don't try to second-guess each other. I'm responsible for formulating the program, market identification, and all aspects of the design and function. Mike handles all the real-world financial dealings. He and I are close in age (I'm three years older) and come from similar backgrounds: two Brooklyn boys who share parallel memories of growing up in that enchanted borough at that enchanted point in time, served in different branches of the military at about the same time, and then lived through both very good years and real down years. We agree that very good is a lot better.

Mike and I first crossed paths in Atlantic City nearly thirty years ago, when it was a small town and everybody knew everybody. Back then he was "doing deals," like a lot of people in the Atlantic City of that era. We've kept in touch because we have so much in common. Mike hails from President Street in south Brooklyn, where the Irishers lived. He's a thin, wiry guy, about five foot eight, as charming and full of the blarney as Paddy's pig and with the map of Ireland stamped on his face, as the saying goes. Growing up he was in the rough-and-tumble world of kids whose favorite recreation was rumbling. But Mike also has an inquiring mind; as a youth he spent his Saturday mornings at the Brooklyn Museum, where they had free art classes for children (gifted, he became an artist, in addition to his many other talents), and then he would go over to the gym to train for the Golden Gloves. He's one of the most interesting people I've met, an individual who's extremely intelligent but wasn't turned on by schooling. Mike never had much use for formal education, but he can do a ten-year flowchart and hotel pro forma better than most professionals in the field. I've always been impressed by his grasp of financing and knowledge of the hotel field, as well as his many contacts with developers, moneymen, and hotel professionals.

When I approached Jay Furman about putting up the money for the Wall Street hotel, it was my concept and Mike Callahan's financials that sold the project. Now, as the Holiday Inn was nearing completion, we were on the lookout for our next development. Newark Airport was expanding, well on its way to becoming a major New York–area hub. Rapidly increasing air traffic had overwhelmed the modest inventory of hotel rooms near the airport, and Mike found an opportunity to build a modern airport hotel that would fill the need. We negotiated a long-term contract on seventeen acres of unzoned land in Elizabeth, convenient to the port of Newark and the airport. We knew that zoning this piece of property would take a minimum of three years to satisfy all of the environmental concerns (it wound up taking four years), but winning the right to build a major hotel at this locale would justify the effort and expense.

Finally, after those years of intensive effort, we secured our zoning approval. The demand for a big airport hotel was greater than ever. We planned both an eight-hundred-room ten-story (the maximum height permitted adjacent to the airport) Crowne Plaza containing full meeting and conference facilities and a two-hundred-room extended-stay motel-hotel chain to be determined later. Occupancy at the existing airport hotels was in the low 90 percent range and the rates that could be charged for rooms were on the rise. We arranged for $140 million in financing and held a press conference on the site to announce the project. Closing date on the mortgage was set for September 23, 2001.

My architectural practice had been maintaining itself at a steady, if unspectacular level. I wasn't making any great profit, but I was able to pay my bills and draw a salary. One job was designing a Crowne Plaza hotel in the Dominican Republic. It was located on the north side of the island, and I enjoyed learning about this relatively unknown Caribbean vacation spot, which brought back pleasant memories of my early days designing island resorts in the 1960s. Word came that the project had received its financing, permitting us to proceed to the next phase.

At my shop we were also working on our bread-and-butter project, the Flatotel on West Fifty-second Street. A high-rise was converted from an apartment building to a hotel in gradual stages, and we had been working on it every now and again for ten years. At the moment we were redoing several floors of rooms along with the ground floor, where we were creating a proper lobby and a restaurant and cocktail lounge. It was dull but steady work.

Things were beginning to look positively rosy.

The World Trade Center was a complex I knew very well because it was designed by the firm of Emery Roth, headed up by my friend Richard Roth. In 1977, I spent an evening at Windows on the World, the restaurant atop the North Tower, with an unforgettable Texas personality named Billy Bob Walker. My knowledge of the twin towers might have come in handy that night, if anyone had listened to me.

Billy Bob Walker was a Dallas wheeler-dealer who drove a monstrously huge gold Lincoln with actual steer horns actually mounted on the hood. I rode in this modest little vehicle when I visited him in his home territory to discuss his plan to have me design a ski resort near Elkins, West Virginia. Billy Bob once flew me over the site of the resort in a single-engine Navion, a plane flown both in the military and by civilians. Billy Bob had been an army pilot in Vietnam. He flew as if the Vietcong were dug in down in the coal mines. As he clipped the tops of trees he grinned broadly and reminisced about the "good old days" flushing out the VC.

When Billy Bob came to New York to continue discussions about the project, I wanted to impress him. So I took him to dinner at Windows on the World. I bribed the headwaiter to seat us at a table facing north. The date was July 13, 1977.

Suddenly, about 9:30, the twinkling lights spread beneath us to the horizon stopped twinkling. As soon as I saw the city going dark sector by sector, marching northward until the entire region was without light, I understood what was happening: The Great Blackout of the Northeast had begun. Billy Bob was duly impressed: "Alan," he drawled, "y'all put on one *hell* of a show!"

Based on my familiarity with the design of the World Trade Center, I also knew that the floor plate for the building was exactly one acre, with the kitchens in the center of the restaurant. The building was what is known as "tight"—meaning totally sealed, with the only ventilation provided by mechanical equipment. I knew that without electricity to operate the ventilation system, there was no way to bring air into the room. And now the restaurant was packed with people smoking and drinking. In terror, I approached the harried maître d' and explained that I was an architect who knew a lot about the design of this building. I explained that the air was going to get stale very fast, which would only add to all the more obvious problems.

I also pointed out that since we had lost electricity, the hoods over the stoves would have automatically closed (a lack of electricity is the same to a kitchen hood as a fire, and the hoods close down to prevent the fire from venting and gaining force), which would further deplete the oxygen supply and radiate heat throughout the room. Moreover, I added, at least three of the fire stairs went to the roof directly above us, so if we blocked the fire doors open, we could vent the space. And, I told him, although the passenger elevators were sealed tight, the service elevator shafts were comparatively "loose." In fact, I pointed out, you could hear the wind whistling up their shafts. So if he also blocked open the doors between the service areas and the restaurant, enough air for decent cross ventilation would be brought into Windows on the World. The guy looked at me like I was an idiot, assuring me that the situation was under control and that there were very strict laws against opening the fire doors. Why didn't I just return to my seat and enjoy the view, he suggested.

I kept pleading with him to ask people not to smoke, but he insisted that he could not inconvenience his customers that way. At that moment

I noticed that the waiters were setting out *candles* on the floor, to help everyone see the steps that separated the different levels. Literally grabbing the maître d's arm, I screamed, "Are you nuts? Half the people in here are tipsy and getting more so, the air is about to get foul, and you're putting candles on the fucking floor! If we have a fire up here, we can all kiss our asses good-bye!" Seeing that I was so distraught, he was kind enough to offer to buy me a drink. I declined.

When the lights went out that night, I was afforded a great view of the whole Northeast starting to go dark, except for an occasional burst of light from a few buildings. After the blackout of 1965, the city mandated that certain buildings such as hospitals have emergency backup generators. Unfortunately, the framers of this law neglected to require that these generators be maintained properly or run periodically. Without being used and recharged at regular intervals, generators won't work. As I watched that night, the few buildings that did have generators would light up for a few minutes and then go dark as the unmaintained generators failed.

I was well aware that the twin towers had their own emergency generators. They finally kicked in, and the spacious passenger elevators arrived at our floor. Billy Bob started to go over to the elevators, but I held him back. I knew that these big beasties sucked electricity like a cyclotron, and I didn't think the generators were sized to run them. The first load of people got in. The doors closed and the car started down. And soon halted. From our spot up top, we could hear the passengers in the stalled car screaming for the next four hours. Someone finally thought to use the freight elevators, which did not consume nearly as much electricity because they ran much more slowly. Soon the firemen took charge and made sure that no more than twenty-five people got in each freight elevator and that just one car at a time was running.

People had started passing out from lack of oxygen, combined with fear and shock, about two hours after the blackout began. Fortunately, the first firefighters were able to give them oxygen and revive them, and no one died inside the twin towers. That night. Six hours after Billy Bob and I arrived for our festive dinner, we made it back down to ground level, found a gypsy cab, and went our separate ways. Billy Bob never again visited me in New York.

———

One day when I was four years old our housekeeper had taken me to my nursery school at the local yeshiva, as she customarily did. She briskly disappeared, expecting the gates to be opened in a few minutes, as they customarily were. What my mother, eternally clueless about our religion, had overlooked was that it was a Jewish holiday and the school was closed. None of the teachers or other kids showed up, and the gates never swung open. People swirled around me, but I didn't know where I was, where I lived, or what my telephone number was. Nor did I have any identification that would have provided answers to any of the above. Before long I started to whimper, and when that effected no remedy, I began to wail at great volume.

Eventually a great big man in a blue uniform arrived and knelt beside me. In what I have since come to realize was an Irish brogue, he put his huge hand on my cheek and started talking soothingly to me. Then he took me by the hand, and he and I started walking down the unfamiliar-looking streets. He asked me if I lived on a street with big trees. Yes. Did I live in a house or an apartment building? A house. Did it stand by itself, or was it attached to another house? By itself.

As we walked, with my tiny hand in his great big comforting one, he headed in the direction of the detached single-family houses in my homogenous Brooklyn neighborhood. Walking down Coney Island Avenue, he kept asking if I recognized any of the shops. At last I saw the candy store where my mother sometimes bought me an egg cream. Under the cop's gentle questioning, I recognized the drugstore, then the imposing mass of the Dime Savings Bank of Brooklyn. As the landmarks appeared, I stopped whimpering and started recognizing familiar houses. The cop asked me to describe my house. "It has a red door."

Recognition! He was that stalwart fixture of New York that has all but disappeared: the beat cop. And he remembered a house with a red door. Soon I was back in the arms of my mortified mother. It was my first experience with blind terror.

Now, nearly sixty years later, I decided to help keep my city a welcoming place by joining the NYPD auxiliary force. After attending police training for four months at night, taking qualifying tests, being fingerprinted, passing background checks, and having our photos taken, my classmates and I journeyed to the Police Equipment Bureau at One Police Plaza, near City Hall, to be outfitted in "the blue suit." The entire package consisted of a winter and summer uniform, utility belt, baton, handcuffs, and more. Early one spring evening in 2001 (I had already been on patrol for a year, but, hey, it's municipal government!), about 150 of us new auxiliary cops from every precinct throughout the city gathered at One Police Plaza for our induction ceremony. There, in the spacious auditorium, we viewed a film about the NYPD. Then the department's top brass filled the stage. We took our formal oaths en masse, then lined up in groups of ten at the stairs up to the stage. As our names were called, each of us mounted the stairs, marched smartly across the stage, snapped a crisp salute (at least I did, a talent I had acquired after serving in every branch of the military), looked up at the photographer in the balcony to have our picture taken, and then received a certificate, a police shield, a police ID, and a handshake.

My duties included going on foot patrol one night a week, usually from 6:30 to 10 o'clock, when there are the most people on the streets and the need for police presence peaks. After reporting for roll call in a basement room at the Twenty-fourth Precinct at 100th Street and Amsterdam Avenue on the Upper West Side, I was assigned my post, which could be anywhere from West 86th to 110th Street. I also augmented the full-time cops on weekends for street fairs, parades, and other special events. We auxiliaries were also subject to being called in for emergencies. Most of my work involved providing an enhanced police presence on the street, calling in any suspicious activity, and actually helping people. As my training officer, Anthony Maresca, was fond of saying, "It's more fun *being NYPD Blue* than *watching NYPD Blue.*"

Maresca also drummed into our heads that if we observed anything serious going down, we were instantly to call for backup. During a class on the different types of commendations, he gestured toward the department's most prestigious award, the Order of Valor. "If anyone here ever gets the Order of Valor," Maresca promised, "I will personally give him the Order of Stupid."

In other words, we were not to try to be heroes.

———

When the sun went down and the city changed into its nighttime persona, I changed with it. On designated evenings I walked into the locker
room at the Two-Four—which looks exactly like the one on *NYPD
Blue*—and traded my Harris tweed jacket and black turtleneck for a blue
suit with a shield bearing NYPD number 11556, and the tools of the architect's trade for a nightstick and handcuffs.

On numerous occasions, including the predawn hours of November
7, 2000, I worked a later shift, because I had an opportunity few auxiliary
policemen receive: to ride with the night watch commander for all of
Manhattan. This was Detective Sergeant Wallace Zeins, a fellow Jew
and the brother of one of my friends. Not to mention a legend in the
NYPD. Starting out as a patrol officer in Brooklyn in 1973, Wally advanced steadily to the undercover narcotics squad, then internal affairs,
and next organized crime investigator focusing on the Gambino family.
After graduating from the FBI Academy in Quantico, Virginia, he
taught undercover techniques to FBI agents there, and, since 1996, he
had been commanding officer of all the detectives investigating homi-
cides and other major crimes throughout Manhattan on the midnight to
8 A.M. shift.

Wally Zeins is a man of average height, about five foot ten, with a
pleasant, earnest, unprepossessing Jewish type of face, the way you wish
your favorite uncle looked. When I rode with him he was in his late forties, ten years or so younger than me, with a low-key manner and soft
voice and a typical New York accent and "working stiff" demeanor that
other cops, bad guys, and everyone else found easy to relate to. When
Wally arrived at a crime scene, he instantly took charge with both authority and sensitivity but without raising his voice, and everyone de-
ferred to him. He was meticulous about thanking witnesses for their
time and inconvenience, as well as expert at organizing an unfolding
crime scene to make sure that procedures were followed and evidence
was not tainted. Wally clearly loved New York and knew the city, especially the way it functioned under cover of the late night, the way most
mystery writers could only wish they did.

He delighted in showing me some of Gotham's architectural landmarks

I had only read about or was totally unaware of, including the oldest Russian Orthodox church in the city, and some after-hours S & M bars (both gay and straight) where he had an easy live-and-let-live rapport with the staff. During our travels, he and I talked about anything and everything, from our marriages (my second marriage had failed and I had moved out) to the proper way to "go through a door" at a suspect's hideout. It was truly a great experience.

At 1:30 that morning, I took the shotgun seat in Wally's unmarked car, and the two of us set out on patrol. He had asked to see the Holiday Inn Wall Street that I had designed and developed, and shortly after 3 A.M., when we were just two blocks away from the hotel, a call, urgency dripping from each word, came over the division radio: "Man shot on the Number Two train, William and Wall. This is confirmed!"

Sergeant Zeins had been amiably chatting with me about Manhattan's nighttime landscape. Instantly he became all business. Grabbing the division radio, he said, "Let's go." Then he keyed the mike: "Watch Commander responding to Wall and William."

Strobes and flashers became the visual accompaniment to the siren, as we sped though the empty streets of Manhattan. The radio broadcast the first description of a suspect: white male, red jacket, tan pants. My head started swiveling, as I looked down the side streets, trying to spot him, while we were on our way to the Wall Street subway station.

As we ran down the stairs, Wally ordered, "Hang with me. Take the radio."

The change booth attendant shouted, "Last stairway—uptown tracks!"

Wally and I tore through the station at a dead run. I had a passing thought: "Damn! I've seen this situation on *NYPD Blue*."

But this was no television show. Reality awaited us at the bottom of the stairs. A human being was frantically being worked on by a team of emergency medical technicians. That bullet hole in his stomach was for real. The bright orange of the plastic board that he was being strapped to contrasted cruelly with the dirty subway floor. Professionalism was on display as, for the first time, I watched the resources of our city going into gear to try to save a life and find a shooter.

For a quasi civilian like me, this was an awe-inspiring drama that was unfolding. Wally was sorting through the few people who had been present. He quickly found the one who was to be the crucial witness. At the same time he was monitoring the police calls as possible suspects were spotted in Manhattan and Brooklyn, and he dispatched "uniforms" to seal off possible crime scenes so potential evidence could be found, preserved, and left uncontaminated. The subway car that was the scene of the shooting had to be moved—somewhere—in order to get the system back on line, but the car itself was the crime scene. Wally conferred with the motorman and quickly handled this problem, too, ordering that the out-of-service train be moved to a siding and secured by a uniformed officer.

Detective Zeins was like a symphony conductor—calmly, professionally, and unemotionally orchestrating his forces. Get the victim the best and quickest care. Swiftly apprehend any suspects. Keep the crime scenes uncontaminated, so if evidence was recovered it would hold up under the narrow strictures of our legal system. By now there were three crime scenes to be cared for: the subway station; Battery Park, where plainclothes cops had apprehended a possible suspect hiding behind some garbage cans; and a Brooklyn subway station where another potential suspect was being detained. Transit police were arriving in increasing numbers. The victim was being quickly but carefully carried up the stairs to a waiting ambulance. I stayed with the passenger who was the crucial witness.

Detective Zeins was on the radio, calling for the K-9 unit to check out Battery Park. More detectives streamed in. Wally took the time personally to thank the secondary witnesses for their help before they were escorted upstairs to a police van. His manner, in the midst of this hectic and fast-developing drama, was sincere and soothing. It became obvious why Detective Sergeant Wallace Zeins was also New York City's lead hostage negotiator.

The pressure was intense. Time *was* of the essence, both to try to save a life and to apprehend a predator. But none of these pros showed any sign of stress. I was being given a fly-on-the-wall's view of a smoothly operating team as it worked with awesome efficiency. I stuck with Wally as we raced to New York Downtown Hospital. Images of the TV show *ER* flashed into my overloaded mind as I watched a doctor kneeling on a gurney, respirating the victim while fluids in tubes flowed, a sonogram showed its gray and ghostly images, and a portable X-ray machine was wheeled in.

After personally making sure that anything that could be done for the victim was being done, we sped off to Battery Park and the suspect who was being held there. The K-9 unit had already arrived and a German shepherd named Shawn had started the events that were to break the case. Shawn went over to a trash can that was half hidden behind some construction equipment. Bingo! Out came the "throwaway" jacket that matched the description of the one a perpetrator was wearing, along with a backpack containing handbags and other items from previous robberies, and the clincher—a Beretta .25 automatic, recently fired. Zeins called for another K-9 unit. The second unit arrived as we rolled away.

Before long word came over the radio that the victim, a twenty-eight-year-old Haitian immigrant named Louis Nixon, had died. Looking straight ahead as he drove, Wally advised his units that the case was now a homicide. Meanwhile, in Battery Park, the second dog nailed it. She sniffed the "throwaway" jacket and she followed the scent of where the suspect had fled when he had tried to escape. The dog stopped cold at the spot where the police had put him in the squad car. As we traveled uptown, I asked Detective Zeins how the dog would be crucial to the case. With a slight smile he glanced at me and answered, "Every court admits police canines as expert witnesses." Sorting out the evening's extraordinary events, I flashed on the bizarre image of a defense lawyer trying to cross-examine our expert.

A good man, on the way from his home in Brooklyn to work his shift at UPS in Midtown, who used some of his pay to help support his mother back in Haiti, had been senselessly murdered. Two career criminals had been going through the train, robbing people at gunpoint. The victim was asleep when the perps tried to wake him with a gun and ordered him to give them the gold chain from his neck. He had woken up with a start, instinctively pushed back, and been shot in the abdomen. For a gold chain! The city's finest had reacted instantly, expertly, and compassionately. Within two hours, his probable killer was locked up.

The shooter, the man found hiding behind garbage cans, Michael Amuso of Staten Island, also twenty-eight, was on parole for a previous robbery and had a rap sheet with at least fourteen convictions for robbery, burglary, drugs, and larceny. He was convicted of first-degree murder for killing Nixon and sentenced to life in prison without possibility of parole. He led officers to his accomplice, Ali Carrington, twenty-five, of Queens, who was convicted, too, and given a fifty-year term.

I was born in New York and had lived there for all of my sixty-five years, except when I was at Trinity College and in the military. Never before this incident, though, had I truly appreciated how well cared for all of us New Yorkers are.

Wally was taking something of a risk by inviting me to join him as he patrolled the city. As an auxiliary, my role was very much in the margins. I was technically a "ride along," like reporters and other civilians the department wanted to impress. Yet Wally, as a "D," or detective, made no such distinction in our dealings with the other Ds with whom he and I interacted. The other detectives always addressed me as "Detective," and Wally made no attempt to disabuse them. About a week after the capture of the subway killer, one of the other Ds slapped me on the back and congratulated me on "the nice collar" I had made.

I had many chances to accompany Wally Zeins and witness him in action. I was with him once when he confronted a handcuffed, armed-robbery suspect at the New Jersey end of the Lincoln Tunnel, where Wally and I had sped on a "hot pursuit" that allowed us to go beyond the boundaries of the city. Two suspects had been captured, but two others had gotten away.

"Do you believe in God?" Wally asked one of the prisoners.

A nod.

"Do you remember the story of Noah and the ark?"

Another nod.

"Do you remember that Noah got to save two of each species, while the waters rose and everyone else perished in the flood?"

A confused look.

"Well, I am going to give you the opportunity to get aboard the ark and save you from the rising waters." With a sweeping hand, Wally indicated the growing police presence. "If you give up your two associates that fled the scene, I will let you aboard the ark. I will speak to the DA and I will save you from the rising waters. I'll give you some time to think about it, but you must make your decision soon." Wally also informed the subject that if he refused to cooperate, he would find himself in New Jersey's notorious Rahway State Prison, where, Wally promised him, "You go in as a tight end and come out as a wide receiver."

With that, Wally walked away from the prisoner. As he talked to other law enforcement officers, I watched the suspect. His eyes followed Wally; clearly, he was afraid he might be left to the flood. Wally approached a tall detective, who, like the suspect, was black, and told him, "He wants to give them up. After a few minutes, talk to him." The prisoner gave them up.

One night my background as an architect came in very handy. About two dozen of us, including agents from the U.S. Treasury Department and members of the city's Emergency Services Unit (ESU — more commonly known as SWAT), along with detectives and uniforms, prepared to raid a counterfeiting operation in an apartment at 145th Street and St. Nicholas Avenue in Harlem and execute a no-knock search warrant. One young cop, clad in the full body armor ESU personnel wore during potentially ultradangerous operations, had drawn up diagrams of the building and the neighborhood. Recognizing that the apartment was in what is known as an "old law tenement" that usually had stairwell exits, I was able to add to details in the diagram during the preraid briefing. "If there are shots fired, *do not enter the building!*" Sergeant Zeins commanded all of us. "ESU will take care of that." I personally was removed from the most likely source of danger, assigned to cover one of the rear exits. By the time I entered the apartment, all the drama was over, and three very groggy-looking suspects were handcuffed and sitting quietly.

To bring the circle 360 degrees, on a bitter cold evening, January 2, 2001, I was able to do for an elderly and disoriented lady what that beat cop had done for me back in Brooklyn when I was a mere lad of four. About 8:30 that evening, at the corner of 103rd Street and Broadway, a young woman approached my auxiliary partner and me and told us the older woman with her was lost. The older lady was clad in a well-worn fur coat, and no stockings, gloves, or hat. She was coherent enough to tell us her name was Helen, but when I asked her where she lived, she replied, "I was born in Germany."

I got on the division radio and called it in. While I was asking for a patrol car to come pick up the woman, another voice cut in on the radio: "This is the two-zero. Send description of disoriented female."

"Gray hair, light brown fur coat, approximately five feet four inches tall," I answered.

"That's her! Twenty supervisor responding to call—we have a missing persons out for her. Her husband is frantic."

It was over in a few minutes. I could see flashing lights coming down Broadway. I put my arm around Helen and said, "It's okay, Helen, don't be frightened. We'll have you home soon."

She looked at my partner and me with a sweet smile. "How could I be frightened with two handsome policemen helping me?"

It wasn't until I got home that I started crying.

After Helen was safely reunited with her husband and I returned to the station house, around 10 P.M., the CO (commanding officer) of the Twenty-fourth Precinct, who like most COs rarely spoke to individual auxiliaries, approached me and said that the CO of the Twentieth Precinct had called and asked our commander to compliment "the patrolman" responsible. (The Twentieth's CO thought I was a regular cop.) My commanding officer was quite proud, of course; in fact, all the cops at the Twenty-fourth took pride in the fact that the precinct's auxiliary officers dressed and bore themselves like real cops, as opposed to auxiliaries in some other precincts who were sloppy looking like a bunch of bozos. Actually, the Twenty-fourth's auxiliaries had been named the best in the city for the last nine years in a row. As a result of my actions that night, I was recommended for the NYPD's Award of Merit. Since it wasn't the Order of Valor, no doubt even Training Officer Anthony Maresca would have approved.

My usual night for auxiliary cop was Tuesday. Tuesday, September 11, 2001, was a bright, glorious end-of-summer morning. I carried my police shield and ID to work in a wallet on a neck chain, since I was scheduled to work that evening. My offices were now at Sixtieth Street and Broadway, on the eighth floor, with large windows facing south. I lived five blocks away, in the apartment house Trump owned, and I arrived at my office about 8:30 every day. Shortly before 9 o'clock, one of the people who worked for me burst in and asked, "What the hell is that?"

Billowing in the sky from downtown was a huge cloud of smoke. We could not actually see the twin towers because of high-rises between our building and Lower Manhattan, but the smoke cloud was front and center. Over a radio, amid the horrifying newscasts, boomed an urgent announcement: "ALL OFF-DUTY FIRE, POLICE, AND AUXILIARY PERSONNEL—REPORT TO YOUR COMMANDS!"

Stunned, I rushed down into the street, where traffic was slowed to a crawl. I approached a cab with a passenger in it and showed my shield. "Can you take me to the Two-Four Precinct at One Hundredth Street?"

Cabbie and passenger both nodded, and we took off.

The "house" was a scene of controlled chaos. In the locker room, as I suited up, an officer ran in, banged on the lockers with his baton, and screamed: "EVERYONE OUT OF THE HOUSE—NOW!"

As we rushed into the street, I learned that some sick son of a bitch had called in a bomb threat.

Of course it was a day like almost no other, except for December 7, 1941, and November 22, 1963. I was just old enough to remember Pearl Harbor. Five years old then, I couldn't fathom exactly what was happening, but I remember my parents' stricken faces and the neighbors pouring out of their houses, shouting and crying.

Now it was happening all over again, except that this time I was all grown up and in uniform. Mayor Giuliani, who will forever be my hero for his actions and eloquent words on that day, had sent a city bus and driver to each precinct house, in order to transport us to wherever we were needed. We were needed a lot.

The mayor, with Solomonic wisdom, had ordered there to be two "uniforms" at every subway entrance during the evening rush hour. As my partner and I stood at the West Eighty-sixth Street station that dreadful afternoon, I could see the look of relief on people's faces when they saw two police officers standing there. Our uniforms, obviously, were reassuring. One woman was ascending the stairs with her eyes lowered, staring down in front of her. As she looked up, she smiled sadly and approached me. Putting her fingers on the mourning band that we all wore on our shields, she said, "I'm so sorry for your loss."

Tears still come to my eyes when I think of that moment. It was New York City during its worst time but also at its best.

By the end of that awful week, I returned to my office and started making preparations for the end of my existence as a New York architect. All the projects we had had under way had come to a halt. When I called the owners of the Flatotel about the sixty-five grand they owed me, their answer was, "The hotel is down to 40 percent occupancy. We can't pay you anything." Another example of an age-old truism in architecture: When a project is successful, your fee gets paid; if it doesn't make money, you suddenly and unwillingly become a partner. The owners of the Crowne Plaza in the Dominican Republic did pay me for my pre-liminary design work, but that hotel was put on hold because of justifiable fears that tourists would be reluctant to fly from the mainland to the islands. I never heard from the Crowne Plaza developers again.

As I watched the horror unfold on September 11 and over the next few days, I realized that my architectural career, at least in New York City, had just ended. That didn't seem very important in the context of the times. I wound up my business, closed my office, and moved with my new wife first to her home on Martha's Vineyard and then to a small town in Maine.

Here is where I will continue my work. And my life.

On a sunny spring day in 1963, I received my architectural degree from Columbia University. On a sunny fall day in 2001, I closed my office.

It had been a richly varied thirty-eight years.

21.
Ryokan

Everyone has a secret fantasy. With some it's sex, money, power, or losing ten pounds. I am kinky for hotels. After spending years designing hospitality facilities to fulfill other people's ideas for the perfect vacation, I started to think about creating a hotel at which I would like to stay. I didn't have to think very hard to find it.

While still an architectural student, I had discovered the Japanese architectural magazine *Shinkenchiku*. The first part of the journal was devoted to contemporary architectural design, but the second half always featured a thorough essay on one of that country's architectural gems from the past. I was enthralled by the beauty and elegance of these ancient wooden structures. Just as my wife, a concert cellist, can listen to a piece of classical music and hear nuances and cadences that are largely lost on my untrained ear, I looked at these structures and was amazed by the subtle interrelationships of form and proportion. The details of this type of wood joinery were as mystifying as they were beautiful. Wooden beams seemed to pass through each other without any metal fastenings, and a sense of serenity and harmony pervaded every square inch of the buildings. This type of ethereal design was echoed in every aspect, from the gardens to the richness of the simple but elegant materials. Then, one fine day, I read about the Japanese country inn, or *ryokan*.

Although these facilities were originally designed for travelers on the Tokaido Road, that connected the eastern capital of Tokyo to the ancient capital of Kyoto, they gradually assumed a different function in Japanese life. They became places to restore ones soul, or *wa*, with immersion in peace, tranquillity, and beauty. Not bad for a start, thought I.

I started to read about and study this type of facility. It seemed ideal. I decided to go and check it out. But first I had to become conversant in the language, since this was part of the closed world of ancient Japan and not readily accessible to a gaijin (foreign barbarian) such as me.

After years of self-teaching, sketching out ideas, and immersing myself in that ancient culture, I came across a hotelier who had similar feelings. Bob Burns was a midwesterner who was not only hip to the concept but had married a Japanese woman. He had also started the five-star Regent hotel chain, utilizing several of the hospitality concepts of the *ryokan*. At the time, I was designing a Regent hotel in Florida, and while Bob was sitting in my office, he noticed on the wall my sketch for a theoretical Japanese inn. His eyes lit up and we started discussing the concept. He graciously offered to recommend a number of authentic *ryokans* in Japan and to help me get accommodations in them. By then I was able to communicate (badly) in the language, so I headed out to see if the actuality of the concept was as good as the theory. It was far better.

In Japan, courtesy is carried to lofty heights, tipping is nonexistent, and beauty is revered. I had found my perfect hotel. I realized it was completely transportable. The structure itself is a one- or two-story heavy-timber building, finished in stucco. Physically it was something any good carpenter could build. If he was Japanese. Or if it was prefabricated in Japan. This type of building was subtly designed to address all the senses: the look of the building, the sound of strategically placed waterfalls and fountains, the varied texture of the materials, the smells of the wood and the gardens, and the varied and wonderful tastes of the exquisite *kai sekai* dinners that are traditionally served. Another delightful feature is that your complete wardrobe is provided for you. In the closet was the traditional soft cotton wrap robe or *yukata*, one of the most comfortable garments ever devised, in which it is impossible not to look great. This robe, with the graphic logo of the facility on the back, is worn by all the patrons. There is a selection of silk overmantles or vestlike garments, tied in the front, that are worn over the *yukata* for evening dress. There is also a selection of toiletries, including real razors, brushes, toothbrushes, and a variety of lotions and creams that are the best money can buy. In short, you don't have to bring any of your own stuff.

I met Bob in Tokyo when I was staying at the Hotel Okura, a luxury facility that combines the best of traditional Japanese design with the best of contemporary facilities. In discussing the adaptability of the *ryokan* to America, he commented that it would be difficult to replicate the service available at the *ryokan*. He said that at best, I could get only the type of "commercial" available at the Okura. This commercial service consisted of women stationed at the elevator whose sole function was to bow to you when approached, maids who would put their carts against the wall and bow as you passed in the hall and, upon initial arrival at the facility, being greeted by an assistant manager in a cutaway respectfully welcoming you to his hotel. I figured that commercial would be just fine. Later, when visiting the Tawaraya Ryokan in Kyoto, I found out what he meant. When the maid entered the room, she was on her knees, and her head bowed down until it touched the floor. That probably wouldn't be a hit with Gloria Steinem. Commercial would definitely be just fine.

Another feature was the *ofuro*, or Japanese bath, a ritual whose object is not to get you clean. (You wash thoroughly before stepping in.) These wooden tubs are set next to a window that looks out on a small private garden with raked gravel, decorative stone lanterns, and bonsai trees. When I first put my foot into the bath, which had been drawn for me by the "room woman" who is in charge of you during your stay, I thought I was about to do myself a great injury. I thought back to the chapter in James Clavell's *Shōgun* when the local lord boiled alive some of the English sailors. But research is research, so I immersed my delicate body parts into the tub. I soon felt a delicious floating sensation as the intense heat permeated my body and I gazed at the serenity of the exquisite garden. It was a great legal high. Then, feeling limp, relaxed, and blissfully peaceful, I had a Japanese massage. It was incredible. The Japanese originally developed their art of massage utilizing blind samurai. I realized that the *ryokan*, transported to the West, could incorporate this into a seriously delightful spa experience.

When I returned to the States, I started looking for a site and financial backing. The resort would be a five-star facility with a glorious spa, an executive meeting facility (they are used for this in Japan), and a variety of restaurants featuring Japanese specialties but with Western dishes available (again as they are in Japan). In short, a luxury resort where you don't have to wonder what outfits to bring, the service is the stuff of dreams, neither servile nor obsequious, just attentive and respectful, you don't have to wonder whom or how much to tip, and you are pampered and taken care of every moment.

It would not be a Disneyesque experience; it would be as close to the real deal as I could make it. I found a location within an hour's drive of New York City, in the Catskill Mountains town of Mamakating, ironically, about ten miles from where my father had designed some of the old borscht belt hotels. I put together a group of professionals with whom I had worked and a young Japanese-born businessman who had lived in this country for over twenty years. He showed me that New York City has a sizable population of young bilingual Japanese who would love to get a green card by working here. Hospitality and service are still regarded by the Japanese as honorable professions, not as stepping-stones to a career in the theater.

In the *ryokan*, one is a guest and not a customer.

I look forward to seeing you there.

Epilogue

When I entered the profession more than forty years ago, the only rich architects were the ones who had inherited money, married it, or been born with it. No one I knew ever became an architect to get rich. Architecture isn't that type of field, nor are the folks in it those kinds of people.

It's the part about getting seriously poor that I hadn't counted on.

My father was one of the most commercially successful architects of his time. He retired after practicing for nearly sixty years, an icon of his times, with a net worth of $2 million. He never lived lavishly. His home for the last forty-five years of his life was in a second-floor condo in a middle-income building in Miami Beach that he purchased in 1961 for $25,000.

Two million dollars today would be a fairly insulting Christmas bonus for Wall Street types, but Morris thought he had done very well indeed. And for an architect, he had.

Architecture is a seductive field, and like any good seducer, the courtship is long and sensuous, a world of promised delight opened by the initial encounters. But the long-term relationship can be fraught with peril, and the pleasure-pain ratio in architecture is in constant flux.

When I was in army basic training, we were taught how to use our night vision (in the days before all the electronic gadgetry) by always looking at the periphery rather than staring straight ahead. It turned out to be in the little "sidebars" of my career where I often found some of the most fascinating uses for my skills.

One example was work I did for the Michael Reese Hospital in Chicago. During the late 1960s while I was in Puerto Rico working on the Conquistador, I met a couple from the Windy City at dinner. Both of them were psychologists, and we enjoyed talking about our respective fields. One morning I woke up unable to move. (This would turn out to be the precursor of a major back problem, later to result in surgery.) Hearing that I was incapacitated (Conquistador was still a small resort, and news carried fast), the husband came to my room to see if he could help. Before becoming a shrink, he had been a physical therapist. He helped me a lot with stretching and manipulating my back. In the week of recuperation that followed, we became quite friendly.

A couple of years later he called about a problem he and his colleagues were having with their new space at Michael Reese. They had just been given a floor there to establish a center to study and treat severely autistic children between the ages of two and ten. The challenge was to establish conditions in this space that were sympathetic to these kids. Autism is a terrible affliction that to one degree or another reduces children, regardless of their intelligence, to reacting only to sensory input. In order to understand this malady and deal with it in architectural terms, I worked with this autism team as a therapist for a week. Their patients were solely in the world of tactile sensations. I learned about holding the children close to your chest in order to make contact and the use of such stimuli as water play and bright colors to get their attention.

The experience helped me redesign the waiting area. This was to be an outpatient facility, and the children needed an inviting place to occupy them while they waited to be treated. But this was a typical hospital, with high ceilings, institutional green paint, and dark gray linoleum floors. The doctors did not want to create a cage around the area, but most of their small patients were crawlers who did not respond to verbal commands. How to keep the kids in one area without resorting to physically restraining them? Just to make the whole thing even more challenging, the budget was minuscule.

Architecture, in its purest form, was the answer. I demarked the waiting area by placing six-foot-high freestanding wardrobe closets on either side of the space. I created a sense of enclosure and shelter by threading bright yellow maritime rope through screw eyes on the tops of the closets. By weaving this rope back and forth between the two wardrobes, I developed a bright latticelike "roof" over the space. I bought a garish bright orange shag carpet to place between the closets and put several beanbag chairs around the space. No child ever crawled past the soft warm carpet or left the shelter of the "enclosed" space. I did this work pro bono, and never have I been more richly rewarded.

Architecture has, historically, been the pride of its civilizations. Does anyone feel proud of the stuff being built nowadays? (Aside from the architects who designed it.) I don't mean to rag on just the contemporary stuff. A classic example of architecture gone wrong in a traditional vernacular is the World War II memorial in Washington. It is just plain bad. Lousy design is not restricted to avant-garde design.

Compare the World War II memorial to the magnificent Vietnam and Korean War memorials and the Marine Corps memorial nearby. To me, monuments are important because they represent architecture in its purest form. I especially like Maya Lin's design of the Vietnam Veterans Memorial. A close friend of mine who is a thirty-year veteran and served two tours in Vietnam, a tough-as-nails, unemotional hard case, cried like a baby when he visited it. That's the point of successful architecture: construction that causes an emotional response.

One reason for the proliferation of junk like the World War II memorial and the march of soulless glass boxes down New York's Sixth Avenue is the proliferation of architecture critics. Yes, I certainly do disdain this group of pompous scriveners, but I also have contempt for the system that led us architects to abdicate our own good sense and place our judgment in the hands of the "experts."

Architecture critics are like eunuchs: They can't do it themselves, but, my, they certainly can tell everyone else how to do it. I've never been able to understand why we think we need some pundit to explain to us what we can see for ourselves. I can understand the need for theater, movie, and book critics. Before you lay down your money for one of these forms of recreation, it's nice to have someone advise you if it is worth the price of admission.

But architecture? The building is right there. Just look at it! It either works or it doesn't. You either like it or you don't. None of these critics are architects, and they do not have the slightest comprehension of the financial reasons for a building's existence.

During a boat tour around Manhattan, I once had the privilege of listening to a prominent architecture critic give a lecture on urban architecture. When we passed the section of the FDR Drive along the East River that had been covered over, he commented on how lovely the shore looked without the exposed highway and lamented that the urban planners had not had the vision to cover all of it.

Hello! It costs a fortune to cover a main highway with a deck and landscaping. Government officials may have felt they could afford to do it to protect the tender sensibilities of denizens of the wealthy Upper East Side, but economic reality does come into play somewhere along the line.

Years later this same commentator would disparage Bill Zeckendorf's Worldwide Tower, designed by Skidmore, Owings & Merrill, because the granite facing was "thin," and the windows were one sheet of glass rather than being subdivided in a classical manner. The critic apparently had no comprehension that this was a speculative office building that had to make a return on its investment rather than a corporate icon built solely for "image." Skidmore and Zeckendorf did a terrific job of showing that one can actually develop and design an elegant contemporary masonry office building and still have it return a profit. Worldwide Tower is a remarkable achievement that does not need the smart-ass nitpicking. It is that sort of gratuitous and ignorant criticism that can discourage others from taking a chance on erecting quality commercial buildings. The critics have yet to learn that there are two categories of buildings: expensive pets and buildings that have to work for a living.

It is absurd to compare a building like Frank Gehry's Disney Concert Hall, a monument to ego, status, and bravado, to a speculative office building. I think the concert hall is a pretty nifty piece of heroic urban sculpture, which happens to have a concert hall stuffed into it. But I do not believe that any structure where the outside has no relationship to the inside can be called architecture.

So what have I learned on this thrill ride?

I am intensely committed to people liking my work. Not as an abstract concept fraught with arcane symbolism and subtle social connotations but as a place, as Shakespeare had Mark Antony declaim, for you "to walk abroad, and recreate, yourselves." In short, I have tried to design structures that people will enjoy looking at and being in.

I have always felt that if you had to write a doctoral thesis to explain your building, you failed. No one has ever had to explain the Parthenon, Chartres Cathedral, or any of Frank Lloyd Wright's buildings. And no one ever laid eyes on the Fontainebleau and wondered about its "context."

Architecture is a visceral, not an intellectual art. As I mentioned earlier, I have never forgotten the dean's welcoming speech when I entered the Columbia Graduate School of Architecture and he stated that architecture should "speak to generations yet unborn, in a universal language." But I did not have to go to architecture school to learn the most valuable lesson of all, which was instilled in me at home from childhood on by my father: "Always design for your clients' clients." In other words, everything by design.

When I read some of the verbose pomposity spewed by a few superstar architects, I wonder what they are really saying and whom they are saying it to. I am old enough (seventy) to have seen the unadorned glass box hailed as the zenith of architectural style. The glass box, as epitomized by the Seagram Building, can indeed be a striking structure. But the appeal of that particular structure has as much to do with its physical context, in a position opposite the wonderfully ornate classic edifice that is the New York Racquet Club, as with any intrinsic beauty.

The Seagram Building itself is a living lie. Mies van der Rohe, the guru of the Bauhaus, pasted phony I-beams all over the façade and placed green marble in the window openings when he had to accommodate the inconvenient necessity of a concrete fire wall. His final product is an ornament of the Machine Age, but it is every bit as uselessly decorative (and a lot less attractive) as any cartouche or egg-and-dart molding. Personally,

I prefer the adornments James Bogardus placed on the true Machine Age icons, his lyrically beautiful prefabricated cast-iron buildings. Compare the harmony and interest found in the rows of buildings in New York's glorious cast-iron district in the NoHo (north of Houston) neighborhood of Lower Manhattan with the soulless boredom of the glass boxes that line Manhattan's Sixth Avenue. I have lived through the architectural craze of the New Brutalism, wherein unadorned raw concrete was considered an ode to joy for our civilization. Now these grimy, crude structures have become an embarrassment and an eyesore.

As long as I am on a rant, I might as well offend the American Institute of Architects.

When I was young, idealistic, and in architectural school, I was president of the school and its AIA chapter. Upon graduation, I was active in the organization and became a committee chairman. There were several aspects of the organization that I thought were dead wrong, and I thought by working through the institute I could effect some changes.

Wrong!

The first thing that struck me as slightly crazed was the licensing exam, which can be taken only after three years of "apprenticeship." Now, your school has had you for either three, four, or five years. They graduated you, so presumably you met the academic requirements. Yet the licensing exam is a test on the history of architecture and six other purely academic subjects. What is so crucial, for your licensure, about remembering the exact date of the construction of the Parthenon three years after you graduated?

This form of torture is unique to the United States. In Canada, you're also required to "apprentice" for three years, but the only exam is on the legal responsibilities of your license. That makes sense. You don't want someone signing a set of documents without fully realizing the legal ramifications. By the way, ironically, that critical aspect of the profession is not part of the U.S. licensing exams.

Having lost on that issue, I raised the delicate topic of making a living in architecture. I pointed out that, as far as I knew, not a single building code required an architect's seal on a set of construction documents. The seal of a professional engineer will do just fine.

This may be a reason that close to 90 percent of the building in this country is done without the involvement of an architect. It is also a pretty good reason why many architects are often in bad financial straits. Again, the United States is unique among countries in the Western world in this regard.

I was told, rather huffily, that the AIA was not a "trade organization" that would lobby for anything so crass as the ability to make a living. At the time, the federal office of the Architect of the Capitol was held not by an architect but by an engineer.

I pointed out that the American Medical Association and the American Bar Association had done a pretty fine job of making sure that their members could ride in Mercedes-Benzes. They had done this by ensuring that only an MD can treat or prescribe for a sick person, and that only a lawyer can represent you in court. I also pointed out the absurdity of having foisted the idea that architects should append AIA after their signature. Doctors don't put AMA after their names; they put MD, because that is what they are. An architect is an RA, registered architect. Putting AIA on the letterhead or after your signature is about as meaningful as putting down that you are a member of the Elks. All it means is that you have paid dues to an organization that has absolutely no legal standing.

My buildings are my babies, my legacy. When I watch one of them going up, or when I pass a structure I designed, the sense of awe and wonder is always indescribable. I marvel that it all started with a pencil sketch on a piece of coarse yellow paper. Like children, some of my buildings have turned out better than others, but each and every one of them I conceived, and I was there at its birth. They will be there long after I am gone to explain in a universal language to generations as yet unborn how we lived.

It is a feeling unlike any other.

For this I am grateful.

accountants ("bean counters"), 140–41
acerola juice, 232
Actors Studio, 5–6
Adachi Steel, 216, 221
air conditioning, 235
aircraft design, 189
airport hotels, 270
Albert S. Bard Awards for Excellence in
    Architecture and Urban Design, 88
Algiers hotel (Miami Beach), 70
Allen, Woody (Allen Konigsberg), 5, 33, 204
Amazonia, 229–37
Americana (now Sheraton) Hotel (New York
    City), 73, 110, 202
American Bar Association, 295
American Institute of Architects (AIA), 51, 70,
    294–95
    "not a trade organization," 295
American Medical Association, 295
Amuso, Michael, 279–80
anti-Semitism, 34, 38–39
Aoki, Rocky, 2, 116, 118–19, 138, 150
Aoki Construction, 191
apprenticeship, 57–58, 294
architect(s)
    and absolute rulers, 127–29
    apprenticeship, 57–58, 294
    dress style of ("chic"), 62, 145, 186
    vs. engineers, in building design, 294–95
    glamorous life of, in films and novels, 3, 21,
        179
    God-like feeling of, 167

number of, in U.S., 3–4
own-designed houses, 28
registered, 3–4, 295
skills required of, 57–58
successful ones, 289, 295
as "victim and fall guy," 5, 255–56
what they do, 2–4
women, 223
architects' earnings and fees, 18–19, 43,
    73–75, 216, 258, 289, 295
"fancy," 11
ownership share as part of, 7, 284
standard 4 percent, 74
unpaid, 284
Architectural Honor Society (Alpha Rho
    Chi), 55, 63
Architectural Record, The, 88
architecture
    a "chronicle of mankind," 2
    degrees in, 43
    delayed gratification in, 6
    emotional, visceral response from, 291,
        293
    employment in, 50–51
    financial hazards of the field, 7, 216,
        227–28, 256–59, 284, 289, 295
    as pride of civilizations, 291
    psychology of, 126–35
    reputation of, 24
    retiring from the field, 257–58
    "second oldest profession," 2
    Vitruvius's definition of, 133

architecture critics, 65, 87–88, 141, 250, 252–53, 291–93
architecture firms
    dress code at, 62
    letting people go, 181–82
    management practices, 222–23
architecture schools
    curriculum, 43–51
    degrees, 43
    new technology in, 43
architecture students, 21, 53
    in eighteenth-century France, 186
Arlen Realty and Development, 248
Army, U.S., 39–41
Art Deco architecture, 260, 262
Atlantic City, N.J., 142–43, 149, 151, 253–55, 269
    beginnings of, as resort, 15
    Donald Trump's interest in, 10–12, 17–19
    gaming in, 116, 155
    planning agency, 152–53
    rules for casinos, 119–20, 123, 155, 254
Atlantic City Convention Hall, 152, 157–58
At Play in the Fields of the Lord, 231
autistic children, architecture designed for, 290–91
Aventura condos (North Miami Beach), 104–5
average daily room rate (ADR), 174
Avery Hall, Columbia University, 42–43
Award of Merit (NYPD), 282

Back Street Hong Kong restaurant (Puerto Rico), 108–9
Bally chain, 157
bankruptcy, builders', 196, 224–26
banks, loans from, 220–26
Barbizon Plaza Hotel (New York City), 147–48
Bard Awards, 88
Barzun, Jacques, 54–55
bathhouses, 128
    Japanese, 287
Batista, Fulgencio, 90
Bauhaus, 46, 61
beach resorts, 96
beat cops, 274
Beatty, Warren, 192–93
Bedford-Stuyvesant pool and recreation center project, 77–89, 253
Belém, Brazil, 232–33
Benihana Steakhouses, 2, 116

Berkeley, Busby, 73, 97
Berner, Dr., 30
Best & Co., 249, 253
Beverly Hills Hotel (Calif.), 188
Big Apple Wrecking Corporation, 210
Bikel, Theo, 49
Biltmore Terrace (Miami Beach), 70
biodigester, 236–37
Birmingham, Stephen, *Our Crowd,* 12–13
blackouts, 272–73
Bloomingdale's, 220
Bogardus, James, 294
bonuses, 223
Boullée, Étienne-Louis, 187
boutique hotels, 263–64
Bowstead, John, 180, 212
bow ties, Morris Lapidus's wearing of, 25, 145
bow tie shape, 25, 145
"boys with interesting backgrounds." *See* mobsters
brand consciousness, 70–71
Brazil, 229–37
Broadway theaters, 198
Brooklyn, N.Y., 26, 153, 269–70
Brown, Courtney C., 52
building codes, 82–84, 199–201
building envelope, 199
buildings
    collapses of structures, 106–12
    designed by engineers not architects, 294–95
    high, "mine is bigger" motivation for, 3, 254
    ownership of, 7, 284
    profitability of, vs. aesthetics, 292
    unusual shapes of, for variety (e.g., bent), 174
Bunshaft, Gordon, 62
Burns, Bob, 286–87
business cards, 118
business hotels, 264–68
business travelers, 7, 262–68
Butcher, Susan, 191
Byrne, Brendan, 143

cacao, 234
CAD (computer-aided design) machines, 43, 57–58
Cadillacs, given to big losers, 137–38
Caesars (Atlantic City), 141
Caesars Palace (Las Vegas), 118–26

Caligula, 142, 254–55
Callahan, Michael, 269–70
campus protestors, rare in early 1960s, 52–55
cantilever, concrete, 106–8, 154
Cantor, Irwin, 201, 203
Caribbean, hotel and resort construction in, 96–112, 114–15, 117
Carmel, Calif., 40
carpeting, 158–59
Carrington, Ali, 280
cartoons, Disney, 133
casinos, 116–38
    layout of, 119–20
    men's vs. women's reactions in, 132
    psychology of, 119, 126–27, 129–38
    security and money-handling arrangements of, 121–26
    state rules for, 119–20, 123, 155, 254
cast-iron buildings, 294
Castro, Fidel, 100, 109
Catholic church, 128–29
Catskills, the, 100
    author's spa project in, 7, 288
Central Intelligence Agency (CIA), 3
Central Park Garage (Atlantic City), 150
Central Park West (New York City), 257
charrette, 186
Chartres Cathedral, 128–29, 293
cheaters, in casinos, fate of, 124–25
Chicago, 216–18
children, architecture that appeals to, 129, 173–74, 290
Chrysler Building (New York City), 206
Churchill, Winston, 129
Churchill Hotel (London), 104
cigars, Cuban, 241–42
City Club of New York, 88
city planning, 198–99
Clark County, Nevada, 124
Clavell, James, *Shogun*, 287
clients
    architects' relation with, 1–2, 238
    designing for "people like me," 97
    kinks and twists of, 1–2
clients of clients, designing for (Morris Lapidus's rule), 73, 208, 264, 293
Clinton administration, 238–39
cocktail waitress costumes, 130–32
Cohen, Leon, 223
Colanzi, Commissioner, 153
Colbert, Charles, 53–55
color
    and emotions, 135
    of high-rises, 207–9
    tasteful, from light gray to black, 207
Columbia condominium (New York City), 197
Columbia University, 35, 197
    campus design, 42, 51–55
    School of Architecture, 2, 4, 21, 42–55, 58, 72, 261
    School of Business Administration (Uris Hall), 52–53
columns (structural), 201
combat engineers, 40, 49
competitive bidding, 98
completion bond, 157
Concord resort (Catskills), 7
concrete, 46, 106–8, 294
Conquistador. *See* El Conquistador
"consigliere," 113
construction
    coordination of architect, engineer, and subcontractors in, 98, 102
    Latin American way of, 101–12, 211–14
construction documents ("blueprints"), 50–51, 57, 212
    coordination of, 102
    seal on, 294
construction financing, 216
construction projects, on hold, 182
Contemporary hotel (FL), 171
contractors, 71, 157
    bidding and building practices of, 79–86
    in Russia, 244–45
convention centers, 176–83
Cooper, Gary, 3
corridors, 173–74, 187
Cosentini Associates, 217–18
Cosmopolitan Hotel (Atlantic City), 151
cost cutting, unnecessary and cheapening, 140–41
Coursey, Almira, 86
Crédit Lyonnaise, 216, 221
critics, 291–92. *See also* architecture critics
Crocker Bank, 149
Crowne Plaza hotels, 148, 270–71, 284
Crowne Plaza Times Square (New York City), 48, 140–41, 200–210, 215
Crusinberry, Richard, 40
Cuba, 90, 100, 109
    author's secret visit to, 238–42
Cuban-Chinese restaurants, 109
Cuban missile crisis, 241
Cubans, 99, 146
    exile community, 240

curves and corners, 133, 174
  and emotions, 126–27, 133–35
Custer's last stand, 41

Dalí, Salvador, 133
Davis, David, 31–32
Davis, Sammy, Jr., 157
decoration, architectural, 293–94
de la Torre, José, 98–99
demising walls, 201
design
  bad, 291
  practical vs. aesthetic issues in, 102–5
  vocabulary of, 135
design presentations, 160–61, 190–91
designs, architectural
  cancelled, 218, 221
  changes to, during construction, 140–41
  that never get built, 5, 168–69, 182, 237
DeSimone, Vincent, 153–54
DiLido Hotel (Miami Beach), 59, 70
Dime Savings Bank, 11
Dinallo, "Babe," 253–54
Disney, Walt, 133, 171, 181
Disney characters, 193
Disney Concert Hall (Los Angeles), 292–93
Disney Corporation, 2, 123, 129, 133,
    160–69, 180–94, 215, 227
  aesthetic control exercised by, 183–84
  financial control exercised by, 181
  hotel projects, 171–78
Disney Corporation Downtown Hospital, 278
Disney Design Studio (Hollywood, Calif.),
    184
Disneyland (Anaheim, Calif.), 165, 171
Disney World (Orlando, Fla.), 133, 140, 160,
    163–69, 171–94
  autonomous government of, 165–66
  "the tunnels" (underground city), 164–65
Dolphin hotel (Orlando, Fla.), 140, 187–94,
    215
Dominican Republic, 271, 284
Domino the dalmation dog, 30–31
Donaldthink, 152
draft board, military, 39
drafting, 57–58
  a lost skill, 57–58
drafting tables, 46, 53

Easthampton, N.Y., 238
East Side (New York City), 198
ecohotels, 230–37
Economou, Gus, 43

ecotourism, 229–37
Ed (contractor), 81–82
Eden Roc Hotel (Miami Beach), 59, 73, 90,
    114, 153
Eighth Avenue (New York City), 217
Eisenhower, Dwight, 51, 192
Eisner, Michael, 2, 162, 168, 171, 180–85,
    187–88, 190–94
El Conquistador hotel (Puerto Rico), 91–100,
    104, 105–8, 117, 175, 211, 213
electric power, eco-friendly, 236–37
elegance, and "good taste," 73
elevators, 155, 173, 187, 272–73
Elizabeth, N.J., 270
Elkins, W.V., 271
El San Juan hotel (Puerto Rico), 100, 108–12
Embassy Suites (New York City), 208
emergency backup generators, 273
Emery Roth & Sons, 257–58, 271
Empire State Building (New York City), 206
Empire State Development Corporation, 11
engineers
  interaction with architects, 47–48, 294–95
  mechanical, electrical, and plumbing
    (MEP), 98
Epcot Center (Florida), 161, 171
Equitable Insurance Company, 11
escalators, 155–56
European travelers, 263
exclusivity contracts (not to take on other
    work), 147, 176
eye, the
  keeping it interested, 134–35
  view from level of, 156

Fajardo, Puerto Rico, 91
Farrell, Frank, 65–66
Farrow, Mia, 154
fast-track construction, 98
Feder, Abe, 206
federally subsidized housing, design of, 10
Feldman, Robert, 66
fiberglass, 189
Fiestaware, 28
Fifth Avenue (New York City), 252–53
Financial District (New York City), 7, 262–68
financing/raising money, 146–50, 216, 263–64
fire alarms, 177
fire ants (Brazilian), 234
fire codes, 166–67, 177
fire doors, 272
fires, high-rise, 177, 272–73
Fitzcarraldo, 236

flashing (windows), 156–57
Flatbush/Flatlands section of Brooklyn, 27,
204
Flatotel (New York City), 223, 271, 284
floor area ratio (FAR), unused, 199–200
Floyd, Jerry, 158
Foerderer, Norma, 149
folded plate construction, 110
folksingers, 48–49
Fontainebleau Hotel (Miami Beach), 7, 25,
97, 104, 114, 117, 158, 293
critics' dislike of, 88, 250
design elements of, 126, 174
Morris Lapidus chosen as designer, 68–70
Morris Lapidus's design and building of,
72–75
opening of, 20
as postmodern architecture, 4
recent "improvements" to, 153
food deliveries, 103
Ford Ord, Calif., 41
Ford Town, Brazil, 236
"form follows function," 72, 179, 184
Fort Dix, N.J., 39
Forty-Second Street (New York City), 11
Fountainhead, The, 3
Four Seasons Hotel (New York City), 175
France, architecture studies in, 186
franchises, 267
Freeman, Harvey, 12
"fronting" the design fees, architects asked to
do, 216, 258
Furman, Jay, 263–64, 268, 270

gamblers, 132, 137–38
compulsive, 136
gaming, 116–38
and human nature, 136–38
legalization of, 100, 136, 137
psychology of, 130–32, 135–38
gaming areas in casinos, location of, 155–56
gaming licenses, 144–45
Garfunkel, Art, 49
Gehry, Frank, 292
general manager (GM), 267
gentrification, 197
Gere, Richard, 3
German Jews, in New York City real estate,
12–14, 170
Gerstman, Milt, 172, 176
Giuliani, Rudolph, 283
glass boxes (buildings), 50, 61–62, 207, 291,
293–94

Goldberger, Paul, 141
Goldfinger, 97
Goldman, Andy, 16
Grand Floridian (Orlando, Fla.), 168–69
Grand Hyatt hotel (old Commodore) (New
York City), 11, 18, 147
Graves, Michael, 183–94
Great Blackout of 1977, 272–73
Greek architecture, 251
Greenberg, Shelly, 32–36, 44–45, 93, 114
Greene, Aaron, 261
Greene, Gael, 109
grenades, design of, 47
Grossinger's resort (Catskills), 7
guard dogs, 86
Guccione, Bob, 2, 142, 253–55

Hanlon, David, 131
Hannah, Daryl, 231
Harrah's Casino (Atlantic City), 148–50
Harrah's Casino brand, 148–50
Harrelson, Woody, 3
Haskins, John, 46
health clubs, Russian, 246
Heilbron, Susan, 16
Helen (lost old lady), 281–82
Hell's Kitchen (New York City), 217
Helms-Burton Act, 239, 242
Helmsley, Harry, 13
Helmsley, Leona, 13
Hench, John, 133, 161, 167, 187
Hernandez, Gregorio, 106, 111–12
Herzog, Werner, 236
high-rises
fire danger in, 177, 272–73
standard configuration of, 201–2
Hill, Jimmy, 118–26, 130–33, 137
Hilton at Walt Disney World hotel, 175–76
Hilton Hotel Corporation, 143, 266
historical preservation, 150, 261
hitchhiking, 39
Hohauser, Henry, 70
Holiday Inn Corporation, 147–48, 200, 205,
208, 265–68
Holiday Inn Wall Street, 7, 277
Holidex, 267
Hollander (DeVries), Xaviera (the "Happy
Hooker"), 64–66
Hollywood, business practices in, 181
homes, custom-designed, 1
Hope, Bob, 157
Hopkins, Jane, 94
Hopkins, O. D., 93–96, 105

hospitality industry, 288
hotel architecture
    aesthetics of, 104–5
    construction costs, 174–75
    inside terminology of, 163
    layout of kitchens and laundries, 103–4
    overbuilding in the eighties, 175
    as participatory theater, 3
    security and efficiency as main issues, 102–4
    small rooms craze, 263–64
    standard dimensions of, 110, 201–2
hotel chains, 171, 265–68
hotels
    employees of, 103
    guests of, catering to tastes of, 73
    management contracts and franchises,
        266–67
    money made from, by owners not
        architects, 7
    operators of, 265–68
    pilferage in, 104
    profitability of, vs. aesthetics, 104–5,
        174–75
    test of success of, 7–8
Hoving, Thomas, 66, 76–77, 86–88
Howard Roark character, 21
Hughes, Howard, 130
Hutchins, Robert S., 52
Huxtable, Ada Louise, 4–5, 65, 86–88,
    252–53, 255

imagineers (Disney), 161–62
Indecent Proposal, 3
InterContinental hotel chain, 100
interior designers, 102, 109–12, 158–59
International Style, 44, 61–62
Intersection, 3

James Bond movies, 97
Japanese clients, 142, 221
Japanese corporations, 162–63
Japanese country inns (ryokan), 7, 285–88
Japanese culture, 101, 285–88
Japanese economy, 221
Japanese language, 286
jet plane travel, and vacation resorts, 96
Jewish holidays, 34, 274
Jews
    in Cuba, 240
    German Jews, in New York City real estate,
        12–14, 170
    immigrants, German vs. Eastern European
        differences, 12–13

minority status of, 33–34, 73
    Orthodox, 260
John F. Kennedy Space Center (Cape
    Canaveral), 62
John Hancock Center (Chicago), 171
Jurassic Park, 231

Kahn, Louis, 44, 52
Kalashnikov rifle, 245
Kallmann, Gerhard, 4, 46–47
Kendis, Sherman, 151–52
Kenin, Mike, 5
Kennedy, John F., 51
Kerkorian, Kirk, 117–18
KGB, 245
Kimonos restaurant, 191–92
Kirk, Grayson, 52
kitchens (hotel), location of, relative to
    restaurants, 103
Koch, Ed, 85
Komarin, Leo, 49, 56–57
Korea, 40
Kornblath, Leo, 63–65
Kouzmanoff, Alexander, 54
Kremlin, 244
Kwan, Chef, 108–9
Kyoto, Japan, 287

labor, cost of, 103
laminene, 46, 53
landmarking, 260–62
Lanigan, Al, 109–13
Lansky, Meyer, 146, 154
"Lapidus," as pejorative, 87
Lapidus, Adam (son), 55, 114, 185
Lapidus, Alan (author)
    apprenticeship, 56–63
    architectural schooling, 2, 4, 42–55, 60
    bankruptcy filing (1992), 16, 224–26, 257
    called "Donald Trump's architect," 9
    and the casino business, 118–27, 129–33
    childhood, 24–32, 274
    college years, 33–35, 42–55
    cooking avocation, 27, 109
    draftsman work, 35, 39, 56–58
    early schooling, 5
    famous clients of, 2
    financial dealings, 113–14
    firm of, 222–24, 258–59
    flying avocation, 12, 219
    folksinging avocation, 48–49
    friendship with Trump, 145
    hotel architecture business of, 3, 215, 285

Japanese cultural studies of, 101
laborer jobs in hotel construction, 58–60
management practices of own firm,
    181–82, 214–15, 222–23
marriages, 35–37
media descriptions of, 3
mentors of, 133
in the military, 35–36, 38–41
on the NYPD auxiliary force, 274–84
offices of, 258–59, 282, 284
personal traits, 194, 224
professional relations with father, 4, 67
retirement wish, 257–58, 268
shuts down office after 9/11, 284
small ego of, 194
social life and dating, 150
Spanish speaking skill, 90, 99, 114, 237,
    239
volunteering as auxiliary police officer,
    195
Lapidus, Beatrice Perlman (mother), 20,
    24–31, 64, 71, 274
Lapidus, Ben (uncle), 23
Lapidus, Caroline (third wife), 37, 284
Lapidus, Evelyn (aunt), 22, 37
Lapidus, Leon (grandfather), 21–24, 243
Lapidus, Morris (father)
    architectural style, 50, 65, 87–88, 249–50
    architecture training, 72
    asked to design a municipal bathhouse,
        76–77
    brownstone office of, 56–57
    disparaged by critics, 65, 87–88, 250,
        252–53
    fame of, 4, 43
    as father, 20–21, 24–29, 89
    firm of, 63–65, 222
    hotel work, 68–70, 72–75, 91, 110, 146,
        153, 186, 250
    large ego of, 194
    as mentor, 133
    on-the-job personality of, 64
    personal traits, 25, 64, 145, 194
    praises Alan, rarely, 157–58
    shuts down business and retires moderately
        wealthy, 222, 289
    store layout work, 70–72, 134
    theatre career, 71–72
    Too Much Is Never Enough (memoir), 22,
        63, 64, 89
    and Trump Village, 9–11, 17–18
Lapidus, Nancy (second wife), 36–37, 147,
    194

Lapidus, Richard (brother), 21, 24, 29–31,
    214, 224–26
Lapidus, Sol (uncle), 22, 37
Las Vegas, 178
    convention centers, 178
    gaming industry, 116–33, 143
Las Vegas Hilton, 118
Latin America
    construction practices in, 101–12, 211–14
    hotel and resort building in, 114–15
Latin lunch, 99
Latin spirit, 114–15
laundries, hotel, 103–4
lawsuits, developers', 181–83
lawyers, small-town, 142–43
Lebed, Alexander, 246
Le Corbusier, 44
Lever Brothers, 62
Lever House (New York City), 62
Levien, Arthur, 248–49, 251
licensing exam, 294
life drawing classes, 44
light and air requirements (New York City),
    199
lighting
    and human behavior, 72, 126
    new technology of, 206–7
    outdoor, 205–9
    stadium, 78–82
lightning, 188–90
Limelighters, the, 49
Lin, Maya, 291
Lincoln Center (New York City), 260
Lincoln Square Synagogue (New York City),
    260
Lindsay, John, 2, 66, 76–77, 83
linoleum, 28–29
loads, 49–50
lobbies, 9–10, 203
Loews chain, 104, 176, 185
Loews Monte Carlo (Monaco), 151
London, 104
Loquasto, Santo, 204
Lordi, Joseph, 132, 155
Loren, Sophia, 2
Los Angeles International Airport, 62
Lubyanka Prison, Moscow, 244
Luckman, Charles, 62

MacArthur, Douglas, 192
Machine Age architecture, 294
Madison Square Garden, current (New York
    City), 62

magic carpet ride effect, 156
management contracts, 265–68
Manaus, Brazil, 236
Manhattan, 18
Maples, Marla, 16–17, 148
Maresca, Anthony, 275
Marine Corps, 38–39
Marnell, Tony, 131
Married to the Mob, 153
Marriott, Bill, 217
Marriott Corporation, 216–17, 221
Mary (parents' maid), 26
Mass, Marvin, 217–18
Mayflower Hotel (Atlantic City), 154
McCrory store chain, 249
McKim, Mead & White, 42
Mediterranean Village project (Orlando,
    Fla.), 133, 162, 167–69, 172
Meisner, Addison, 168
memorials, war, 291
MEP construction firms, 98
Mercer, Leonard, 151–52
Merrill Lynch, 136
MetLife, 185, 193
Metropolitan Museum of Art (NYC), 66, 87
Miami, Fla., Cuban exiles in, 240
Miami Beach, Fla., 68–70, 72–75, 100, 250
mice, in hotels, 193
Michael Reese Hospital (Chicago), 290–91
Midwood High School (Brooklyn), 5, 33
Mies van der Rohe, Ludwig, 44, 293
Miller, Irwin, 177
Minos, Crete, architecture and costumes of,
    251–52
mirror glass, 250
Mitchell, Joni, 207
mixed-use structures, 203
mobsters, 6–7, 101, 146, 153–54
    as author's clients, 2, 113–14
    socializing with, 151–52
    word of, good as gold, 114, 255
money
    and keeping score, 130
    made by owners, not architects, 7
    other people's (OPM), 216
Moore, Demi, 3
Moore, Robin, 65–66
Moore & Hutchins firm, 52
Morgans Hotel (New York City), 263–64
Moscow, 243–47
Moses, Tom, 166–67
Moskva Hotel, Moscow, 243–47
mountains, building on top of, 91–96

movies, architects in, 3
Municipal Art Society, 204, 210
music, and emotions, 135

National Westminster Bank (NatWest), 216,
    221, 224–26
Nature Conservancy, 230–31
Newark Airport, N.J., 270
New Brutalism, 4, 46, 294
New Jersey
    Casino Control Commission, 119–20, 130,
        142, 143–46, 150, 155
    Coastal Area Facilities Review Agency
        (CAFRA), 142
    gambling legalized in, 136, 137
    Gaming Commission, 132
    regulating agencies, 142
    State Historical Preservation Office, 150
Newman, Paul, 3, 6, 21
New Orleans, La., brothels in, 155
New York City
    building code, 82–84, 199–201
    Building Department, 78, 82–84
    city planning, 198–99
    Emergency Services Unit (ESU), 281
    Landmarks Commission, 260–62
    Lindsay era, 76–88
    mid-1970s near-bankruptcy, 11
    municipal construction rules, 80–86
    Parks Department, 78
    real estate developers of, 12–14, 170–71,
        227–28
New York Police Department (NYPD)
    auxiliary force, 274–84
New York Racquet Club (New York City),
    293
New York Times, 53, 65, 69–70, 86–88, 141,
    206, 250, 252–53
    headquarters building, 198
Nicholas, Frank, 268
Nixon, Louis, 279–80
NoHo district (New York City), 294
Novack, Ben, 68–70, 72–75
Novack, Ben, Jr., 69
Nunis, Richard, 161

ocean views, 1–2, 157
O'Connor (architecture student), 43
office buildings
    boring, 207
    unrented, 207–8
ofuro (Japanese bath), 287
Okura hotel (Japan), 287

Olympic Tower project (New York City), 248–53
Onassis, Aristotle, 2, 65, 248–52
Onassis, Jacqueline Bouvier Kennedy, 252
Order of Valor (NYPD), 275
Orlando, Fla., 140, 178
Orman, Herman "Stumpy," 151–52
OSHA, 59
other people's money (OPM), 216
Outlaw, The, 130

Pagano, James, 225, 226
Palais Royale (New York City), 6
Palm Beach, Fla., 168
Pan American Airways, 100
Paradise Island Hotel (Nassau), 146
Paramount Theater (New York City), 203
Park Avenue (New York City), 61
parking garages, 149–50, 259
Parnass, Harry, 43, 51
Parthenon, 293
Pearl Harbor day, 283
Pei, I. M., 53, 175
pencils, and drafting, 57
Penthouse Hotel and Casino project (Atlantic City), 253–55
Penthouse magazine, 254
Perelman, Ronald, 263
Perini Construction, 157
Perlman, Rose, 29–30
Perlman grandparents (author's), 26
pharmaceutical industry, research in rain forests, 235, 239–42
piles (construction), 153
pilferage, 104
pink buildings, 207
Pirelli tire company, 229–30, 233, 237
plan, architectural, as God's eye view, 135
Plaza Hotel (New York City), 85, 227–28
plumbing, 45
pneumatic vibrators, 108
police dogs, 279
police work, 274–84
  beat cops, 274
political correctness, 204
Polynesian hotel (Florida), 171
Ponti, Carlo, 2
porn theaters, 198, 200, 209–10
Port Authority Bus Terminal, 198
Portuguese language, 237
Postmodernism, 4, 69
preservationists, 150, 261
pro bono work, 290–91

"protection" (Russian), 245
Prudential Center (Boston), 62
Puerto Ricans, 99
  Spanish of, 109
Puerto Rico, 90–115, 211–14
  as vacation paradise, 100–101
Puro, Lou, 90–92, 97–98, 100, 101, 111–14
Pussycat Theater, 200, 209–10

Quesada family, of Cuba, 90

Radio Days, 204
Rahway State Prison, N.J., 281
rain forest
  Brazil, 229–37
  Puerto Rico, 213
Ramada Renaissance hotel (New York City), 208
Rand, Ayn, The Fountainhead, 21
Rapid-American Corporation, 249
Raskin, Eugene, 47–49, 54
Raskin, Francesca, 48
RCA Building (New York City), 206
real estate
  hyperbole in selling, 15
  public's incentive in buying, 13–14
  recession of 1989–1990, 207, 220–26, 257
  recession of the mid-1970s, 216
  "when it gets a cold, architects get pneumonia," 222
real estate developers
  bankruptcies of, 196
  bottom line paramount with ("nothing personal"), 218–19
  dealmaking and political connections by, 13
  lawsuits as part of doing business, 181–83
  New York City dynasties of, 12–14, 170–71, 227–28
  secrets of success, 139–40
  shafting the architect as standard operating procedure, 227–28, 257, 258–59
rebars, 106–8
recessions
  1929, 259
  1975, 216, 221–22
  1989–90, 207, 222–26, 257
Redford, Robert, 3
Redi-Mix trucks, 107
"Reds" (mobster), 151
redundant design, 236
Reedy Creek Improvement District (RCID), 165–66

Regent hotel chain, 286
registered architect (RA), 3–4, 295
regulating agencies, staff at, 142
Rehnquist, William, 137
reimbursables, 18–19
remote control cameras, 121
Renault, Mary, 251
reservation systems, 266–67
Resorts International, 146
restaurants (hotel), location of, relative to
    kitchens, 103
retail stores, architecture of, 70–72, 134
Rexach Construction, 98–99
Rickover, Hyman, 23
RICO charges, 182
Riklis, Meshulam, 249, 251
Rio casino (Las Vegas), 131
Rio Mar project (Puerto Rico), 211–14
Ritz-Carlton chain, 59
Rocha, Edo, 229, 237
Rockefeller, John D., Jr., 196
Rockefeller Center, 170–71
Rodriguez, Juana M., 69
Romans, ancient, 128
Rosc, Mike, 147–49
Roth, Richard, 257–58, 271
rubber industry and plantations, 229–30, 232,
    234, 236
Rubell, Steve, 263
Rubenstein, Howard, 15
Russell, Jane, 130
Russia, 243–47

Saarinen, Eli, 52
St. Patrick's Cathedral (New York City), 249
San Juan hotel. See El San Juan hotel
San Juan InterContinental hotel, 100
Sans Souci hotel (Miami Beach), 9, 70
Santa Fe, NM, 200–201
Sayers, Charles, Jr., 193
Scheadel, Bob, 43
Schrager, Ian, 263
Seagram Building (New York City), 293
security
    casinos, 121–26
    hotels, 102–4
Segal, Erich, 5, 33
September 11, 2001, attack, 282–84
setbacks, 199, 262–63
set design, 6, 71–72
sex
    gambling as form of, 132
    and tourism, 100–101

sexism, 132
sex shops, 198
shape, and emotions, 135
Shawn (German shepherd), 279
Shelburne Hotel (Atlantic City), 150
shell structure, 110–12
Sheraton chain, 140, 176, 185, 216–18, 266
Sheraton Hotel (New York City), 110
shifts, hotel employee, 103
Shinkenchiku (Japanese design magazine),
    285
shootings, 277–80
Siegel, Bugsy, 6, 151
Sierra Cardona Ferrar, 211
signage, 204–5, 208
signifier forms, 126
Silberstein, Michael, 208
Silverstein, Larry, 208
Silverstein family, 12
Sinatra, Frank, 154
single-room-occupancy hotels, 196
Sixth Army, U.S., 40–41
Sixth Avenue (New York City), 61, 291, 294
Skidmore, Owings & Merrill, 35, 61–63, 161,
    207, 253, 292
ski lifts, 92–94
Sklar, Marty, 161
sky exposure plane, 199
skyscrapers, lighting of, 206
slavery, 234
Smith, Kenneth, 2
Sofia, Mr., 258–61
Sofia Bros. Moving and Storage Warehouse
    (New York City), 258–62
Solomon, David, 218
Solomon architectural firm (Chicago),
    218
Sopranos, The, 3
sound systems, 179
Soviet Union, 244
spa, Japanese-style (ryokan), 7, 285–88
specifications, architectural, 51
Speyer, Jerry, 171
sprinklers, 166–67
stadium lighting, 78–82
stained glass, 128–29
Stalin, 244
Statler chain, 266
Stone, Sharon, 3
Strasberg, Lee, 5–6
stresses, 49–50
structural elements, loads and stresses on,
    49–50

structural engineers, 106
subcontractors, 156–57
Summit Hotel (now Metropolitan) (New York City), 59, 252
Sunoco building (New York City), 61
supporting columns, 108, 201
surveying tools, 105
Swan hotel (Orlando, Fla.), 140, 187–94, 215
swat teams, 281
swimming pools, in hotels, 202
synagogue, author attending, 40

Taj Mahal casino (Atlantic City), 14, 139
taste, "good," vs. glitz and glamour, 13–14, 204, 207
Tawaraya Ryokan (Kyoto), 287
Temple Emanu-El, 12–13
Terminal Construction, 253
termination clauses, 147
texture, and emotions, 135
theodolites, 105
thermae (Roman baths), 128
thievery on construction sites, 86
3-D computer modeling, 190
tidal dam power, 237
"tight" buildings, 272
Times Square (New York City), 198–210
  hotels in, 208–9
Times Square Redevelopment Zone, 200
Tisch, Bob, 202
Tisch, Larry, 151, 202
Tisch Brothers, 151
Tishman, John, 2, 140, 200–201, 211–15, 216–20, 224, 226, 227, 261
  cancels author's project, 218
  Disney projects, 170–94
  personal side of, 170, 219
  speech omitting praise of author, 194
Tishman, Robert, 171
Tishman Building (666 Fifth Avenue, NYC), 218
Tishman Caribbean Holdings, 211
Tishman Construction, 171, 172
Tishman family, 12, 170–71
Tishman Speyer Realty, 171, 172
tourism, 100–101, 229
Towering Inferno, The, 3, 21, 80
trams, 94–96, 105
transfer beams, 202
Traymore Hotel (Atlantic City), 151
Trinity College, Hartford, CT, 33–35
Trocadero (London), 25
Tropicana chain, 157

Trump, Donald, 2, 9–19, 139–59, 200, 205, 215, 220, 226, 227–28, 243–47
  applying for a gaming license, 144–45
  Atlantic City venture, 10–12, 17–19
  as builder, 142–59
  as celebrity and "brand name," 14–16
  as friend, 159
  honest dealings of, 159, 255
  skating rink success, 85
  as youth, 10
Trump, Fred, 9–11, 17–18, 19
Trump, Fred, Jr., 10
Trump, Ivana, 158–59
Trump, Julius and Eddie ("Trump Group"), 14
Trump, Robert, 14, 142
Trump International Hotel (New York City), 15
Trump Marina Hotel and Casino (Atlantic City), 143
Trump Organization, 14
Trump Parc (New York City), 85, 148
Trump Place (New York City), 15–16
Trump Plaza (Atlantic City), 9, 18, 135, 140–59
Trump Plaza (New York City), 147
Trump Tower (New York City), 11, 18, 85, 147, 148
Trump Village (Brooklyn), 9–11, 17–18
Trump World Plaza (New York City), 200
Twenty-fourth Precinct (New York City), 275–76, 282, 283

Unbuilt America (book), 253
underscaled buildings, 129
Union Square (New York City), 197
United Nations headquarters, 196
up-front financing, 216
Upper West Side (New York City), 195–97
Uris Corporation, 51–53

vacation paradises, 96
  sin, sex, and forbidden delights in, 100
vandalism, 78
ventilation, of high-rises, 272–73
Vermillion, Dick, 163–65
Vietnam Veterans Memorial (Washington, D.C.), 291
Village, the (Orlando, Fla.), 171–94
Vitruvius, 133

Walker, Billy Bob, 271–73
Walker, Card, 161, 162
"walking the dirt," 172

Wall Street (New York City), 199
Walters, Barbara, 7
Walters, Lou, 6–7
war memorials, 291
Warren & Wetmore, 158
WASPs, 12, 26, 34, 61–62, 150
weather, 156, 188–90
WED Engineering, 161–62, 167
Wells, Frank, 185
Westin chain, 140, 185
West Side (New York City), 198
White, Stewart, 43
Wickes Law, 84–85
Williams, Frank, 197
Williams Island (Miami Beach), 14
windmill power, 237
windows, 156–57, 174
Windows on the World (World Trade Center),
    271–73
Wollman Skating Rink (New York City),
    85
women
    as architects, 223
    as casino visitors, 132
World Trade Center (New York City), 171,
    258, 271–73
    9/11 attack, 282–84

7 World Trade Center (New York City), 171
World War II, 22–23
World War II memorial (Washington D.C.),
    291
Worldwide Plaza (New York City), 215, 217,
    292
Wright, Frank Lloyd, 43, 293
Wright, Professor (at Columbia), 45
Wurlitzer jukebox, 209

Yale University, campus, 52
Yamasaki, Minoru, 258
Yankee Metal Products, 22
Yarbrough, Glen, 49
yukata (Japanese robe), 286
Yurok Indian tribe, 213

Zeckendorf, Bill, 2, 175, 200–201, 205, 210,
    215–26, 227, 257–58, 292
    cancels author's project, 221
    personal traits of, 196–98
Zeckendorf, William, Sr., 196
Zeckendorf family, 12, 258
Zeckendorf Towers (New York City), 197
Zeins, Wallace, 276–81
Zen archery, 101
zoning districts (New York City), 199, 260